TWO LIVES IN TWO WORLDS

To Tioore
Best Wishes.

By

Iacob Lascu

1stBooks – rev. 12/28/02

I dedicate this book to Maria Lascu,
whom I loved and who loved me
through good and bad times
all her life, and without whom
this book couldn't have been written.

TABLE OF CONTENTS

ACKNOWLEDGMENT

I received a lot of help in writing this book from a large number of people, but most of all I am grateful to and I would like in particular to thank:

Suzan Chalom, who wrote the detailed summary of Two Lives in Two Worlds, helped me review the manuscript and corrected the spelling and the grammar. Traian Lascu, who provided advice and corrected the spelling and grammar of the initial manuscript. Eugen Gal, who accompanied me in Romania during my research and shared some episodes from our time in the army, the Ciocirlia Artistic Company and our friendship. He also gave me Cernocan's (the orchestra drummer) diary from the Chinese tour. Emilia Ocico, for sending me her invaluable letters about her friendship with Maria. Ana Micu, who generously handed me her detailed diary, which she took during the Chinese tour. Alycia Hutchison, who shared with me her writing experiences and gave me practical recommendations about the copyright process. Mary Jane Doerr, who helped me prepare my manuscript for publication; she has been a freelance writer for the *Observer and Eccentric Newspapers,* the Royal Oak *Daily Tribune,* the Petoskey *News-Review* and the *Oakland Press,* all well-known Michigan newspapers. Peter Diggins, for providing names, phones and addresses for some of the principal dancers, who performed in my productions.

Also many thanks go to the Bogdan, Boer, Faur and Nica families for their hospitality and support during my research in Romania; to all the parents and dancers who set aside time to meet with me and share memories of our various collaborations and for encouraging and prompting me to write this book; and to Shinsei Hoshitsuki, Allen Chen and Ben Chang for sharing their expertise of China.

Last, but not least, to my son Eugen Lascu, who in addition to recommending many positive changes to the summary and manuscript, enhanced and edited the pictures prior to placing them within the text.

FOREWORD BY CYNTHIA HARVEY

When Iacob Lascu asked me to write the foreword to his book, I half expected the manuscript to read with great deal of familiarity. My association with Mr. Lascu, as he is respectfully known, goes back to the early 1980's when I appeared in Mr. Lascu's production of *The Nutcracker* for Dance Detroit and Detroit Symphony Orchestra. Many guest appearances followed for me, so you can imagine that in my estimation I believed that I knew the history of Mr. Lascu and the beautiful Maria, his beloved wife.

What surprised me was the rich tapestry of the Lascu's life before they immigrated to the West. They struggled for their art, family and existence. Theirs is not simply a love story, but a story of the hardship of the strict Communist regime that threatened to suppress their love for everything that they believed in.

Later, when in the West, the struggle to find work brought many moments of frustration. These lows were only temporary and a small price to pay for freedom. After a time, their joy was shattered by the news of Maria's illness. Here, Mr. Lascu describes his emotions like the artist that he is. He had to deal with the doctors and hospital staff in a very pragmatic fashion, which often irritated him. Finally, Mr. Lascu had to deal with Maria's death.

In the end, it was their integrity in so many situations that saw them through their difficulties. It is integrity that continues to imbue everything that Iacob Lascu does today and which endears him to those who have crossed his path.

You will find his story a journey through so many emotions. Mostly this is a journey beginning and ending with love.

Cynthia Harvey
Former Principal Dancer with the American Ballet Theatre

FOREWORD BY EVELYN CISNEROS

I was born in California, a third generation Mexican American and dance has always been a part of my life. After twenty-three years with the San Francisco Ballet Company, I am now retired from the stage and I am enjoying my newest role as a full time mother. I work part time as an Artistic Consultant with the Outreach and Education Department of the San Francisco Ballet; I host KQED's "Bay Window" program, which is aired on our local public broadcasting station; I stage ballets for choreographers Val Caniparoli and Michael Smuin, and teach the occasional master class.

As an American, I am proud to live in the most ethnically diverse country in the world, where an estimated 630 different languages or dialects are spoken. Growing up in America it is sometimes very easy to take our freedoms for granted. The ability to pick up and read any literature, to speak our minds freely in public or private, to chose were we work, purchase almost anything we desire and practice any religion we believe, are an integral part of living a free and fulfilled life. These were the very opportunities that tempted the founders of our nation to reach out and begin anew. Such freedoms continue to capture the imagination of the oppressed people of the world. It is very important to look to our neighbors and listen to their stories of emigration to the United States of America. Our diversity is what makes this country great. We are able to share our similarities, and unite our differences, while guarding our liberty. Although the fire to pursue "The American Dream" burns passionately in some more than others, we maintain the freedom to choose, and when we see someone achieve the dream it empowers everyone with hope.

It was this passion for freedom that drew Mr. Lascu to America. In this book he is able to share with his readers in a very sincere and concise way, the events of his life and of his family's lives during the Second World War. How the persecutions he survived and the losses he experienced, didn't embitter his heart is astonishing. The ability to study the arts and pursue the development of the soul through music and dance, while serving time in the military, is quite impressive and demonstrates a remarkable determination to improve his standard of living. During those chaotic and fearful times it was essential to have artistic outlets, as an emotional escape from the hideous realities of war. Ballet was an art form the country of Romania valued deeply and they took pride in cultivating and supporting it financially. Artists of that era were respected and honored as ambassadors who represented the finer cultural aspects of their country. While we are learning about the structure of the ballet world experienced by our author, his descriptions are carefully non-technical, enabling the reader to share the experience without hindrance. In the ballet world, it is often said that for a man to be surrounded by beautiful ladies in top physical condition wearing only tights and a leotard, which doesn't leave much to the imagination, is similar to a child being left in a candy store with a pocket full of money. Of course, our Iacob is no different and as fate would have it, a lovely lady who affects his heart and life forever smites him. While it is expected for a male dancer to be elegant on stage when Iacob commences to express the emotion of first love we are mesmerized by the eloquence and sincerity of pure love and truth that is indisputable and can only be envied.

With young Iacob, he shares with us the successful times on stage, in the rehearsal studios, on tour and his choreographic experiences as well as the inevitable disappointments for which the theater world is so famous. The artistic direction of the company is soon compromised. Bigotry and politics are subtly, but firmly rooted in the company's structure so that working there any further becomes unbearable and impossible. We learn how the decision to leave one life by sacrificing everything was a decision that was confirmed more by circumstance than by conscious choice. His emigration and genesis in a new world, from learning the language, culture, and customs to establishing an art form in the desert of an artistic wasteland was truly a monumental achievement that required constant perseverance.

What Mr. Lascu has to share with our generation is inspiring and encouraging to all who are willing to listen. His life demonstrates the potential for success, if sacrifices and commitments are made. As a ballerina performing nationally, as well as internationally, I am well aware of the struggle, constant commitment and sacrifices that were made in order to achieve the legacy which Mr. Lascu now leaves behind in Detroit. I have had the opportunity to perform with his company many times in his full-length productions of the *Nutcracker* and *Cinderella*. A professional atmosphere exuded from his productions, while being technically demanding, they were always artistically fulfilling. Maintaining this standard gave dancers, as well as the public, a local treasure, of which they could be proud.

I am saddened for the Detroit community and the ballet world, for the loss of their local treasure. Perhaps with the inspiration of his story someone new will pick up the reins and share the dream of a professional ballet company in the Detroit Metropolitan area. Dreams do come true!

Evelyn Cisneros
Former Principal Dancer with the San Francisco Ballet

PROLOGUE

Sometimes, after a couple of rainy days, it is an intense pleasure to inhale the fresh morning air during my daily walk. Each season has a special kind of magic that can lift me up, help me to maintain continued health, and grant me the strength to hold on. This magic is crucial to my life: it gives me wings to fly above the emptiness created by my wife Maria's unforeseen and untimely departure. Coming home from work each day during my married life, I always had felt great satisfaction in sharing everything with Maria. I miss Maria; she was the most precious thing in my life.

For me, the love I had with my wife was a beautiful world in itself, a combination of commitment, sharing, dedication, joy, fun, and a feeling of everlasting ecstasy. Her eyes captivated me and mine captivated her.

In the past, on the many occasions when Maria and I were interviewed, the journalists were always very impressed by our life stories. Maria told me many times that I should share that story with the world and she promised to help me write the book. But writing this book took a long time without Maria to help me; I lacked the courage to start.

The way we lived our lives made us celebrities to the people who surrounded us. Our happiness, love, contentment, closeness, joy, peace and the excitement of our successes were admired. Our past was a series of lessons that propelled us to higher levels of living and loving. We emerged from the most painful circumstances with strong insights about who we were and what we wanted.

At the beginning the desire to write swept over me, but only in random intervals and then it came more often. Maria's permanent presence in my thoughts placed me in a positive emotional state. She always admired me, trusted my talent, and encouraged my initiatives.

It took me some time, with so many false starts, dead ends, and dashed hopes, to begin writing this book. Then the time came when I dared to really try. I decided to write down my experiences, imagining that I was talking to her. I was desperately in need of projecting my thoughts toward her for the clarity of my own understanding of our life together. I wrote this book for Maria, to depict our wonderful life spent together. My life-long journey through this complex world has given me an infinite number of salient moments with her, some of which I now share with my fellow humans.

Now I am retired and living in a condominium in a northwestern suburb of Detroit. I love living here. Memories come flooding back. I find myself filled with thoughts of her from the past when we used to walk together. Now, after my walk, I sit on the balcony; I admire the lake surrounded by trees and flowers with a fascination that is tinged with the sadness that Maria, my wife, is no longer near me. Wow! I wish that she could see this fantastic view. From both my bedroom and living room, looking south, I have a beautiful view of Fox Lake and the line of trees hiding the houses on the opposite shore. The view is breathtaking, seeing the fantastic panorama of the trees surrounding the lake. I just have to glance out of my window to see the wild geese floating on the water.

Men in small engineless fishing boats can be seen. When the weather is nice, I rest in my armchair on the balcony, reading a book or contemplating nature, listening to the wild ducks or watching the majestic floating swans on the lake, seeing the rabbits and the squirrels running in the backyard or imagining Maria dancing in the mist. With her love of gardening I can only imagine the beautiful flowers she would have planted around the backyard. When it gets dark, my eyes try to penetrate the infinite space through the glittering stars, imagining that possibly my dear Maria, is somewhere there.

When my twin grandchildren, Marie and James, were younger, they would ask.

"Where is grandma?"

My daughter-in-law, Mihaela, would answer.

"She is out there among the stars."

For me, reality is that she is nowhere among the stars; she is gone, forever; but she is still in my mind. I lost her and I miss her. Since then, I have been alone. I have empty days and deep silence in my house, surrounded by an idle feeling.

My life experiences have made me feel that I am a minuscule part of the vast history of mankind. I am a 76-year young senior citizen who has survived much turmoil in the world. The thread of my life passed through the glories of scientific and medical discoveries, the destruction of natural disasters, and wars and conflicts between nations and social systems: capitalist versus communist. I like everything that I had a chance to see on this planet Earth, except injustice, war, and the countless disputes among religions.

Why was there hatred against the Jews and why was there hatred between people in general? All these questions have remained with me since my childhood. They are with me now as I write about my experiences in this book. Is hatred a consequence of the differences in so many religions or races? Why does this hatred unfortunately dominate today's world? In my heart and mind, I will always believe that we are all equally created creatures of this world and that we have by birth the right to live in peace and freedom whoever we are or wherever we go.

I recall traumatic moments during World War II. I survived, but the memory of that war is still in my mind. When I read or hear the word "war", I become frightened. War is such a small word but it has an immense apocalyptic significance. Different politics, ethics, and philosophies that govern a society have their pluses and minuses, but they all tend to exploit the individual who believes in doing his best. I grasped the opportunities offered me during my lifetime, to embrace the art of dance achieving great personal satisfaction and recognition from various people, institutions, and governments. Often, however, I was deprived of the fruits of my creations as others took credit for them. It happened twice that my professional and personal life was wrecked by political and financial powers. It became my singularly strong belief that a free, rational society should recognize and reward the best in every human being. I have not yet found such a perfect social system and probably never will.

I was fortunate that our ways crossed and that we stopped to become one, to continue the route through life together. After I met Maria, I fell in love, she became the sunshine that gave unlimited strength to my life. We had the pleasure of hugging and kissing each other at every opportunity. Seeing her, being with her, touching her, was enough to make the surroundings disappear into a fog. For us, love was "A Beautiful, Everlasting World!"

Now, as I write these words, I feel that I am with her, talking to her, and she touches my soul with a magical glow. Maria's love was the invisible thread that tied the two of us together. The relationship with her was unconditional. We cared for each other at any given moment or situation. The strength of her character was in her gentleness, which conquered everybody around her. A woman can be your neighbor and, for one reason or another, you never meet her; or she can live miles away and destiny attracts her to you like a magnet. This was my fate. She, Maria from the village of Paloş, and I, Iacob from the village of Beclean, miles away, found each other one day and never left one another. The story of our lives unfolds as we traveled through two vastly different economic and political systems. This book is about us, Maria and me, "Two lives in two worlds."

THE FLIGHT

On January 29, 1972, we emigrated from Romania and joined the ongoing Melting Pot of the New World, becoming naturalized citizens of the United States by 1978.

My wife Mary, (Maria) my son Eugen and I departed from Romania on the Tarom Airline (a Romanian airline company) for Detroit, Michigan via a transfer flight to the United States on PanAm Airlines in London.

We were very excited because for us this was the flight to freedom, but our excitement was overshadowed by the fear that at any time, the Romanian plane could be called back to Romania. It had happened before with other people. They were returned from the airport or sent back on another Romanian airplane. There was no escape because on each plane there were state security agents.

The time passed very slowly between Romania and London; fear was still with us thinking back to Romania where we had lived so many years in a totalitarian state. We had lost everything that we had gained with very hard work, and now we could only take forty pounds of luggage with us. But at the same time in our minds, we were optimistic. We believed that nothing bad would happen on this flight, and that we would arrive safely in London.

Fate was with us. When we arrived at Heathrow Airport in London, patient people who understood our universal mime and hand signals guided us to the Pan American gate. We kept repeating over and over the magic word "PanAm" until we found ourselves in front of the right desk. Quickly, we presented our tickets and boarded the plane, constantly vigilant to see if any Romanian security agents had followed us, eager to take us back to Romania.

Excitement, freedom, no more fears. Thinking about the past and the life we were leaving, I had no regrets, no bitterness. Maria and I had pulled ourselves up from our roots, out of the fertile fields we had so carefully cultivated in Romania with so many years of hard work and devotion. Now we were walking into unknown territory; an unfamiliar forest lay ahead of us.

Despite the language barrier, we enjoyed the service on the plane and especially the orange juice and the champagne. The in-flight movie was in English, but we were intrigued with the acting.

My thoughts drifted more and more into a sentimental recollection of my national country Romania, the small silver screen images of the in-flight movie faded gradually and I visualized the map of Romania, my childhood and the migration from the small village of my birthplace to the large cities

1

like Timişoara and Bucharest, which imprinted my lives evolution. I realized that I abandoned that country where I was born, grew up, learned and flourished in my profession. I always enjoyed exploring, hiking in the mountains, cruising on the Danube and bathing in the water of the Black Sea.

Romania lies mainly north of the Balkan Peninsula in the lower Danube River basin. Romania's total area is 237,500 square km. (91,800 square miles). The climate is warm in the summer and cold in the winter. The population is about 23 million. The official language is Romanian, which is of Latin origin. Besides the Romanian language, you can hear Hungarian, German, Serbian, and Yiddish, spoken by the corresponding minorities of the Romanian people.

I was born on March 19, 1926 in Beclean, a little village situated in the northern Transylvania province. It is the province most well known to the world because of the famous story of Prince Dracula, Vlad Dracul of Romania (1431-1476), nicknamed the Impaler. He was surely one of the most intriguing figures to have stalked the corridors of European and Asian capitals in the fifteenth century.

On my recent return visit to Romania, I stopped by at the house were I used to live before moving to Timişoara in 1937. The layout of the house hadn't changed; the only thing missing was the brick kiln in the kitchen where mother baked the bread and other goodies.

"Where is the synagogue now?" I asked the owner of the house. "I didn't see it when I passed the site where it was before," I asked.

"The Nazis burned it down," he said, "and the ruins were demolished to make space for other new constructions."

I was the youngest; Iacob (Yacob) was my given name, but my parents called me Iancala. I had two brothers, Zolty, 7 years older, and Eugen, 4 years older. My birthday was on a Friday night, the Seder evening of the Passover holiday (the feast of Passover was observed in the home on the eve of both the first and second day of the holiday). My parents were disappointed;

Iacob as a toddler

they didn't want a third boy. But since they didn't have a choice, they accepted me with joy as I was.

2

My mother Malca was an Orthodox Jew fishing lady, and during the Passover holiday it was forbidden to consume bread or other leavened foods for the duration of one week. She told me that they had expected my birth to occur well before Passover, and that they had prepared a lot of goodies: ciorba de perişoare (soup with meatballs), ceapă cu ou (a mixture of onions, eggs and goose-fat), sarmale (stuffed cabbage) knesiglach (chicken knishes), piftie de peşte (fish jelly) and piftie de gîscă (goose jelly); there were also many sweets and drinks for the event such as găluşte cu prune (prune dumplings), torte de mere (apple tortes), dulceaţă de pepene roşu (watermelon jam). But Mother Nature changed the plan; therefore, all the goodies, sweets and drinks prepared for my birthday were given away to non-Jewish friends and neighbors who were not celebrating Passover.

We had two bedrooms and a big kitchen with a brick kiln where my mother baked the breads, knot shaped breads special for Sabbath, and the traditional cholent, a meal made of beans and stuffed gooseneck. I liked it very much. Just to the north of the house was the stable for the cow and nearby was the barn. The backyard was pretty big and in the front of the barn was a little house for our dog. The garden extended north of the barn where my mother and my grandparents cultivated all kinds of legumes and vegetables.

My parents were both born on February 10, my father in 1894 and my

mother in 1897. My father, Samuel Brűmmer, was born in a small village called Midyodofka, nearby Kiev in the Ukraine. My mother Malca Abraham was born in Săsarm, a very small village close to Beclean. Her photo shows that she was a beautiful girl with dark brown eyes about 5 feet 4 inches tall and long hair that almost touched the ground. I always admired her beautiful hair and could not understand why she had to cut it.

Iacob's mother

"It is a requirement of my Jewish orthodox religion that when I got married I had to cut it and make a wig out of it, and wear it," she explained.

He was a soldier in the Russian army during the First World War and was captured as a prisoner by the Romanian army. In the meantime, the Russian Revolution had broken out. They got married on December 18, 1928 in Beclean.

When the war ended, my father didn't return to Midyodofka but instead asked for political asylum in Romania. My father was a good tailor and he enjoyed a good reputation in our village and in the district. However, the Romanian government refused to grant him full citizenship status. He was residing in Romania based on a decision made by the International Convention in Geneva. The convention awarded a special passport called the Nansen, named after the initiator, for all the prisoners from the First World War who didn't want to return to Russia.

My father liked to play poker and gamble. Unfortunately, this habit followed him all his life. Being a child with my own dreams and fantasies, I didn't notice the growing tension between my parents due to gambling. My mother was locked up in herself; she never complained to me. Her everyday activities didn't suffer so I couldn't tell that something bothered her. Later on, when I grew up, I remember asking my brother Zolty why my father was missing for so long every day? He explained to me that my father was a gambler; he liked to play poker and rummy.

I received an orthodox religious education well before attending elementary school by attending the chaider, which was a Jewish Hebrew school where you learn the Bible and Hebrew at an early age. I liked the stories from the Bible.

Elementary school opened a new door in my life. The school was about one mile from my house situated in the plaza behind the church. I walked in any weather by myself or with other children from my neighborhood. At the Hebrew school, I had known just Jewish boys, but when we had breaks during our prayers, sometimes I spoke to the girls in the synagogue's courtyard. At the elementary school, however, I met both boys and girls from different ethnic groups. We became friends and shared our after school time, playing together.

I found out bitterly that their religious education was unfavorable to the Jewish people. During the Easter holiday they avoided me and I asked them why? They didn't answer; they just walked away. A very good friend of mine, a Romanian boy, one-day confessed to me the reason why the others avoided me:

"They are afraid that you will take blood from them comparing the situation with the time when the Romans crucified Jesus."

I didn't understand the meaning of his explanation and I asked him to elaborate. He did, and I found out that it is written in the Christian New Testament that all of Jesus' disciples were Jews and one of them betrayed him. The findings saddened and confused me. I was not able to make a connection between what happened in the past with me in the present. I didn't argue with him; I thanked him and left puzzled.

I went home crying and told my mother that the non-Jewish children don't want to play with me and they avoid me. She let me know that this happened to my brothers, too, and I should not pay attention to it. She thought that it was just a temporary reaction of my Christian peers during Easter when they learn the story of the crucifixion from the New Testament. In my opinion, I didn't consider it a temporary reaction and it frightened me. My first reaction was not to return to school. My mother was shocked by my reaction and told me that it was mandatory for all the Romanian children to attend school. Grudgingly, I returned to school, confused with fear and frustration.

I was selected for the school choir and I enjoyed it. The teacher told me that I had a nice voice. I had never paid attention to the Jewish cantor before (the cantor sings some of the prayers in the synagogue), but since I discovered that I had a nice voice, the cantor became my main purpose for attending the prayers in the synagogue. At home I tried to imitate the cantor, repeating the songs. My parents liked this new hobby of mine. Sensing that I had musical inclination, they bought me a fiddle, and encouraged me to study. I started to take special classes, but I didn't like them. I never practiced. When my parents asked me to play something from what I had learned, I found an excuse to refuse. I said that I was not ready yet.

The truth was that I never practiced and I found the classes boring. Instead, I spent more time singing. I loved singing. I would put my father's thalles on my head (a white or light beige colored shawl ornamented with black lines, which married men use when they pray) and imagined that I was the cantor, singing in the synagogue for the congregation. The fiddle was always at hand just in case my mother would surprise me. After a while my mother understood that I didn't like the fiddle and they sold it and let me enjoy the singing.

Every Wednesday in Beclean was market day, gathering people from all the smaller villages in the proximity. At that time the main street and side streets were over-crowded with carts pulled by one or two cows or horses. The carts were full of all kinds of agricultural products or various merchandise. Some people carried their produce or products with yokes on their shoulders. The female peasants had the dexterity to carry them on their heads. Lots of people came, some to buy and sell; some just to buy and some just to sell. They arrived either mounted, in their carts or on a bus that passed by only once a day.

My father had his own booth displaying and selling ready-made clothes for men. After school, I liked to stroll through the market and stop at my father's booth. I kept an eye on the booth when my father took his lunch, brought by my mother. I liked the market, seeing so many people moving in

5

an unorganized flow not even noticing that they bumped into each other. Each individual would only be concentrating on finding a particular item before sunset when the market disbanded.

This tumult allowed my creative imagination to invent new games with the other children. We ran to catch each other or to find other children hiding behind people, booths, merchandise, and carts. My favorite game was to climb from one cart to another, as fast as possible without being caught. Once I miscalculated the distance between the carts and I fell with my forehead hitting the axle of the wheel. I was told afterward that I lost consciousness, fainting and bleeding a lot, till the people around took me to my father's booth and then my parents ran to Dr. Fried across the street. He stitched up my wound and bandaged my whole head so that I looked like an oriental with a turban. The wound was above my right eye. We always said that I was lucky that it wasn't worse. My mother prayed and thanked God that I was alive, that I didn't lose my eye. For me it was a lesson (for a while). After my wound healed I looked forward to the next market day and continued to play but a bit more carefully.

My middle brother Eugen wanted to learn a trade and he very much liked to spend his time after school in my father's shop. He asked my father to teach him tailoring. My father was happy to teach him; he would have liked to teach all of us, but my big brother Zolty and I didn't want to learn. The shop was a good size and it was divided into two rooms. In front of the south windows facing the street were two Singer sewing machines. On the north wall was a huge mirror with built-in hangers on both sides and shelves for storing fabrics of different colors. In the middle of the room was a big table on which my father cut out the parts for coats and pants.

At the west side was the door leading to the smaller room where the ironing of the suits were done. This room also had a door leading to the street. The reason that ironing was done in a separate room was that the flat iron functioned with burning coal, which emanated toxic coal gas. Very often it was necessary to open the windows and doors for ventilation. Even so, my father often came home with a bad headache.

Every October, when communist Russia celebrated the anniversary of its revolution, my father incurred the displeasure of the Romanian government. The police would enter my father's shop and search for so called communist fliers, turning upside down the fabrics, the suits and chairs. Certain that they wouldn't find anything, they always threw under the table their prepared fliers with communist content and then accused him of conspiracy against the Romanian government. He was annually arrested and kept in jail in a city called Dej about 60 km from Beclean, and then he would be released as soon as the October Revolution anniversary celebration was over in Russia. This was a big inconvenience for him, as well as our family and our business.

Communism as an ideology was beyond my comprehension at that time. I knew nothing of the fliers with the communist content purposely thrown under the table by the police. Unfortunately, I found out much later the cruelty of the communist ideology.

We decided to move. Not far from my new house lived one of my best friends Mojşi Kohl. His father was the owner of an oil factory. I was happy that I could play more often with my friend. He invited me to visit the factory and he guided me through the process of producing the oil that was extracted mainly from sunflower seeds. I especially liked the part when the sunflower seeds were peeled. The smell of the freshly peeled seeds stimulated my appetite but I didn't dare take any. Fortunately my friend noticed my craving and offered me plenty. The seeds were so good that I could have eaten them forever if my friend hadn't taken me away from there. He told me that I had eaten enough for one day but that I could come back every day and he put some in a paper bag for me to take home. Those peeled sunflower seeds became a favorite treat for my whole family Mojşi was nice to me and taught me how to ride his bicycle. I enjoyed it and learned fast which made me desire to have my own bicycle. I asked my father to buy me one, but he refused, saying that he didn't have the money for it. I was mad and went home pouting. My mother was cooking and looked at me and asked what had happened.

"You want a bicycle? Are you crazy? You want to have an accident? You want your head broken? Who will teach you to ride it?"

My mother was a gentle-spoken lady, so I was perplexed by her sudden eruption. I looked into her face and I understood that her eruption was genuine. Her face expressed that she was really worried. But in her last question I sensed a hint that she would like to help me and that gave me hope.

"I already know how to ride a bicycle; my friend Mojşi taught me."

She looked at me with her warm eyes and said, "Tomorrow, bring your friend over and ask him to bring his bicycle. I want to see you demonstrate what you have learned."

The next day I passed the bicycle-riding test. My mother was satisfied with my bicycle-riding skills and promised me that she would be my advocate with my father. My father finally reluctantly agreed to buy me a bicycle, but not a new one. I had to wait until the next weekly market. Several weeks passed and nothing showed up.

I was disappointed and resigned, but kept up my hope that we would find one in the near future. As weeks passed by I finally gave up hope. My mother prayed for me and said that I should never give up hope, and that you never knew from where and when the bicycle might pop up. She was right.

One day that summer, one of my friends, Bubi, celebrated his birthday and invited me to his house. My mother dressed me in my holiday clothes and she was proud of the way I looked. Looking in the mirror, I, myself, was pleased with my outfit. I knew that Bubi had a big house but I had never been inside before, so I was shocked once I entered through the main door. Their living room was bigger than our entire house. The floor was covered with a huge beige-colored carpet, and the windows were decorated with beautiful drapes. The furniture also held my gaze; everything was amazing to me. I found myself in another world, uncommon for me, and different from mine. Mojşi and other children from school were invited, too. Bubi warmly welcomed me and introduced me to his parents.

"This is my friend Iancala (my Jewish name in Beclean) which I told you about; his father has a tailor shop."

I was pleasantly surprised when his father said, "I know your father; he is my tailor and he is a good one." Maybe that was the one moment in my life when I was really proud of my father.

All the children were invited to the table and the maids served us goodies: ficat prăjit (fried goose-liver); jumere (fried goose-skin) with white bread; lapte de pasăre (bird's milk—a combination of milk, eggs and sugar); pure de castane (roasted chestnuts); and a variety of ice creams and chocolate milk. Later Bubi opened his presents. I had given him a book about butterflies; he liked to chase them and to catch them, but he never knew what kind they were. I thought that this would help him to sort them out. He liked it and thanked me. One of his major presents was from his parents, a brand new bicycle. At that moment, I envied him and at the same time admired the beauty of the new bicycle.

It was a wonderful birthday party; I enjoyed it tremendously. Then, at my departure, as we stood at the door, I plucked up the courage to ask him what he would do with his old bicycle.

"I don't know yet; it is in the garage," he answered.

"Would you ask your parents if they would sell it to me?"

"I will talk to them and give you the answer tomorrow," he said, Bubi kept his promise and talked to his parents about the bicycle. He told me at school that they agreed to give it to me.

"How much are they asking for it? I have to tell my parents to see if they can afford it."

"I told you they are giving it to you; they won't sell it to you. They allowed me to give it to you with all my heart as a present from me."

This act shocked me; and my heart filled with joy. He asked me to stop by his house and take the bicycle. Later that day I stopped by to thank him and his parents and to ride the bicycle home. First, I stopped by my father's shop and showed him the bicycle. He liked it and asked me to whom it belongs.

I said with pride, "It is my property."

"How did you get it? Did you steal it? I didn't give you the money to buy it!"

"I didn't steal it. I received it as a present from Bubi Eidinger. His father is your client. You can ask him if you don't believe me." "O.K. I shall ask."

One day coming home from school I rode as usual, speeding on the sidewalk, instead of on the street. This was against the traffic regulation as well, but I was proud that I had a bicycle and looked right and left and neglected to pay attention to what was in front of me. As I was passing in front of our former house, suddenly a little child ran out from his yard. I applied the brakes of the bicycle but it was too late and I hit the child and I fell and rolled over him. Fortunately, he was not injured, but he cried and his parents came rushing out of their house. My elbows and knees were injured but nobody paid any attention to me. The parents were concerned, with good reason, for their child's well being.

I rushed home and told my mother what had happened. She took care of my wounds and told me that I couldn't use the bicycle anymore. I didn't answer her, but I was depressed, thinking about what the child's parents would do about the accident. They reported the accident to the police, and I was arrested and kept in jail. My father was mad at me, but my mother went to the child's parents and begged for forgiveness. The child's parents were happy that their child wasn't injured and told my mother that they would withdraw the charges.

I was released from jail and my parents bought a present for the child. My father punished me, forbidding the use of the bicycle for an unlimited time. My mother was happy that I was alive. She said that material objects don't mean anything; they can be replaced anytime, but the body cannot be replaced.

The Jewish Middle and High School in Timişoara (Liceul Israelite din Timişoara) offered my brother Zolty a full scholarship. Zolty was a brilliant student and the scholarship was to include tuition, books, board and lodging, as well as the uniform of the school. Our parents were worried about having their first son live away from home in a big unfamiliar town, but my brother's strong desire to go to school and his passionate appeal to my parents prevailed.

Zolty finished every year of high school in Timişoara with *magna cum laude* and received a substantial financial reward. From his letters we understood that he was doing fine and was well appreciated by the school administration, his peers and professors. In all his letters he complained just of one thing, that he was homesick and missed us all and that he could hardly wait to come home for summer vacation. We all missed him, too. For me, he had become a role model because of his determination to do well in school.

It was a hot, but sunny beautiful summer day when he returned home from high school. The whole family welcomed him at the railroad station. He looked so good in his uniform, that I was impressed. He had become handsome and taller. In one word, he had become a gentleman. We all bombarded Zolty with a lot of questions about the city of Timişoara, the school, the dormitory, the canteen, etc. We listened very attentively to his stories and he was a good conversationalist, describing the places, people, and events in great details.

Zolty's stories captivated me. His opinion was that studying was the most important thing in his life. My mind flew away to the city that he enjoyed so much, and I wondered if I would like to be there myself. I had the opportunity to be alone with him. I shared with him my accident with the bicycle and he shared with me how much he loved the French and English languages "It would be wonderful if you could come to Timişoara and attend the same school," he suggested.

"With my marks I couldn't get a scholarship and our parents couldn't afford it," I answered.

"I will do my best to find out what other possibilities of financial aid are available for children whose parents can't pay the tuition or maybe for a partial scholarship."

Saturday my father's shop was closed and the whole family gathered at home. After we returned from the synagogue and had our lunch, my brother opened the discussion about the school and how wonderful it would be if I could go to the same school. My father was immediately against my leaving. My mother just listened and looked at my brother as if to encourage him to go on and try to persuade my father.

"Father, listen to me. Sooner or later there will come a time when all your sons will choose their own destiny. I have the feeling that you would always like to be with us or, at least, in the same city with us. We are together now as a united family. Until your sons will go their own way, why can't we stay together? I suggest that the whole family should move to Timişoara."

I had never traveled on a train before and I had never seen any other city. Our seats were in the economy class and I was curious to see the other cars, so I asked permission from my parents to go. We went through all the cars and could see the other passengers through the glass windows of their compartments. I was impressed by the luxury of the first class car and in the

In Beclean with my parents and older
brothers, Eugen and Zolty

sleeping car; all the doors were closed, so I couldn't peek inside. We returned to our parents and we ate the lunch that had been prepared by my dear mother.

The train sped through fields, small villages, small cities and big cities. On many occasions I saw grazing horses and cows. We crossed bridges over rivers and I noticed that the train stopped at city stations but never in small villages. My oldest brother Zolty left some time ahead of us with the purpose of finding a place for us to stay in Timişoara.

After traveling all night we arrived at noon at the North railway station of Timişoara City. As we entered the outskirts, I comprehended the grandeur of the city as my brother had described it to me. The railroad station was huge with several tracks and platforms. The crowd pushed one another, and it was difficult to pick out my brother Zolty, who was waiting for us. He was the one who spotted us and yelled and waved his hands. I saw on his face his pleasure over our arrival.

Zolty told us he had found a modest apartment at a very reasonable rent. We had lots of luggage and handbags, so we were concerned about how far we had to carry them. My brother informed us that the apartment is pretty far but we should not worry because we would be taking the streetcar. He guided us through the station toward the exit, which led to a streetcar station. Dragging my luggage, I followed my family.

The streetcar was crowded but I found a place near the window so I could take a peek at the city. The huge buildings amazed me and there were many cars, bicycles, trucks, buses, but no horses or cows. Throughout this ride, I saw trolley buses with two steel bars on the roof, which were connected to two parallel wires supported by huge poles similar to a streetcar. The difference was that a streetcar runs on two parallel iron rails and a trolley runs on tires, as does any regular bus.

Zolty said that we had to get off at the next streetcar station, so I looked around at my new surroundings; this was where I would be living. We crossed a grassy field and found ourselves on the street where the building was. On the wall near the right side of the gate was a sign with the address Iulian Grosescu Street Number 2.

Our apartment was on the right side of the courtyard; luckily we had to climb only a few steps. The first room was the kitchen equipped with an oven, which was heated with wood, and there was a sink with cold water. The bathroom was far back in the courtyard. The next room was a very big room with two windows facing the grassy field. I knew that Zolty would stay at the boarding school dormitory so I asked where Eugen and my rooms were. The answer came from my brother Zolty:

"None of you will have separate rooms. This big one is the only room."

I made a somber face, as did the rest of my family, but Zolty continued to tell us that the rent for a two-room apartment was very high and even this place had been difficult to find for the price. Then he told us his plan for arranging the room. We could divide the room into two sections, with two well-placed armoires. Our parents could sleep in one section and I could sleep in the other with Eugen. He continued to elaborate further, saying that after my father started working, we could afford a better place.

We resigned ourselves to the situation with hope for a brighter future and my father sold some of the furniture from our house and from the tailor shop but he kept the two sewing machines. These were shipped by the postal service together with other heavy items from our house and the tailor shop, that night, however, we improvised and slept on the floor in the spots where our beds were supposed to be.

We started our new life in the big city by addressing ourselves to problems that stood in front of us. My parents went to look for some furniture and other items necessary for the house and shop. My brother Eugen, who achieved the rank of journeyman tailor, was fortunate to be offered a very good job that he found advertised in the local newspaper.

Zolty took me to the school and I was enrolled. On behalf of my parents, he applied for a scholarship for me. Being an "A" student Zolty had won his scholarship on merit. But in my case, the board of directors of the school took into consideration that we had just arrived in the city and that my father hadn't had a chance yet to find a job. To our surprise the board of directors approved me for a full scholarship and we were all happy.

My parents were relieved that their children's major problems were solved; now they could concentrate on looking around for clients for my father's business. The leaders of the Jewish community warmly welcomed my parents and promised that they would let the community know of our arrival. They also would spread the word of my father's tailoring business.

The school was a block long building. The main entrance, a wide one, was in the middle of the structure. In comparison with the school from Beclean, it was as huge as a dinosaur. It was a group of buildings with two distinct wings; the right one was for the girls and the left one for the boys. On the second floor were the classes for the older boys like my brother. During breaks we played soccer in the huge school courtyard, or we tried to converse with the girls from the other side of the wire fence that divided us.

My favorite subject was physical education and especially the high jump, (a jump over a horizontal pole placed on two vertical poles). At the time, I didn't envision that this skill would be later helpful for ballet. During the first French language class, the teacher, Mr. Kardos, introduced himself and asked the names of each student. I told him that my name was, Iacob Brűmmer.

"In French you are Jacques, Jacky," and so from that day on, my fellow students, colleagues, friends and everybody else called me Jacky except for my parents who called me Iancala. Discipline in the school was rigorous. We had to wear our uniforms all the time. The teachers were proficient in their subjects and strict in demanding the maximum from the students' potential. We had to greet the director or any teacher very formally whenever we met them even when we were just passing by. It was mandatory that we sew our registration number on the left sleeve of our school uniform.

Since I couldn't afford the streetcar I walked to school every day. It was a pleasant walk and I was already used to walking to school in Beclean. On my way I had the opportunity to see my neighborhood from my district. Basically it was a workers' quarter with one or two-story apartment houses and four or five-story office buildings called The Fabric District. During, the second half of my walk, I passed another quarter where the scenery radically changed. There was a beautiful park named "Parcul Rozelor" ("The Park of the Roses"). Wherever my eyes wandered I saw only flowers, roses of many kinds and colors arranged in a variety of designs.

Through the park flowed the Bega River, which crosses the entire city in a serpentine-like manner. The river serves as a port and flows into the Danube. As I exited the park I entered the nicest and richest district of the city of Timişoara: wide streets and gorgeous single family, two-story villas with their own gardens, garages and some with tennis courts and swimming pools.

I loved Timişoara. It opened the door for endless possibilities in knowledge, sports, entertainment and dating. Most of my fellow classmates were sons of rich people. They lived in big apartments or houses with big courtyards. Morel was one of them and we very often-spent time together playing ping-pong in his family's courtyard not far from our apartment. Sometimes we played doubles or we organized mini-championships. Others were invited too, among them my friend Jancsy Taub. As a mater of fact, Jancsy invited me to his house where I met his sisters Gaby, Eve and Klary as well his parents. They welcomed me as if I were one of the families. Their house became my second home. Jancsy's mother always offered me something to eat and my favorite was goose-liver.

I continued to frequently visit Morel's courtyard where there was also a tennis court. He was kind to lend me one of his tennis rackets and taught me the game. He was a terrific friend and was always willing to help me. He had a bicycle and let me ride it many times.

Unfortunately, we lost him at an early age. He liked to ride his bicycle while holding onto the handle of the door of a moving streetcar. One day as he was enjoying this trick, a dog ran in front of his bicycle. He hit the dog and lost his grip from the door handle. He fell backwards hitting the ground with his head and died instantly. It was a great tragedy, which affected all of us.

ARRIVAL

I was still lost in my sentimental recollections of my homeland when my wife touched my hand telling me that she liked the in-flight movie. I told her that I could not express my opinion because my attention had drifted in to the past. After a while we heard the captain's voice calling our attention to fasten our belts for arrival in Detroit.

A fear of the unknown wrapped me suddenly. This time my thoughts drifted to the future. How long would it take for me to learn English? Would I be able to find a job? Would I be able to earn enough money for my family to enjoy a decent life? Would I be able to afford an apartment or own a home or a car? Would I be able to adapt to a new life, new culture, new laws, new customs, and new food? Would I be able to make friends and adjust to a strange city and a different climate? Maria, as she would be known in this new country, and Eugen, as he would insist on spelling his name, were both deep in their own thoughts. As I looked upon their faces, I could see they were happy and so was I.

The landing was smooth. Deplaning, we proceeded toward the exit, passing through a corridor that connected the airplane directly to the terminal. This was new to us. In Romania and London we were taken to and from the plane by bus. At the end of the corridor, we followed the crowd to the baggage claim. Passing through customs with ease, we found ourselves in the main lobby. Then, for the first time since we left Romania, we saw smiling, familiar faces, those of Maria's brother and sister-in-law, Traian and Olga.

Traian was elated, so pleased that his efforts to help his sister and her family were successful. Our laughter was a mixture of hugs, smiles, and tears. These exciting moments were filled with a barrage of questions and answers as we inhaled the atmosphere of freedom. On the flight to Detroit, I had been so thirsty for more orange juice, but having no money, I hadn't dared ask for refills after the complimentary drinks. Since it never occurred to me that refills were free, I endured my thirst until we landed in Detroit. Now in the middle of Metropolitan International Airport, my thirsty mind was being quenched in the atmosphere of freedom. There are no words to describe that feeling; it was something that made me feel like floating in the air as in a dream. I could not believe that it was real. We were free and nobody was following us. In this airport we could speak our minds freely without risk of being arrested should we happen to say something against the communist regime or its leaders.

Traian and Olga took us to their home near Greenfield Road on Outer Drive in Detroit, where a "Welcome to America Mary & Jacky" cake was awaiting us. The layout of the house impressed me as they guided us to a guest bedroom and Eugen to a sofa-sleeper in the downstairs recreation room. Would I be able to afford a house like this?

It was almost lunchtime before we emerged from our rooms the following day for a brunch of eggs, hotdogs, baked ham, all kinds of cheeses, juices, cereal, milk and this strange kind of white puffy bread. Everything was terrific except the white puffy bread. Even when it was toasted, it tasted like cotton.

Olga, Mary, Jacky and Traian Lascu
with the welcoming cake

After brunch, eagerly and impatiently, I asked Traian when we were going to look for a job. He replied kindly, "You have just arrived. Rest, look around, and start to learn English. There are many things to do before we can look for a job. First of all," he continued, "we have to go to the Social Security Service to apply for Social Security cards for all three of you."

I couldn't understand why I couldn't work and I replied impatiently that I could work until then. "No, dear Jacky, in the United States you can't legally work without possessing a Social Security card." But, I did not give up.

"How long will it take to get the Social Security card?" He knew that my interminable questioning was because I was nervous and hadn't yet found my place in this new society.

"I don't know. Just have patience and everything will be O.K. Your assignment right now is to wait and relax, watch TV and concentrate on the English language."

For me, patience has always been a silent killer, shattering my brain and giving me headaches. Maria and Eugen were far more understanding about our situation and advised me to calm down. Turning on Traian's TV, the first program I found was *The Price is Right,* on Channel 7, a show I still enjoy watching today. As I watched the program, I thought of more questions that I wanted to ask Traian, but he was at work. So was Olga. Alone in the house, I felt trapped with nobody to help me.

I was wrong, Traian had thought of everything having been an immigrant himself. The next day he took off from work and took us to the Jewish Community Center in Detroit where he registered us in an English class. The class was filled with immigrants from all over the world. Mrs. Gilman, the teacher, impressed me instantly. She was patient with all of us but required daily homework. After a few classes she noticed that Maria, Eugen, and I were serious students who came prepared with our homework finished while the others did not. She began giving us special attention.

In the meantime, all three of us received our Social Security cards, and Traian took us to the Jewish Foundation to apply for jobs. There, we were surprised when the foundation gave each of us a coupon for $100 to buy clothes at the Federal Department Store and additional money to make a deposit on an apartment. We rented a two-bedroom apartment on Santa Maria Street in Detroit near the Jewish Community Center. The apartment was nice but unfurnished. Traian and Olga then gave us a sofa, chairs, and recliner and we bought two mattresses to sleep on but we couldn't afford any beds at this time. Walt Lazar, Traian's good friend who owned a Chevrolet dealership, gave us some chairs.

At the Jewish Foundation, we were introduced to a gentleman who was in charge of finding us a job. Interviewing me first, he asked me what my profession was. Proudly I answered.

"I am a ballet master and choreographer."

A funny smile came across his face and he said, "I am sorry, we don't have such a job. Maybe you can do something else."

At that moment neither Maria nor I cared what kind of jobs we found. Ever since we decided to leave Romania, we had been preparing ourselves for the possibility that we might never practice our profession again. We were so desperate to leave that totalitarian state to create a better future for Eugen; we were ready to accept any reality.

Sitting in that office at the Jewish Foundation, I looked to Maria for direction. She lifted her shoulders as if to tell me she didn't know what to advise me. I knew I had to think fast. My parents' joint effort brought me into this world and gave me life, but they didn't give me a survival pass. I had to find one and struggle for it. Here in our new land I had to become independent of my brother-in-law: to earn my own salary in order to provide food for my family and myself. I told the gentleman to give me some time to think and that he should talk further with my wife and my son about their jobs.

■■■

I started to search into my past to find something that I had learned besides my dance profession. I continued to rack my brain going through my memories. The city Timişoara popped out in my mind.

I remembered how my father succeeded slowly, but steadily, more and more clients came to my father's tailor shop, which was improvised in our apartment. My father's business started to prosper with a sizeable clientele. One of them, Mr. Fuchs, had a store with ready-made men's clothes. He liked my father's work and asked him to make clothes for his store. He accepted Mr. Fuchs's offer and completed the first delivery on time with great success. The two hours round trip my father had to spend with each delivery put a heavy burden on him. As the demand for more ready-made clothes substantially increased, the idea to move near his store became a reality.

The district called The Iosefin District was a commercial one, with large boulevards and streets lined up with trees. The houses were well maintained and their style was similar. Mr. Fuchs's store was located on the main boulevard across from the Notre Dame School and Church.

After many days and weeks of looking for an apartment we finally found one, two blocks from Mr. Fuchs's store. The building was on Constantin Brincoveanu Street No.2. The apartment was similar to the one from where we had just moved, but it had the advantage of being close to Mr. Fuchs's store. We still divided the room with our furniture. After about a year or so we moved again into a two-room apartment on Boulevard Carol No. 22 just one block from Mr. Fuchs's store. The building had three stories and our apartment was on the north side of the second floor, with windows facing the interior square courtyard. This was progress! My parents had their own room, and my father's shop was in the other room where Eugen and I slept. The common bathroom was still outside near the stairway for the use by all the tenants on the second floor.

In the kitchen there was a wood-burning oven, and each room had its own wood burning tiled stove, for use in the winter. The stoves needed a lot of wood to even moderately warm the rooms. My father bought the wood cheaper in summertime and stored it in our basement. Most of the time the pieces of wood were too thick so I was in charge of splitting them into thinner pieces. This work was also done in the basement. We had a stump on which I placed a log of wood, and with the axe I cut the log into many thin pieces. I was skillful, but one day I didn't pay enough attention and I cut my left palm very badly I still have a scar today; Bleeding, I ran up the stairs to my parents. My mother bandaged my hand as I fainted.

Not long after, one of the other apartments on the west side of the first floor became vacant. It was a one-room apartment with a kitchen, but it had a bathroom with a bathtub. My parents bought beautiful new furniture and Eugen and I moved into our own apartment. My father's business went well. He needed help to be able to deliver the ever-growing orders on time. My mother offered to teach me how to do the easiest parts of tailoring. I didn't like that idea but my mother didn't give up and she gradually persuaded me to help my father. So, after I finished my homework, I became a tailor's apprentice. There was so much work to do that even my brother Eugen helped my father after he came home from his regular job. I had hated the tailor work but he taught me to sew basic things so I could help him.

■■■

Now, in the New World I had to choose between two alternatives: to exist on my own with dignity or to fall into a continuing existence depending on Traian's generosity and welfare. I selected the first option. The need of survival had pushed me into action.

In the meantime Maria went through the same questioning. She told him she was a ballerina but would take any job available. Eugen told him that he was an architectural draftsman.

It was my turn again, with much hesitation and a low voice; I answered the gentleman that I had been an apprentice tailor with my father. The job-placement counselor was satisfied with my answer, and said.

"That's O.K. I will find you a job as soon as possible."

The next day, the Jewish Foundation called me and sent me to my first temporary job. It was at a cleaning establishment at the corner of Curtis and Livernois, the "Earl Ruby Cobo Cleaner" at 18135 Livernois. The boss, Mr. Ruby told me that I didn't need to do the work at the cleaners but could take it home. He handed me a fur coat and explained to me that I had to change the lining. Not knowing what to say since I have never worked on fur before, I thanked him and took the coat home.

"You can't do this" said Maria, laughing at me.

"But I have to do it."

Knowing how determined I was she helped me remove the old lining, copy a new pattern on newspaper, cut a new lining and insert it into the coat. Since I knew nothing about working on fur, I didn't know that we needed special needles. Not only did we not have the right needles, but also we didn't have a thimble either. It took us all day to finish the fur coat. I was only paid for three hours of work since that was the actual time necessary for such work. In spite of this, I was very happy because it was the first money I had earned in the New World. But Maria and Eugen still did not have jobs.

■■■

We continued studying English at the Jewish Community Center. The teacher was very satisfied with our progress and advised us to continue watching the news on TV and listen to a special English language tape. Lowering our heads in despair we thanked her for her advice and told her that we didn't have a TV to watch or a tape recorder to listen to." Silently she left. We had no idea what she was thinking.

The next morning, a car stopped in front of our apartment. Through the window, Maria recognized Mrs. Gilman as she stepped out of her car. Excitedly, she told Eugen and I who was coming. Why was she coming to visit us? Did we do something wrong? Did we offend her? Living under the communist regime so long, these ridiculous questions filled us with fear as we answered the doorbell.

"How are you?" "We are fine," we answered simultaneously.

Mrs. Gilman asked us to follow her to the car. We weren't sure what it was all about but we soon found out as she opened the car doors.

"I brought you a TV and a tape recorder so you will be able to learn English faster and better." Then she told me to grab the TV from the car and Maria the tape recorder. Mrs. Gilman grabbed pans, pots, plates, dishes, and all kinds of spoons, forks, glasses, and cups. With tears in her eyes, Maria hugged her and thanked her for the gifts. In the European style, I kissed her hand. Mrs. Gilman was always very nice to us in class but her arrival that morning at our apartment overwhelmed us emotionally and taught us that she was not only a teacher but now a good friend as well. She had sensed the difficulties we were experiencing in our transition to our new life. Her help encouraged us to speed up our English practice and to have more hope for the future in our newly chosen life. What a good feeling that was! A boost, a trust, a sense of encouragement went through our hearts.

Life went on. The Jewish Foundation found another job for me as a tailor. My new employer was Mr. Guttman whose name I soon learned reflected his good character. He realized right away that I really didn't know much about tailoring. Patiently, he helped me to do better.

With this new job, I soon realized that to be truly independent of Traian, I needed to buy a car. As always, Traian helped us. He talked with his friend the car dealer Walt Lazar who sold me a brand new Chevrolet Nova. He understood that we did not have established credit and arranged with the bank to give me loan.

With this new car, I became the chauffeur for my family. I was so proud of myself. In such a short time, a half a year, with the help of such good people, I had accomplished so much. I had rented an apartment, bought a new car, and was earning $5 an hour, a good wage in the early 1970s.

Meanwhile, through his friends in the Romanian community, Traian found Maria a job in a leather factory. Every morning, I drove her to work before I went to work. It was tiring for me, but I did it with pleasure.

Traian then decided to give Maria his second car, a Volkswagen Beetle. Maria was impressed and excited by this large-hearted gesture. Later, she was laid off from the leather factory. Through his same connections, Traian found her another job at a Chrysler auto factory, working on the assembly line. This was difficult work and every night Maria came home exhausted. I didn't like it and asked her to quit and stay home until she found a more suitable job. She was determined to work though and stayed with it. Eugen found work as an office boy at the Redstone Architecture Company. Happily, I drove him to work daily.

We all had jobs now and every Friday we all came home with paychecks, very satisfied with ourselves. Our monthly earnings were more than a year's income in Romania! Gradually, we began making improvements in our lives, buying clothes, and necessities for the apartment.

Eugen registered at Wayne State University in Freshman English to improve his English before taking other classes. His schedule conflicted with Maria's and mine so we decided to buy him a car. He chose an MG, an English midget sports car. It was a neat car that always drew lots of attention, especially from the mechanics. It constantly needed repairs.

One Friday evening, Traian invited us to dinner. After Olga's meal, while we were enjoying our dessert and coffee in the family room, he asked me a question.

"How are things going at the tailor shop?" "Fine." I could read on his face that my answer did not satisfy him.

"Jacky, I have the impression that you are not happy with what you are doing."

I had to admit to him that working in my own profession would give me more pleasure than this job; but that I understood that it was too difficult to find a job in the dance field in the Metropolitan Detroit area. I maintained to him that I was happy with my life here in America and that the main purpose in coming to America was to ensure a better future for Eugen. Traian said he understood and suddenly changed the subject.

"Jacky, I don't know exactly what you did or where you worked in Romania."

He knew that I was a ballet teacher and a choreographer, but he wanted to know more information more details about our life. What did I do during and after the war? How come I chose the dance profession? How did I meet Mary (Maria)? Where had I worked and for what companies? What dances had I choreographed? And so on he discharged his questions.

"Traian, it is a long story. I don't want to bore you." "Jacky, I am really interested; you will not bore me."

I unfolded my story for him.

21

■■■

Dear Traian, in Timişoara as I grew up, my voice matured into that of a baritone, and I was glad that I was selected for the school choir and, later, for the synagogue choir. As my musical knowledge broadened, I developed a strong desire to learn even more about music. Every week our school organized a variety of activities for the students. Some chose different sports like volleyball, soccer, kayak, swimming, tennis and ping-pong. My brother was not sports-oriented. He preferred to read books or to go to symphonic concerts and the opera.

On one occasion when he was going to the opera, he suggested that I join him. Zolty, my brother, told me that the opera he was going to see was *The Barber of Seville* a comic opera by the Italian composer Gioacchino Rossini. He was very persuasive and in the end convinced me to go with him. We did not have the best seats. They were up in the rafters upper most balcony, but from there I could see and enjoy the splendor of the theatre, the big chandelier, the lower balconies with their boxes and the orchestra pit. When every seat was taken, the chandelier's light dimmed, and the conductor took his place at the podium. At the energetic movement of his arms, the orchestra started to play the overture. The music was beautiful. I felt that the sound of the music surrounded me and hit my soul. The three acts of the opera were full of comic moments and the arias were charming. My favorite aria was Figaro's first act aria. The whole opera had a great impact on me. The singers, the scenery, the costumes, and the vibrant music that rose to the rafters impressed me. I thanked my brother for that wonderful experience and I told him that he chose the right opera form to introduce me to the infinite world of aesthetic beauty. I became a frequent and ardent follower of opera and other art forms.

I felt that this experience channeled my mind in a completely new direction, a turning point in my aesthetic education. At home I started to sing the barber's aria, first humming then louder and louder. I was not shy about singing with the windows open. The neighbors complemented me for my voice. In my spare time I sang the melodies that I could remember from the opera. My mother bought a record player and records with very nice arias. I spent all my free time enjoying the beautiful recorded opera arias from the records and some times even during my work. In that period, I paid more attention to singing. My parents were happier now that I was staying home to sing rather than spending time outside playing soccer. I was advised to take canto lessons and my parents agreed to pay for them. I started to take voice lessons and learn new Italian songs and other operatic arias. Simultaneously, I enrolled in rhythmical gymnastics classes. The teacher, Fleischmann Katy, a very beautiful lady and good gymnast, liked my movements. She knew that I took canto lessons and that I wanted to be an opera singer. She told me that I had to learn how to move with poise and be relaxed for the stage. Therefore, she advised me to take classical ballet classes and recommended Ionel Marcu, a very good teacher.

Unfortunately, this idyllic happiness was disturbed by political events in Romania and in Europe; politics invaded our family. As a 14-year old, I was out of touch with the political and social events in my country and abroad. I was a teenager, and my mind was attracted to my relationships with my peers and our extracurricular activities, especially singing, social dances and sports.

The year was approximately 1940. My brother Eugen was arrested and sentenced to prison for communist underground activities. My brother Zolty disappeared. He had often visited us, but now it had been a long time since we had heard anything from him. We were concerned and tried to contact him but to no avail.

At that time King Carol ruled Romania. However, a new fascist-type party arose called the Iron Guard. It was an anti-Semitic fascist group, which sympathized with similar groups in the fascist countries of Germany, Italy and later Franco's Spain. Germany decided that Basarabia and northern Bucovina should be annexed to the Soviet Union, northern Transylvania to Hungary and southern Dobrogea to Bulgaria. King Carol humiliated and under the pressure of national protest led by the Iron Guard, the King of Romania abdicated. His 19-year old son Michael became King Mihai I. He appointed General Ion Antonescu as head of the new military government. Soon after about 500,000 German troops entered Romania. Great Britain severed diplomatic relations with Romania. When Germany attacked the Soviet Union on June 22 1941, Romania had no choice but to join Germany.

My parents were scared and worried. I was scared, too, but I couldn't comprehend entirely what was happening. Our concern was legitimate because a brutal anti-Semitic campaign had started up in the entire country. Jewish owned stores were painted with the Star of David or they were vandalized. Jewish students were advised to go to and from home in groups so they would be better able to defend themselves from an expected attack by Nazi youth organizations. Friday nights and Saturday mornings, the Jewish people went to and from synagogues also in groups. In some cities, especially in Bucharest, the capital of the country, Jewish people were killed. The Germans were everywhere, giving orders to everyone. In the countries invaded by the Germans, the Jews were stripped of their belongings, businesses, and freedom, to be taken to different concentration camps.

Beclean, my Transylvanian birthplace was already annexed to Hungary. My immediate family had left before the annexation so we escaped deportation, but my grand parents, aunts, uncles and their children were taken to the concentration camps. We were scared and expected any day to be taken also. The Romanian government, however, opposed deportation and adopted another policy. Instead of sending us all to concentration camps, they organized labor camps for men over eighteen in various cities throughout the country.

My father was taken to the Tirgu Jiu labor camp. The women were allowed to stay home, so my mother took care of my father's business. I watched her with admiration, how skillfully she managed the tailoring and at the same time prepared the food for both of us. She never forgot about my brother Eugen in prison and my father in labor camp. Periodically, as was allowed, she made up parcels to send them. Later we found out that Eugen was transferred from the Romanian prison to Transnistria in a prison in the Russia area, under Romanian administration.

As a minor I was forced to work. First, I worked in a flower garden and then I was transferred to a hospital where I worked as a janitor alongside some of my former classmates. In the evenings, I was permitted to go home and help my mother. The Jewish High School had to cease its activities and evacuate the building. Ironically, it was transformed into a German military headquarters.

The local newspapers and radio praised only the victories of the Germans and their allies, so we couldn't know what the situation really was. The Romanian government seized the radios from all the Jewish families so we couldn't listen any more to be updated by London's radio broadcasts. When authorities confiscated our radios, one of our neighbors had two and was able to hide one. Every evening, we went to her apartment to listen to the BBC broadcasts. In this way, we found out about the devastation in Europe caused by the Germans as well as their recent disaster suffered at Stalingrad in Russia. We realized that the world was engulfed in a terrifying struggle with death and hunger and that our lives depended on the outcome of the war.

To help the Russian offensive, the Allies launched air attacks against the German army and their allies. Romania was not left out of the attacks and neither was Timişoara. The sound of sirens warned us to go to a shelter. Most of the air raids were at night when I was home and our shelter was in the basement of the building. However, there were many air raids during the daytime when I worked at the hospital. As the hospital didn't have a shelter in the building, the hospital administration was made to dig a deep zigzag trench in the hospital courtyard.

During one raid I jumped in one of the trenches, plunged to the ground, and coiled myself up. It was warm and I could smell the loose earth. I remained in a frightened silence putting my hands over my head in an involuntary move as if to defend myself from a punch. Then the silence was broken by the approaching sound of airplanes. It was a sunny day with a beautiful blue sky. We could clearly see the reflection of the sunlight on the huge heavy bombers that looked like silver birds. It was a tremendous sight, but, at the same time, it was a fearful warning that spread terror of death and destruction.

My pulse accelerated at the first explosion. We never knew where the bomb would fall and waited every minute with horror for the next strike. I could hear the sharp cracks like thunder and lightning, one right after another. But they were neither lightning nor thunder; they were bombs. I could hear the explosions of the bombs grow closer and closer and then a strong whizzing sound followed by a deafening explosion shaking the ground with the trenches. It was an infern. The dirt thrown by the bomb explosions fell over our bodies. I didn't dare move as the bombardment continued. The sounds of the explosions horrified me but then the sounds became dimmer and dimmer until they stopped. The scary sound of the airplanes couldn't be heard any more. The sirens this time let us know that the attack was over. Fate protected me, but it was a heavy blow to some of my classmates who had been in the nearby trench.

In Romania, during 1943 some of General Antonescu's opponents undertook secret negotiations with the Allies with King Michael's approval. In the spring of 1944, the four parties from Romania agreed to form a National Block in order to get Romania out of the war. On August 23, 1944, a coup d'etat overthrew the now Marshall Antonescu and brought Romania into the war against Germany. The armistice between Romania and Russia was signed in Moscow on September 12, 1944. At the end of August, the soviet troops occupied most of Romania. We stayed at home, impatiently watching the door, waiting for my father and brothers to return home.

My father returned home exhausted, weakened, and sick from the labor camp. He cried while hugging us; so did we. Our hearts were filled with joy. It was a mixed feeling for him, the joy of release from his suffering during his detention in the labor camp and the joy of being home again with his family. I barely recognized him. His cheekbones jutted out, his eyes appeared lost deep in his skull, and his skin was dry with deep wrinkles all over his face. I wondered how he had survived. I was happy to see him and forgot that he had neglected me in the past. He was my father and I loved him as he was. What a joy it was to have him for dinner, sitting at the head of the table and celebrating the event with us. After about two weeks of recovery I was glad to see him resume his work in the morning. He worked with more enthusiasm than ever. His desire to rebuild the business caused him to work non-stop. My mother had to beg him to cease work. To our satisfaction, he didn't show any signs of resuming his gambling.

We didn't know anything yet about the fate of my brothers. With heavy hearts we awaited the return of both. Not too long after my father's return, Zolty arrived. We all bunched around him and hugged each other, bombarding him with questions: "What happened to you?" "Where were you during the war?" "Why didn't you write us or send us a message?" "Are you O.K.?" He smiled at us and said, "Yes I am O.K."

Indeed he looked fine, more mature and in good shape. That gave us the idea that he had not been in a labor camp. Then he unfolded his story. When he had found out that my brother Eugen had been arrested he had been frightened that he would be arrested, too, as he was also part of the communist underground movement. At that time he dated a girl that later would become his wife. She had hidden him during the entire war. We hadn't met her yet but we admired her amazing courage. Zolty apologized for not contacting us, but he hadn't wanted to endanger the family that was hiding him.

Friday night my mother lit candles and said her prayers. After we returned from the synagogue, we had our traditional Friday dinner. One seat was empty because my brother Eugen hadn't come home yet. We were concerned about his fate and my parents questioned other people in town whose sons had been in the same prison. They hadn't heard from their sons either. Time passed by, a week, two weeks and so on, and no news about Eugen. Our nerves were cracking.

The waiting stopped suddenly one day when Zolty came running home with a newspaper in hand. He was crying and his face was contorted. He ran to my mother, embraced her and continued to weep. My mother asked him what was the matter. He stepped back and showed us the horrible news written in the newspaper. The Germans, before their retreat from the Ukraine, machine-gunned all the inmates in the Rîbniţa prison. Our brother Eugen was among them. So our waiting ended with a painful blow. My mother tore her dress and my father tore his lapel, as was the Jewish religious custom when a member of the family dies. My brother and I didn't know what to do, so my mother took a knife and cut my brother's and my lapels. The war's merciless touch affected everybody's house in one-way or another. We had lost a beloved member of our family.

But the war didn't end; the Germans and their allies wouldn't yet surrender. The fighting continued on and the Germans who found themselves in Yugoslavia made their way toward Timişoara. We panicked and so did the entire Jewish population of Timişoara. We were afraid that the Germans would kill us all. We hastily packed only the bare necessities, clothes and whatever food we had in the house and rushed to the railroad station to catch a train going as far east as possible. On the platform of the railroad station, there was already a crowd of Jewish people, also hoping to escape by train. The intent was to find a train to Bucharest, but such a train would not depart until afternoon. We didn't have much patience or clear judgment; we just wanted to be as far as possible from the Germans. Luckily, we found a passenger train going to Lugoj City, which was about 100 km from Timişoara. Everybody on the platform in the railroad station had the same idea. I was overcome again with fear, as I was when the bomb had struck in the hospital courtyard. The train departed slowly which spread a temporarily relaxed feeling over my body and I fell asleep on my mother's shoulder. This pleasant moment didn't last long as I was soon awakened by the sound of airplanes. We all rushed to the window and looked up to the sky to see the planes. I heard people yelling.

"They are German airplanes." The train stopped, and people hollered.

"Hurry down from the train and hide under the train."

Everybody stormed the doors; some of the younger people even jumped through the windows. I heard the roaring engine of the plane. I glanced at the sky and saw the airplane descending with incredible speed toward the train. We barely got down from the train, hid under it, and lie on our bellies facing the ground. My mother prayed loudly. I was scared like never before and cursed the Germans and the whole war. Of course, the pilot of the plane couldn't hear my cursing and raked bullets all around us with his machine-gun. Then it stopped, and I could hear just the roar of the plane. The sound of the engine gradually faded and then a long, scary silence followed. We remained, motionless a long time, under the train; nobody dared to leave his or her temporary shelter. When we heard the whistle of the locomotive, we assumed that that was the signal that it was over. Indeed, it was over. The people were relieved. One by one they left the train's temporary shield, got on their feet, and climbed back into the railroad cars. We all ate and soon arrived in Lugoj. They informed us that the Germans had indeed had the intention of invading the province of Banat, but, fortunately, the Allies had landed in Italy and the Germans needed their military forces there. Relieved, we returned home.

On July 26, 1945, the Germans surrendered unconditionally. We joined the whole world to mark with joy the end of the Second World War and hoped that there would not be another one. The Allies liberated all the people from concentration camps. We couldn't predict our future but we were anxious about what kind of government our country would have. What kind of society would it be? We didn't have a magic crystal ball. So we would just have to wait and see.

My brother Zolty went to Bucharest and started his career as a journalist at *Scînteia*, the Communist Party's official paper. I was asked to become a member of the Romanian Communist Party. Because of the racial Nazis' and the Romanian regime's persecution during the World War II, I felt, as did so many others in my situation, that entering the Communist Party would assure us of a future without racial persecution, so I accepted it.

The future, however, would teach us a bitter lesson. The promises made of liberty and freedom from racial persecution made by the Communist Party turned out to be empty ones. We soon realized that we had exchanged Nazi persecution for Communist oppression, which stifled any free expression of thought or artistic creation.

In that turmoil, I resumed my artistic activities. I paid more attention to singing. I was advised to continue take canto lessons and my parents again agreed to pay for them. Simultaneously, I resumed the rhythmical gymnastics and the ballet classes. From the very first ballet class, I realized that it takes a lot of discipline and dedication to accomplish anything worthwhile. The teacher told me that I should have patience and perseverance. In the beginning, I enjoyed that parallel artistic education of singing, rhythmical gymnastics, and ballet. Soon it became obvious to me that I had to give up something to achieve good results in any one of them but I could not yet decide which one I wanted to give up. My destiny had to be decided; which way should I go?

For election campaign purposes, the General Trade Union Council from Timişoara (Consiliul General al Sindicatelor) urged by the Communist Party, formed a propaganda artistic group for the 1946 election. I joined that artistic group, which was named *Scînteia (The Spark)*. Indeed, this group was a spark. It was the first company of that kind established in Romania. The success of that group attracted many young people from different walks of life and I was among them. Vlad Tivadar, the director of the group, cast me in different roles sometimes as a singer, sometimes as a dancer, or both.

I was successful in both dancing and singing, but I preferred my dancing performances. I increased the number of ballet classes to three a week. Ballet bewitched me and became an exhilarating force in my life. My progress was soon noticed and the ballet-master offered me a full scholarship. I enjoyed his classes tremendously six days a week. The classical ballet "bug" conquered my body, and I worked alone for many hours after class to perfect movements.

After the election, the Trade Union from Timişoara decided to change the name of the artistic group from *Scînteia* to *Flacăra (The Flame)*. The director of the company was promoted and left for Bucharest. The new director was Andrei Kollo, a very intelligent man and a good organizer. He appreciated my talent, and on March 15, 1946, hired me as a permanent dancer in the company. Besides dancing, my duties also included administrative work and whatever stage work the director assigned me.

I quit helping my father in the tailoring business, which was something he didn't like and this created a conflict between what my parents wanted for me and what I wanted for myself. I liked dancing and this was the first independent decision of my life. I told my parents that I was starting a new life with a very strongly defined purpose, to educate my mind, body and its muscles. I felt that my body was the most precious possession that I had and nobody could take it away from me. Developing my body gave me a sense of my own endless power. It increased my natural potential to jump, glide, turn, etc. I wanted to do what I liked, to take advantage of what the world could offer me, to fulfill my highest potential, and to never give in to a lesser standard, no matter how hard I had to work.

With Gabriela Darvash in the Bulgarian dance

The ballet classes were my priority, and I would attend them under any circumstances. I felt that I was on my own, that my muscles were my biggest assets, that I could jump and turn freely and was able to conquer the world. Jumping, which I developed as a gymnast, was a marvelous thing in ballet and my teacher was pleased with my leaps across the studio. I felt that my body could do wonderful things. I had the satisfaction of ignoring the law of gravity and holding my body suspended in the air as long as I could. What I liked in ballet was that I could express my feelings with movements, and no words. In the ballet classes, I worked to the point of exhaustion and I would keep on going no matter what. It was important for me to look forward and never return to the tailor's needle again. I felt that I had found the way to freedom, to do what I wanted.

From an initial small group, *Flacăra* became a mature company. Its fame went beyond the Banat province and the city of Timişoara. The Trade Union Central committee in Bucharest decided to send the company on a tour abroad. The production was entitled *Cintecul Nostru (Our Song)*. The content of the show was a divertissement. The dancers presented Romanian, Yugoslavian, Albanian, Bulgarian and Russian character dances. The choir

29

performed folk melodies and songs with the Communist Party's propaganda lyrics and some of the musicians played classical pieces.

With the approved production we toured all over the Balkan countries, Yugoslavia, Albania and Bulgaria. Our first stop in Yugoslavia was Belgrade; from there we went to Zagreb and then we toured Skopje and Ljubljana, two major cities in Yugoslavia. A beautiful chain of mountains named Triglav (Three Peaks) surrounded Ljubljana. We visited the Postoina Cave, a huge cave with colorful stalagmites and stalactites where the large area was used for concerts. From Postoina we traveled to Belgrade where we gave just one performance. With that performance we concluded the first part tour in Yugoslavia.

We left Yugoslavia, on a bus and we headed toward Albania through thirty-six hours of beautiful scenery. It was in the month of May but we were traveling at a 2000-foot altitude with snow on the mountains. By contrast, arriving in Tiranē, the capital of Albania, we found a very warm climate. By bus we toured the cities of Tiranē, Durrēs, Vlorë and Korcë. In Durrēs, we witnessed the dedication of the first 20 km railroad between Durrēs and Tiranē. For the Albanians, the train was a curiosity as if it were the new invention of the century.

On our way back to Belgrade for the second part of our tour in Yugoslavia we visited the thermal bath city of Nish. The Yugoslavs informed us that we would be part of a gala concert dedicated to the 56-year birthday anniversary celebration of President Marshal Tito, Iosip Broz. The next morning, we were invited to view the parade in honor of the president. In the evening, we were invited to a reception in his honor at the Avala Castle. At that reception, the diplomatic corps and members of the Yugoslavian government and other officials from Belgrade and foreign countries were present as well.

We had the honor of clinking champagne glasses with Tito and his charming wife, Jovanka who congratulated us. We wished Tito many more years of life. This was the first time in my life that I had come face to face with a head of state and I was thrilled. For me, everything was like a fantasy or a dream. I was overwhelmed by the magnitude of that event. On the table in front of me was my dinner plate. On one side of the table were countless forks, on the other side, countless knives and spoons. Bewildered and shamefaced, I couldn't decide which fork or knife I had to use first. The waiter behind me, dressed in an elegant tailcoat and white gloves, saw my uneasiness and came to my rescue. He indicated with his hand which fork and knife I should take first. Thanking him I relaxed and helped myself to some butter and caviar, which were new to me, but something I liked very much. Later in my life, I found out that such delicacies are very expensive.

We visited the city of Bled, situated at the foot of the Triglav Chain Mountains around Ljubljana. Bled is a resort city with a beautiful lake, surrounded by villas belonging to dignitaries, high officials, and kings as well as Tito, Iosip Broz.

In the middle of the lake was an island with a small church. There is a cute legend connected with the bell of that church. From time to time girls would take gondolas to the island in order to ring the bell. If they heard the echo of the bell, this meant that they would get married within the year.

From Belgrade, we continued our tour to Bulgaria where we performed in the cities of Plovdiv, Varna, Gabrovo, Bazardzhik and Sofia. In the city of Gabrovo, there was a big industrial complex where all kinds of knitwear in a variety of gorgeous colors were produced. There, we had an amusing event. We wanted to buy some of the knitwear but they told us that everything in Bulgaria was on ration cards. When we asked where we could get the ration cards, we were directed to the city hall. We went to the city hall and asked for an audience with the mayor, which we were granted immediately. We tried to explain that we were members of the *Flacăra* Artistic Company and needed ration cards to purchase some knitwear. Conversing in a little Russian with a lot of gestures, we weren't sure if the mayor understood, but he was very kind and gave us a lot of ration cards. Back at the store we presented our ration cards. The salesmen laughed until they cried. We didn't know why they were laughing but we joined in. After all of us had a good laugh and calmed down, they told us that the mayor had given us ration cards for bread instead of knitwear. Obviously the mayor thought that our gestures meant that we were hungry and needed bread. To our surprise, the salesman accepted the bread ration cards because they really needed the bread.

On June 13, 1948, after the completion of our successful tour, we embarked on a ferryboat at the city of Ruse and crossed the Danube heading back to Romania, and Bucharest the capital of the country.

As we arrived in Bucharest, I was shocked by the news that The International Communist Committee had excluded Yugoslavia from their organization. The reason was that Tito would not obey the Soviet Union. He adhered to the Marshall Plan, which the Soviet Union had strongly opposed. Everywhere on the walls, I was astonished to see Tito's portrait with a hatchet in his hand and blood dripping from it. Written on those posters, were words saying that he was a traitor of the working class. Bewildered, I couldn't tell right from wrong. Just three weeks ago I had shaken hands, and clinked glasses of champagne with Tito and his wife. Now, Tito was being characterized as a traitor. I was to realize later that the idea of friendship between these countries was only a formality and really depended on how obedient a country was to the orders given by the Soviet Union.

This was the first time that I felt that something was wrong in the way the Communist Party was behaving. I was suddenly aware that as an individual under communist rule, I would not be able to express an opposing opinion. Was this a policy to mislead and blindfold the people? Was this a dictatorial power over my own ability to judge right from wrong? I looked for an answer. Did Tito make the right move for independence or not? For the moment these and other questions had no answers. Much later in my life, I was able to find answers through my personal struggle for independent opinions.

We were accommodated in the Atenee Palace Hotel. My hotel room dumfounded me with its elegance and luxuries of comfort. As soon as I had refreshed myself, I left for the newspaper *Scînteia* where my brother worked. There I found him well dressed and handsome. I was proud of him. He asked me about our tour and, proudly, I poured out the details of all the events and our successes. I told him that we were in Bucharest as a reward for our triumphant tour, and we were staying at the Atene Palace.

"Oh!" he exclaimed. "That is an elegant five-star hotel and it is often referred to as the jewel of Bucharest."

He was right. The restaurant salon was glamorous and the waiters were elegantly dressed. The appearance of the members of our company was a marked contrast to the hotel's other elegantly dressed guests. The whole inside of the hotel was impressive. The tables were covered with damask table linens and arranged with sets of silver place settings and crystal dishes, reminding me of the reception given in Tito's honor in the Avala Castle in Belgrade.

Wondering about my brother's opinion of Tito and the Soviet Union, I dared to ask him. He elaborated on the whole theory of class struggle and the Marxist-Leninist theory of the socialist revolution. Yugoslavia's accepting of the Marshall Plan was considered a deviation from the principal ideas of communism, which stated, "Who is not with us is against us." I was not prepared to debate this ideological thorn in my side, but I told my brother that I was very concerned about this situation and, in particular, my individual future.

Our stay in Bucharest was pleasant but very short, and we returned to Timişoara on June 15, 1948 to a warm welcome by the Timişoara Trade Union, an event that obviously my parents didn't miss. They were very proud of me, and no longer opposed my dancing. During the following years, my parents became my companions and strong supporters of me as a dancer.

The leaders of the Timişoara Trade Union valued the success of our tour

very much. They didn't want to show us any less appreciation than the Bucharest Trade Union leaders. Therefore, they sent all the members of the company who toured the Balkan countries for a thirty-day vacation in Călimăneşti.

One of the highlights of our vacation was the series of lectures held by the well-known Romanian composer, critic and musicologist, Alfred Mendelson. The lectures were held every second day with different

With Alfred Mendelson

artistic topics. They were an intense, profound, cultural education for all of us. I enjoyed them very much and had many private conversations with the composer on a variety of topics related to art. This was an experience that had a significant impact on the future of my professional life.

■■■

At home, I received a note that ordered me to present myself for military service. "What a pleasure!" Ha! Ha! Again I was lucky. We arrived at the city of Arad just one hour from Timişoara. There we were ordered to form columns and marched about 12 km west of the city of Arad to a village called Gai. We went to the Center of the Gendarmes Training, which belonged to the Ministerul Afacerilor Interne (M.A.I.) (Ministry of Internal Affairs).

The experience at Gai was despicable, and wretched. First, they cut our hair and then we were taken to a barrack in the middle of the courtyard to the showers. We undressed outside and thirty soldiers entered at a time. We hardly had time to take our place under the shower when the sergeant shouted, "Let the water run, soap yourselves, and get out." Everything was so fast that we didn't even have time to wash off the soap. We entered another barrack where they smeared us with gasoline to prevent or remove any lice.

In the dormitory, we didn't have beds, just some straw spread on the floor and some dirty blankets. We slept in that abject misery, which I lack the words to describe. The food tasted bad but we were hungry and, at least, it was warm.

One day, waiting in the big courtyard for my turn to enter the dining hall, somebody called my name, I turned, and to my surprise I saw my colleague Eugen Gal standing at the back corner of the same table. Of course, we hugged and couldn't believe that we were in the same military training center and so we went through many adventures in that training center together.

My friend and I, having the highest education, were assigned to work in the commanding officers' administrative quarters. For the moment, we were both lucky that we were exempt from field instructions. Our good days didn't last very long though because a captain, the new very soldierly commander, took over the center. The new commander conducted an inspection of the whole center. The new commander ordered us to present ourselves to the company where we belonged. The next day the captain's order was executed.

From that day on we went to the battlefield for training. The sergeant was cruel to us; he was the type who had the desire for a higher rank. He made fun of us in front of the other soldiers and turned the training sessions into ridicule scenes.

At the battlefield, we simulated an attack against an invisible enemy. After the drill, I noticed that I had lost my bayonet. I was scared because one of the provisions of the military rules was to protect your equipment under any circumstances. During my break I went back to where the drill was held. Retracing our steps I finally found the bayonet hanging on the branch of a bush.

I tried to integrate myself into the military, but I was not suited for it. I still remember what happened on one of the night alarm drills. I tried to dress as quickly as possible, but while everybody was out of the dormitory, I was still putting on my ankle boots and wrapping up the lower part of the trousers with the long band from the same material. I was finished with the wrapping of one foot and was starting on the second as the sergeant burst into the dormitory shouting, urging me to hurry, that the whole company was already lined up, waiting for me. With one hand holding the wrapping band I grabbed the rifle and ran. The dormitory was on the second floor and I had a very hard time running down the steps. Finally I succeeded in taking my place in the platoon, still holding the band. The company burst into laughter embarrassing me of my clumsiness.

Winter made our activities more difficult and unpleasant. The most difficult task for me was to stand sentry. The guardroom was a small one and had one wide bed for the soldiers to sleep on when they were not on guard. The mice swarmed all over. My turn was at 2 o'clock in the morning, and that was the chilliest time of the night. Over my regular winter coat I had on a long sheepskin coat and over the ankle boot a pair of huge fur lined boots. On my head I wore a fur cap. On my hands I had fur-lined mittens. In spite of these heavy winter clothes, I was frozen. My fingers, my toes, my nose, my ears were thoroughly numbed, and I trembled with cold. Standing in the snowy dark night, I had the strange feeling that at any moment somebody would attack me from somewhere. In addition, there was a strong blizzard that made the chill unbearable. Guard time was two hours, but it seemed to last forever. That night I felt that time stretched with no limits. I thought that I would die there, but I survived. My mind analyzed this incredible experience, giving me a new perspective regarding the human mind and the body's capacity for endurance.

At that time a new commander of the center, a major, was installed, along with his deputy, who was also a major. He ordered that I should be in charge of the club; and my friend, the library. This was the day that we took over the cultural destiny of the Center of the Gendarmes Training. We found talented people for the choir, dancers and even soldiers who could recite. We had three weeks for rehearsals and worked intensely with enthusiasm and with the cooperation of the soldiers. The new deputy major was a small and slender man, educated, and well informed, and, with all his authority, he ensured that our rehearsals would not to be disturbed. We improvised a stage from some of the tables in the dining hall. It was a good performance and well appreciated. We were proud of our endeavor, to have created a cultural environment at the Center of the Gendarmes Training at Gai.

MARIA (MARY)

After the instruction period ended, the assignment of soldiers to various specialized military units began for tank division, aviation division, etc. The assignment board was all sitting at the table, the commander, his deputy and other officers, awaited for us. I waited for the routine question, "Where do you want to be assigned?" Instead, the deputy major rose to his feet, welcomed me, and told me that they had already made their decision about my friend and me.

"You are going to Bucharest to the M.A.I. Artistic Ensemble. Congratulations and we wish you success."

My anxiety disappeared and was replaced by a great sense of fulfillment. I was deeply impressed when they all rose to their feet and shook my hand. After New Year's Eve, my friend and I were on the train on our way to Bucharest.

We arrived in Bucharest in January 1949 and were taken, to our dismay, to the General Gendarmes Center (G.G.C.) of Bucharest, located in the center of the city. The center was a square six-story building with a courtyard in the middle of the square. The windows looked out toward the courtyard so we were practically isolated, not able to see the streets of the city and only an acre of sky. Because we had no communication with the outside world, it was imprisonment. I was upset and alarmed that I had not been taken directly to the Artistic Ensemble as our documents indicated, any attempt to contact the M.A.I. Artistic Ensemble was rejected. I couldn't understand why. One of the soldiers from the dormitory told me the reason for this was that the G.G.C. intended to form its own Artistic Ensemble and they were holding us for that purpose.

I had to find a way of contacting the M.A.I. Artistic Ensemble. With my friend Eugen I thought about all of the possibilities and arrived at the idea that I should call my brother at the *Scînteia* newspaper. The idea was brilliant but I didn't have access to either a telephone or know his phone number. I became friends with one of the phone operators and asked him for help. He advised me to contact him during the lunch-break when he would be alone at the phone exchange room. I told the sergeant of my platoon that I wasn't feeling well and asked permission to be excused from lunch. As soon as everybody left for the dining hall, I ran to the phone exchange room. In two minutes, the phone operator was able to connect me with my brother.

After our routine greeting and questions about our mother and father, I urged him desperately to do exactly as I asked. I told him the whole story and suggested calling the composer Alfred Mendelson who had lectured us

36

on musical esthetics at the Călimăneşti resort. He promised me that he would do everything to get me out of the G.G.C.

Anxiously waiting for the results I spent my time uselessly. I was tense and my friend had to calm me down. After two tense days of waiting, a warrant officer came into the dormitory and asked.

"Who are the soldiers Brümmer and Gal?" I answered for both of us, "We are."

"Take your trunks and all your belongings and follow me," he ordered.

We willingly took our trunks and followed him leaving behind the rifles, bayonets and shovels. I thanked the phone operator for his help and did farewell to all the soldiers in the dormitory. I couldn't believe that I was out of that bastion and thanked the comrade warrant officer for taking us out.

"I am the warrant officer Roşu and don't thank me. I just follow the orders and I will take you to Excelsior. "What is Excelsior?" was my question.

Comrade Roşu replied, "It is a theatre where the rehearsals of the company are held."

"How did you find us?"

"The composer Alfred Mendelson called our commander who then reported the problem to the highest echelon, which ordered your release."

When we arrived at the Excelsior Theatre, located in the center of Bucharest, the Commander Major Minkievich welcomed us. The commander asked us where we were from and what artistic skills we possessed? We told the commander about Timişoara and about the well-known artistic company *Flacăra*. When I said to the commander, "I am dancer," the ballet mistress, Tamara Cap fixed her eyes upon me and examined me from head to toe. Then she ordered me to go up on the stage to demonstrate what I could do. I was surprised by her order and dared to answer that I didn't have any dance equipment.

"Take off your ankle boots and coat, and dance!" she said.

This was the first formal audition in my life and I dragged myself across the stage to get ready. In spite of the fact that I had danced so many times in front of audiences, I now had stage fright. I noticed the other dancers of the company watching curiously from the wings of the stage. I got excited, lost my presence, and blushed. I asked my friend, Eugen, to accompany me. He asked for an accordion. The time that passed before he was handed an accordion was beneficial to me to regain my composure.

I danced very well using a variety of technical steps and finishing with a double *tour en l'air*. When I finished the dancers from the wings dashed on stage, surrounded me and congratulated me and assailed me with questions. Where and how many years did I study ballet? Who was my teacher? I felt accepted into their collective. I found out later that nobody else in the dance company could execute a double *tour en l'air*.

Double *tour en l'air*

I remember the commander and the ballet mistress had radiant faces and happily accepted me into the company. Eugen, my friend, was happy for my success too and congratulated me warmly. But now it was his turn for an audition. My friend was accepted immediately as was I.

After the auditions, the Warrant Officer Roşu appeared and told me to put my ankle boots and coat on and ordered me to follow him. I was afraid that he would take us back to the center where we could see only one acre of sky. We exited the theatre, and, instead of going to the left from where we had come, he turned to the right and, with relief, we followed him. At least, we were going to another place.

We stopped in front of a beautiful villa were all the non-married, non-commissioned officers, sergeants and soldiers, of the M.A.I. Artistic Ensemble, were quartered. This was also the home of the dancers, instrumentalists and singers as well. Mine was a nice room with ten upper and lower berths. In that room with me were the dancers. Eugen was assigned to the choir room. In that villa, I was well off and could lead the life of a dancer devoting myself to my art. One of my fellow dancers was a special man, Borzea Gheorghe whose bed was above mine. He helped me learn the rules of the villa and the hidden rules of the dance department. We developed a very good friendship that has continued until today.

The day after I auditioned at M.A.I., I returned to the theatre and was welcomed by the ballet mistress into her ballet class. After the class, the ballet mistress told me that I had to learn two dances immediately, a Ukrainian dance and a Transylvanian dance. I was glad that she wanted to use me so soon. She explained to me that one of the male dancers had been injured and I must learn his part for the upcoming performance. I told her that I learn fast and not to worry.

In the theatre I could see a girl with chestnut colored-hair. She was dressed in a white astrakhan fur, and sat in the middle of the theatre, so I wondered who she was. Was she a dancer, a member of the choir, a wife of someone from the company? I didn't understand why I had suddenly become so obsessed about who she was? I had a pleasant feeling in her presence. I forgot that I was rehearsing for the ballet mistress in order to be able to dance in the next performance with the dance company. The girl in the white astrakhan was my focal point. I had developed a desire to dance just for her. I asked myself why but I didn't find the answer, it was just a spontaneous feeling.

My first day in the company, the rehearsal began with the ballet mistress designating a dancer to teach me the Ukrainian dance. In no time, within half an hour, I learned it. The dancer was puzzled by my astuteness and proficiency, and reported the fact to the ballet mistress. She didn't believe him and asked me to demonstrate so all the dancers gathered to watch me. The pianist played the musical introduction and then I danced the entire dance with no interruption. She was amazed at my technique and learning ability. During a short break, I went to sit down in the theatre, but the girl in the white astrakhan fur was gone.

The next day, I was called to learn the second dance a Transylvanian dance for couples. The ballet mistress designated a couple to teach me. Practicing the dance, I learned the day before I didn't notice when the couple came on stage. They were watching me for a while and didn't disturb me. The ballet mistress then called to my attention that she wanted me to stop practicing the old dance and to start learning the new one.

Maria

I turned and faced the couple and this was the moment in my life that I will never forget. I was looking at a girl whose beautiful face and body struck me and changed my whole life. I felt a current cut off my breath and take possession of my whole body for an instant. I hadn't seen her during my audition two days earlier.

She was a natural beauty with no make-up on her face or lips, her hair chestnut colored, and brown with searching, penetrating eyes. Her breasts beneath the sheer fabric with the nipples taut, rising rhythmically with each breath, created an unmistakable attraction for me. Her posture had the lightness of a natural feeling. She watched me practicing until I was interrupted. She made a fantastic impression on me. I had never felt that kind of shivering excitement with any other girl.

39

I am an average, 5′4″ height man with brown hair I am bald-headed now, brown eyes, a proportional body, with wide shoulders and strong legs developed from my sports and dance activities. I glanced at her, trying to understand the riddle of her face. At that moment I was curious what impression I had made on her, but I didn't find out at that time. I couldn't quite capture in my mind what it was about her that fascinated me so. I just felt that, without blinking, her eyes had sent her magic beams into mine. Her glance had been intent and purposeful.

Iacob

I felt that this was my place, my moment, and my world. She looked as if enjoyment was her natural state. She seemed unaware of her body as an instrument ready for dance or to be used in any manner she wished. She did everything with natural talent. It burned me with pleasure, but I was shy and blinked many times. Now, suddenly, it seemed to me that the woman of my dreams was in front of me, a woman who walked with a confident step in her life. I imagined that I was alone with her and had the desire to possess this woman right there on the stage. Then, I returned to reality; I was on the stage in front of the couple that was assigned to teach me a new dance. I was ashamed of my fantasies; I barely saw her and I had not yet been introduced to her. She approached me with her partner Gheorghe, my roommate.

"My name is Maria Lascu, but everybody calls me Mary."

"My name is Iacob Brűmmer, but everybody calls me Jacky."

Gheorghe took the initiative and explained to me that Mary would be taking it easy because she had had a minor ankle injury. I realized that the injury was the reason why she had not been on the stage at my audition. Later I found out that she was the girl wearing the white astrakhan fur in the audience. I wondered why she was in the theatre the day before during the Ukrainian dance rehearsal and I hoped that soon I would find out.

Gheorghe demonstrated the first section of the dance with her, and then he asked me to execute it with her. She walked royally, floating with ease, which derived from her natural anatomical body-structure. When she walked, the slow, fluid motion of her thighs and stomach and pelvis combined into the rhythm of a lyrical dance. Her serene walk was actually more of a gliding one. She offered me her hands, and, as I touched them, tender, lovely hands, I was humbled by such a thrill. It was the most fortunate event in my life. She guided me with the sureness of a professional, with competent confidence, and graceful joy. I was intimidated being close to her and moved clumsily. It took me a long time to learn the dance. The ballet mistress who watched our rehearsal was frustrated that this time I didn't learn the dance as quickly as I had the first one. She asked me, "Is this dance more difficult than the first one?"

"No, and I don't understand why I learned it so slowly," I replied.

But in my mind I knew what the real reason was. Anyway, I thanked Mary and I kissed her hand, feeling that I was in heaven. I don't know what heaven is like, but people believe that it is fantastic.

The ballet mistress interrupted me from my fantasy and brought me back to reality. She told me that I should practice the dances from beginning to end with all the other dancers because the performance was that night. I couldn't believe what she, had said. This sudden, unexpected request from the ballet mistress shocked and scared me. I told her that I didn't think that I could do it. She and the dancers didn't give up and encouraged me to go over the dances again and again to accommodate myself to them and to the patterns of the dance. We went over the dance many times, and I felt that my legs were sore and ready to collapse, so I laid down on the stage to rest.

I had not expected to have to perform so soon after learning the dances. I knew that stage technique was different from class technique, and, watching the dancers around me who had performed these dances so many times, I was penetrated by fear, so scared that I would make mistakes on stage and would burn with shame.

Looking around for something, I didn't know for what. I cast my eyes from one dancer to another, but none of their eyes met mine. They didn't watch me, deeply involved in their own problems. Only one pair of eyes met mine: Mary's. Her eyes reflected confidence in my ability, and beams of encouragement radiated from her. I went to the ballet mistress and told her that I would dance. Mary was right; I danced very well at the performance, and I felt that I had won a place in the dancers' hearts, hopefully in Mary's, too. After that performance my body ached all over and I could barely walk but my mind, was full of joyous dreams about Mary.

In the dormitory I told Gheorghe.

"Mary impressed me. She is extraordinary, and I like her very much. Is somebody courting her?"

"Take it easy, my friend. Nobody is courting her. I agree with you that she is a nice and beautiful girl. Everybody likes her and has tried to court her, but they haven't succeeded."

I had thought that getting a date with her would be as easy as my audition for the company was, which I had accomplished without much effort. Now, I was discouraged by his words and didn't say anything more. It seemed that getting a date with Mary was going to be difficult or impossible. That task became even more complicated because of my bashful, hesitating, and timorous character.

Years had passed since I dated. I had always thought that if I found the right girl, I would like to date her. Now I felt that I was ready to do everything possible to make my way to Mary's heart. I lay on my bed thinking of her and hoping that fate would bring us together. I tried to stop thinking of her but I kept envisioning the way she had taught me the dance, and I wished the morning would come sooner so I could see her again.

I quickly found my place in the company; the rehearsals went well, and every day I learned more about the permanent repertory of the dance department, which basically included character dances. Being cast in new dances was fun. Mary was not my partner in the couple dances because she was one inch taller and danced with her established partner. I was unhappy with that situation because I wanted to be close to her all the time. I was also too shy to ask her for a date being afraid that she would refuse me. I always moved around to look for an opportunity to see her beautiful body and to look into her eyes. When we bumped into each other my eyes happily met hers. She kept looking into my eyes and smiling, scrutinizing me as if she would like to read in my eyes what my real character was and what I thought about her. I tried to keep my eyes directly on her as long as possible without blinking, hoping that she would see that I liked her very much and that I would like to date her. I didn't know what she saw in my eyes or what her thoughts were at that time.

Days went by and I was tormented, thinking about what I should do, how I could find a reason to talk to Maria and ask her for a date? During our breaks, I usually withdrew to a corner behind the wings, sitting on the floor and eating my lunch. It was a modest lunch, which consisted of dark, state bread, salami and jam given to me by the military administration. Every day was the same; I didn't have money to buy anything else. One day, while I was opening my bag and reaching for the food, I didn't notice that somebody had come over to me. I was hungry and too absorbed in preparing to eat my typically unpalatable lunch.

Suddenly, I felt that somebody stood in front of me. First, I saw the feet, then the legs that I instantly recognized. I was dumfounded; they were Mary's beautiful legs. I raised my head slowly and saw her hips, her breasts, her arms, and, finally, I met her smiling face. Her eyes were soft; her expression warm and yet still distant and observing. I lost my head; I stood up silently not knowing what to do. I just glanced at her and admired her. Her body required observation as a prelude to invasion and satisfaction. I wished she could understand and read my thoughts. I felt that fate had already been generous to me when I was sent from the military center at Gai to the company in Bucharest. I didn't know what would be my future in the company, but I knew that I had met and was falling in love with Mary.

She broke the silence.

"Jacky, do you have a knife?"

"Yes I do."

"Can I borrow it from you?"

"Of course, Mary."

I had so many things in my pockets and I was so excited that it took me a long time to find the pocketknife. I handed it to her. She thanked me and left. I followed her with my eyes and devoured her, admiring again her floating, royal walk. She was beautiful; it was the simple truth and needed no elaboration. How could she be unaware of her own beauty? She moved swiftly, decisively. She disappeared into the wings, and I fell into a dream of fantasies and hopes forgetting to eat my lunch. Her return woke me from my fantasy. She was returning the knife and thanking me. At the same time, she handed me a big sandwich. I was surprised and reacted foolishly, stubbornly and rudely.

"Mary, it was my pleasure to lend you the knife. I didn't give it to you for a reward. In the future, I will not lend you the knife, anymore."

She was not offended by my attitude; she was calm and charming and lowered herself down to the floor in front of me, still holding the sandwich in her right hand.

"It is a very good sandwich," she said. "You will like it. I know what kind of food you get as a soldier; we dancers need to eat well. Please accept it. Jacky, it is my pleasure to give you the sandwich and it is not a reward or an exchange."

Overwhelmed and impressed by her generosity, I was pleased to conclude that she was highly intelligent; again, an attribute so obvious that no further comment was necessary and beyond intelligence, she was familiar with the ways of her secretive shadowy world and she was not just a beauty, but also a good person. Her words and her charm disarmed me. Ashamed, I apologized. She took my hand and put the sandwich in my palm. I took the sandwich and kissed her hand. She didn't leave. She asked me to taste the sandwich. She was curious to see if, indeed, I would like it. It was a big, white, sliced roll with boiled ham and liver pâté. I took a bite. She was right. It tasted very good, delicious. She left, pleased that I liked it. I was hungry and I ate it with a voracious appetite. Thrilled by the episode that had just happened I resumed the rehearsal.

From that day on, her sandwich became a habit. She came every day and asked for the knife. I gave it to her, and she returned with the knife and the sandwich. I thanked her every day and kissed her hand. On one of those occasions, I told her that when I get a paycheck, I would pay her back. She didn't like what I said and repeated that she was not doing it for payment. She was doing it without thought of reward, just for joy.

One day, she changed the routine and came with the rolls, boiled ham and liver pâté and suggested having lunch together. Nothing could have pleased me more, and I invited her to sit down on the floor near me. I gave her the knife with which she sliced the bread and prepared the sandwiches. She was so close to me that I could smell the natural freshness of her hair and body as I watched her. She had no make up on as usual. I had the urge to kiss her, but I didn't dare. I asked her.

"How is your injured ankle doing?"

"It's O.K," she said.

"Why did you come to see me when I was being taught the Ukrainian dance if you were injured?" She stopped preparing the sandwich and looked at me.

"The dancers told me that a fantastically good dancer had auditioned, so I was curious to see you and couldn't stay home. I am glad that I came. Indeed, you are a very good dancer."

Her words gave me courage, and my shyness disappeared. I asked her if she would like to go to a movie with me. Yes, she would, she promptly answered. Her quick consent without hesitation made me happy and gave me hope that my life was going in the right direction. Two weeks earlier, I didn't know her. Two weeks earlier, she didn't know me. That was how our journey toward happiness started. After lunch, we agreed that it would be best to go to a movie on the weekend when there were no rehearsals. Asking her for a date was a most daring act, done without thinking because I had no money for the movie.

I called my brother and told him the whole story and he generously gave me enough money for the movie and some extra in case I wanted to take her out for dinner. I loved *Tarzan* movies with Johnny Weismuller, who had been raised in Timişoara. She agreed to go. During the movie, I dared to take her hand, and she didn't withdraw it. I held her hand until the end of the movie. This was the beginning of my long-lasting relationship.

At the villa, my friend Gheorghe later asked me if I was dating Mary, and I told him that I was and that I liked her very much and hoped she liked me, too. He was happy for me and said that everybody liked her. But I should know that some of the dancers envied me. He emphasized that Mary was a very good dancer and respected by everybody in the company.

"You are a lucky man and I wish you a long, lasting happiness with her" he said.

I agreed with him. Indeed, I considered myself a lucky person because fate had given me the chance to meet Mary in that company. I was looking forward to a beautiful, steady relationship with her. My intuition signaled me that this was the girl with whom I wanted to spend the rest of my life.

Mary was born on June 15, 1929 in the village of Paloş, in the province of Transylvania, in Romania. She was one of four children with an older sister Anna and two brothers Traian and Pandele. She also had a stepsister

As a toddler   With her father and brothers   As a schoolgirl
Pandele and Traian

and brother, Lenuţa and Ghiţă. Mary's mother died at a very early age from cancer, a horrible disease. Mary completed three years of elementary school in Paloş. Her father remarried and moved to the village of Ungra, where Mary finished elementary school. Her father enrolled her in a middle school in the city of Sighişoara, not far from their village. She attended the school just two years before her father remarried and moved the whole family to Bucharest where she continued her schooling. There, she was enrolled in the Zoe Ramniceanu High School, a private, religious school under the patronage of the Romanian Orthodox Church. She didn't finish school because after awhile her sister Anna couldn't support her financially and her father had already left Bucharest.

During the Second World War her brother Pandele died from a heavy bombardment by the allies. The whole family moved to a small city Rupea not far from the village Paloş, and later Mary and her older sister Anna moved back to Bucharest. Her brother Traian left Romania. He tried to establish himself in France but didn't succeed. From Europe, he emigrated in Canada and then to the United States.

Mary told me that the M.A.I. Artistic Ensemble was founded on August 15, 1947. The members of the company were selected from the soldiers doing their military service, non-commissioned officers, officers and their wives. It started as a non-professional company, but, in time, it had become a first-rate professional company. At the height of its fame, the company numbered 400 members.

Maria joined the company soon after it was founded. In Bucharest, she worked at the Standard Telephone Factory, which had a dance group of its own. She was a very talented dancer. When she found out that the M.A.I. Artistic Ensemble was auditioning dancers, singers and musicians she auditioned and was accepted. It was my lucky day when I auditioned for the same ensemble and found her.

At the beginning of the year 1949, the M.A.I. Artistic Ensemble was reorganized as a professional company as a result of the minister's decision. A panel was formed to select those members with professional qualifications. Everybody had to go through

Maria flanked by Anna and Traian

another audition. My friends Eugen and Gheorghe, and Mary and I succeeded in being accepted as professionals in the revamped company. However, the bureaucratic system of the army made it difficult for us to remain in the M.A.I. artistic company. Because we were soldiers in the service, nobody could give us a salary. We had to choose between becoming non-commissioned officers with a good salary or they would send us back to an army unit to continue our regular time of service. I was disturbed by their decision and I didn't know what I should do? I had to make up my mind and it was very difficult. To go back to a military unit for eighteen months was not desirable. On the other hand, the contract to be a non-commissioned officer was for nine years, a hell of a long time to be under military orders!

I wanted to talk to Mary, to see her eyes, which would tell me what to do. My relationship with Mary had warmed up. We always left rehearsals together, and we walked in Cişmigiu Park; she lived nearby with her sister Anna. We walked hand in hand and I felt that I was part of her. We kissed when we parted, and we were eager to meet again the next day. We were together almost all the time. She knew the terrible conflict that was going on in my mind and heart. She didn't say anything that would influence me to decide one way or another, but the expression in her eyes was sad, telling me that she was afraid of losing me. I was tormented by the thought that I might never see her again if I left to return to a military unit.

My friend Gheorghe had already signed the contract, but Eugen hadn't. He told me that his wish was to go home as soon as possible. He said eighteen months was shorter then nine years. I didn't blame him; he was right but he was not in my position, tormented by love. The powerful feeling of love for Mary pushed me to the decision to sign the contract on May 1, 1949, and became a non-commissioned officer with the rank of sergeant major. Mary was happy and so was I.

I was free to leave the villa and look for a rented room. My brother had a nice big apartment with a small room initially intended for a servant. He offered it to me until I could find something better. I accepted his offer and moved in right away.

My friend Eugen was stubborn and refused to sign the contract. I took a look at my contract and noticed that the heading on all the pages had the royal emblem. I told my friend that this contract would soon be invalid because the king had already left the country. I had the feeling that the contract that I signed would not be binding for very long. I advised my friend to sign it, and, grudgingly, on August 15, 1949, he signed it. And so life went on.

The M.A.I. administration organized a Sunday trip for their employees. We were free that Sunday so Mary and I signed up for the trip. We took a ship on the Dunăre (Danube River) destined for Marea Neagră (Black Sea) and the major port of Constanța. Mamaia, the most famous and most popular beach resort on the Marea Neagră (Black Sea), was located not far south of Constanța. We decided to visit that resort and took the bus.

Maria at the Black Sea

Mamaia is situated on a beautiful stretch of beach with white sand and dark blue sparkling Marea Neagră (Black Sea) water. As we arrived, we went to separate cabins to change into our bathing suits. It was a hot day and the sun was burning the tourists' bodies. I was on the beach before Mary and felt right away the burning touch of the sun. Mary made her appearance before long and I forgot the burning sun. I remained with my eyes gazing on her. She was beautiful; her breasts were round, medium size; her waist slim, her hips nicely curved, and her legs slender. Her harmoniously proportioned body and her legs attracted the looks of the other people on the beach. All the men turned their heads; following her with their eyes as she walked toward me they were disappointed that she was with me. I was jealous of them; I wanted that sight to be visible just for me. Although I was proud of her beauty, at the same time, I was uneasy and blushed, to see her almost naked. She felt my excitement and asked me what had happened? I told her that her beauty bewildered me and that I wanted to be just with her. She smiled happily and suddenly kissed me. Then she ran to the edge of the sea and plunged into the water. I followed her and caught her. We embraced and I returned her kiss. We swam for a while. The water was cold and she started to shiver. So she exited the sea.

"It's beautiful here. I love it," she cried out loud as she spun with open arms.

I was still in the water when she started to run up the beach calling to me to catch her. I was happy and felt that my heart had been pierced by a beam of ecstasy. She was far ahead of me so I had to run fast to catch her. She changed direction many times and ran around people who were stretching themselves out on the sand. I finally reached her and held her tightly in my arms. We were exhausted and we lay down, gazing into each other's eyes, searching for our future. She caressed my ears gently. She knew that I loved it very much. I saw in her eyes a desire to belong to me, and I hoped that she discovered in my own eyes the same desire. The sun was burning our bodies as we burned inside with the desire to unite. The beach was crowded so our desire couldn't be immediately fulfilled. It had to be postponed for another such beautiful, spontaneous moment.

Absorbed in our dreams we didn't notice that the sun was setting and that fewer and fewer people were on the beach. We had to catch the boat in time to get back to Bucharest so we rushed to the showers, dried our bodies with our towels, and quickly dressed. We missed the bus to Constanța, so we posted ourselves on the road to hitchhike. We were lucky that one of the supply cars stopped and picked us up. We barely arrived in time for the boat's departure. It was a memorable, exciting and wonderful Sunday. It consolidated our relationship, driving us further on an infinite road of exploring each other.

In the past, I had courted many beautiful girls, but I was like an uncertain child, lost in a wonderland of choices. I was always unable to settle down with one certain girl for unexplainable reasons. This time everything stopped for me abruptly. Here she was, the perfect beauty of my choice. Again, unexplainable, yet, it was clear for me that she was the one with whom I wanted to spend my entire life. She was the kind of woman among so many in the world that appears only once in a lifetime. How good it was to see her, to like her, and to admire her. I was madly in love. She could move her ears without moving the rest of her face. I loved everything about her, her legs, her eyes, her eyebrows, her tender sensual lips, and particularly her wonderful character. Nature had just carved her out for me and ornamented her with all the wonderful qualities that made her unique.

My dates with Mary were no longer a secret. Some of the dancers from the company admired us but some were envious that I had succeeded in dating her. We enjoyed being together. We ate in the same canteen and went to movies during our free time. I played tennis at the M.A.I. sports center and she accompanied me, watching the games, and gathering the tennis balls for me.

One day after dating Mary for approximately two month, I accompanied her home after rehearsals. As usual, I hugged her and kissed her. Every time I kissed her, I fell more in love with her and asked her for another date the next day.

"Are you in a hurry?" she asked me with her singing voice. I sat there too astonished to answer. She looked in my eyes, and I saw her burning desire to be alone with me, which echoed my desire to be alone with her. It was the same penetrating glance that we had exchanged on the beach.

"No, I am not in a hurry; I can stay with you forever." I finally hummed.

"Then come up to the apartment and have dinner with me," she whispered.

I accepted her invitation and we went up to her sister's apartment. We had a long kiss in the ascending elevator, not noticing that it had stopped, and we forgot to open the elevator doors. Our minds were occupied by the effect of our lips. The elevator started to descend, being called by somebody else. We exited as another two people made their way into the elevator. We waited for the elevator to descend and took it up again. This time we were alert and opened the door at the third floor.

Mary's sister was not yet home from work. As we entered the apartment and got rid of our rehearsal bags, we forgot about dinner. We both knew that we were dying to be alone. We both knew from the time at the beach that we wanted to belong to each other. We both knew that we were in love with each other. We both knew that nothing in the world could stop us now, to unite our bodies and souls forever. The words were not necessary; it was the feeling of her hands around my neck, her offering her lips to me. I hugged her and started to kiss her. I was excited and teased her sensual lips. She was excited, too, and responded boldly. We both started to breathe harder. We kissed and kissed a long time. After a while, we broke up the kisses. We lay down on the floor and I helped her take off her blouse, shirt, and pants. She stood completely naked; then she lay down on the floor. I devoured her beauty, letting my eyes explore her form.

I was familiar with her beautiful smiling face. I had watched and admired her gracious body, either covered by pink tights and a black leotard and skirt during the rehearsals or on the beach in her bathing suit. Seeing her naked body, I was dazzled by the sight. It was far beyond my imagination. I glued my eyes on her. Her body was a proportionally beautiful one. It was the right moment to belong to each other. I was excited and kneeled down near her. I caressed her face and kissed her passionately. I felt her breath hot and as fast as mine was. We were both out of control. I was consumed by longing for her. She took my face and pulled it down with both her hands. She kissed me with passion and I responded to her kisses. I felt that her pleasure touched the limits of her sexuality. I caressed her face and hair; she hugged me tightly to her, kissing me all over my face. Then I sensed that the pleasure gave way in her body and in my body, followed by a powerful tension release. We remained a long time in an embrace; then I kissed her closed eyes, cheeks and mouth. She opened her eyes and I saw her happiness sparkling in them. Mary had given her body and soul to me. A tremendous feeling of joy and happiness enveloped me. Mary taught me how beautiful life is.

We were not married yet, but our silent commitment of love to each other for better or worse overwhelmed my mind and my body. I felt that her love for me was genuine and that she had surrendered her soul and body to me forever. I had done the same. I felt that we earned complete trust in each other, which I believe is the most valuable thing in life. We became a unity of flesh and soul in a silent oath, an unwritten traditional timeless law of harmony and commitment. I felt that I had kidnapped a lovely woman from the world, and I would never release her for any amount of ransom. For my crime, fate sentenced me to be together with her for life. It was a sentence that I would enjoy all my life. We dressed and sat on the couch; I put my arm around her shoulders as she laid her head on my chest. We remained a long time in that position, dreaming of our future until the arrival of her sister and brother-in-law disturbed us.

From this time on, we wanted to be together all the time. So we started to look for a room to rent. The dwellings at that time in Romania were distributed only by the state through their housing administration, and there was a shortage of houses and apartments. The M.A.I. also had a housing distribution center. We knew that there was a long waiting period and married people or high-ranking officers had priority, but we applied anyway. We made the application separately because we were not married.

Both Mary and I drained our brains, trying to find a solution. I finally asked her if she would move in with me at my brother's place. With no hesitation her answer was a strong "Yes." I plucked up my courage and approached my brother. I told him about my relationship with Mary. I told him what a nice girl she was and asked him if it were possible for Mary to move in with me until we could get an apartment. I was pleased when he answered, "Yes" and told me that he was glad that I had found a nice girl. It was Mary's birthday and we celebrated this event in a restaurant. We clinked our glasses to toast her health and our hope for a bright future. Then we went to our new residence. The room was very small, but our hearts were big, pumping with joy and happiness that we were together.

In the fall of 1949 we went on our first major tour to the city of Ocna in the Moldova province. There was a huge military drill by the M.A.I. military units. In Ocna there was a huge military camp with a capacity of 5,000 soldiers. The soldiers, the non-commissioned officers and the high-ranking officers loved our performances. Our success resounded throughout the countryside and in Bucharest. As a result, in 1950, we were selected to represent the country in Hungary as part of a 10-day cultural exchange.

Our tour touched many cities such as Budapest, Miscolt, Györ, and the Margit Island on the Danube River not far from the center of Budapest. Our residence was in a five-star hotel on the island. We performed in a huge, outside theatre on the Island and in Budapest, traveling back and forth by boat. Budapest, the capital of Hungary, is a beautiful city, situated on both sides of the Danube. We visited Lake Balaton and the famous wineries situated on the shore of the lake. We were treated with different kinds of wines but I was careful not to get drunk. It was a beautiful tour; we were received very warmly and had many successes. It was the first time in my life that people asked for my autograph.

We traveled by train with sleeping cars and a restaurant car attached. We stayed two in each compartment. Unfortunately, I could neither stay with Mary in the same compartment, nor in the hotel room, but we spent our free time together. We watched when our colleagues went into the city and used that time to sneak in one of the empty compartments and make love. At some point during our splendid relationship, it came to our attention that members of the company were gossiping about our living together. Actually, we couldn't consider it gossip because it was the truth. We were denying it because we were not married.

We knew that our parents would oppose our marriage for religious reasons, but we knew that we had committed ourselves to each other for life. But we had to accept the fact that we couldn't continue our clandestine affair. It was a risky moment in our lives. The situation greatly inconvenienced us and became awkward and dangerous, so we had to give marriage serious thought. It was a moment of firm decision.

When we returned home from the tour, my brother gave me the good news that my father had won 40,000 lei in the state lottery. Happy my parents decided to move to Bucharest and asked me to find an apartment for them. I sent a letter to my parents informing them that I was fine and that I had applied for an apartment for all of us. I didn't write about my relationship with Mary since I knew that it would upset my mother. I wanted to tell her in person with the hope that she would understand. I planned to introduce Mary to her when they came to Bucharest. I hoped that she would like Mary as I did, and would not object to the fact that she was a Christian. Marriage between different religious backgrounds today in the second millennium is very common, but in the 1950's, it was an exception.

I was lucky again. The administration, under pressure from my company's director, assigned me an apartment with two bedrooms, a living room, kitchen, bath and two lavatories. The apartment was beautiful and it was situated in the center of the city on the street Calea Plevnei, No. 8. My parents sold all of their furniture in Timişoara and moved to the new apartment in Bucharest. Again my family was reunited in the same city.

Everybody was happy, but I was obsessed with the idea of how and when I should tell my mother about Mary. I always loved my mother from the bottom of my heart. I always felt that my mother's love was like a magnet. I could stay with her endlessly. I could talk to her about anything. She listened and found the right answers for me. She was gentle, affectionate, and caring for her family. A little smile on my mother's face was like sunshine, which gave me optimism and trust in my future life.

One day I came home tired after the rehearsal, when my mother came in from the kitchen I hugged her and she asked me if I was hungry. I inclined my head as a sign of yes. She returned to the kitchen and brought me some delicious chicken soup. She was moving in and out of the kitchen, serving the rest of the food, including the dessert. I was on the verge of telling her about Mary, but my tongue was hushed. I thanked her for the lunch and helped her clear the table. I couldn't stand it any more and plucked up my courage and bared my chest to her.

"Mom I have met a wonderful girl, and I love her. I am very happy and I want to marry her. I would like to introduce her to you." I saw on her face that I had taken her by surprise. Then she poured out her questions.

"Who is she? Where did you meet her?"

"Her name is Maria, but everybody calls her Mary. She is a dancer in the same company where I am."

"Is she a Jewish girl?"

I lowered my head and said, "No."

She was shocked and returned to the kitchen leaving me stunned, alone. It was clear that my mother was against my courting a girl who was not Jewish. I didn't follow her. I had known that because of her strong religious beliefs she would oppose it, but I was not prepared for her to react in such a way. I was discouraged that she couldn't understand me. I was sorry that by telling her I had hurt her feelings. For the moment I regretted that I had told her, but I really had no choice. I didn't want her to find out from some other source. I had to convince her that Mary was a unique, lovely person, and that she would bring into my life a lot of joy and happiness.

My mother felt that I had betrayed her faith. All her life she had tried to transfer her religious faith to her children as she had inherited it from her parents. She told me that I was young and that I had plenty of time to find a Jewish girl. I tried to explain that according to her religious beliefs, we are all God's children; love unites people and discrimination divides people.

I had followed my mother's advice all my life, except at that moment when my instincts told me that she was wrong. I had to act against her religious beliefs. Mary's father and stepmother opposed it also because they didn't want their daughter to be courted by a Jew. Even some of her colleagues had told her that. The ballet mistress advised her to cease the relationship with me for the same reason, but Mary confronted her, telling her not to meddle in other people's affairs.

"You should know that I am marrying a wonderful, handsome man and a very good dancer, and not an ethnic person," Mary told a stunned ballet mistress as she turned her back and left the room.

I didn't argue with my mother because I knew how strongly indoctrinated she was with her religious faith. I just told her that it was not the religion, nor the nationality, nor the nation that determines the character of a person. I believed that there were good and bad people all over the world in any religion, nation or nationality. I strongly expressed my feeling that Mary was one of the wonderful people. I was glad that Mary accepted me. The trusted commitment we had for each other meant more to us than anything else. We were happy and enjoyed our relationship with passion. We talked openly about any topic that concerned our lives. It didn't matter who was right or wrong; we just believed that it would work out in one way or another.

Marriage was and still is the result of fundamental forces of conformity. Church and state, hand-in-hand, have always strongly believed and tried to maintain strict conformity of the "moral" society in which we live. Mary and I had to get married because we lived in that world of conformity. But I was not convinced that signing a paper with witnesses in front of a religious or state representative was any guarantee of a long-lasting relationship. I believed that my everyday commitment to somebody with whom I have sexual relations, sleep, eat, play, dream, go to the movies, watch TV, and eventually work with was more important. That kind of commitment is an everyday act of faith that two previously unknown people make voluntarily. I believed and still do that self-commitment cannot be replaced by a contract.

We knew that a wedding normally had to be planned, prepared, people invited and a wedding dress, bought, etc. But this was not how it was with us. I was in a complicated labyrinth and had to struggle to find a way out. The pressure of the situation was a combination of antagonism from our parents, gossip by our peers about our living together without being married, and the threat from the company's administration to discover us and fire us. I watched the days passing on my calendar. I lost any sense of time and didn't even know what day it was. Our life was too unpredictable. No more waiting, I said to myself. Let's do it, whatever the outcome.

For her birthday, I asked my good friend Şany, who had been a jeweler before becoming a dancer, to make Mary a gold chain and a gold medallion in which I could insert my picture. At the same time I told him that I intended to marry her, and I needed two modest gold, wedding rings. He asked me when the rings had to be ready. I told him very soon and that I would appreciate his not divulging my intention.

During one of the rehearsals, Mary and I were at the practice bar performing everyday classical ballet exercises. Mary was in front of me doing the same thing. She was concentrating deeply on her work. My mind was elsewhere, bothered about my mother's religious conviction that I should not marry a Christian girl and her parents' racial attitude towards me. I had to make a radical decision to end this turmoil in my head. I thought that maybe if we got married our parents would accept us, if not right away, then maybe later.

"Don't you think that it's time we got married?" I whispered to Mary, as we continued our barre exercises.

She turned her head to look into my eyes and saw my smiling face radiating with happiness.

"It's fine with me," she said and gave me a brisk kiss on my lips. "When?" she said.

I took her by the hand and told her the time was now, she followed me to the ballet mistress and the whole class stopped. I told the ballet mistress that we both had to leave to take care of an emergency. The ballet mistress and the whole class stood dumfounded not knowing what was going on. I told Mary go dress quickly and I'd meet her in the hall.

"I don't have a wedding dress, we didn't invite anybody, and we are not prepared." I heard her singing voice clink with concern, as we exited from the dance studio and went to the streetcar.

"I don't have a tuxedo, either, and, sweetie, we don't have a choice. Our parents are against our marriage, society requires us to unite legally, we love each other, and I don't want to continue going home alone without you. I want to be with you all the time. We have to compromise with society and obey the rules. Let's also hope that our parents will later compromise, being confronted with a *fait accompli.*

The clerk who did the registration asked who the witnesses were. We didn't have any witnesses. Since I hadn't thought about this important item, we asked the clerk if he could find witnesses for us. He told us that anybody could be a witness. He suggested that we could ask the two beggars in front of the town hall to be our witnesses and reward them with a good tip. It was a wonderful idea; they accepted. We didn't know their names, and when they were signing the register, I was kissing Mary and didn't care about their names. The wedding ceremony took place on June 19, 1950, four days after her birthday.

After the ceremony, we returned to the company and found them already rehearsing the dances. We changed our clothes again and waited for a break to tell our colleagues the news of our marriage. Mary told the women and I told the men and everybody congratulated us. Even the ballet mistress, who was against our relationship, couldn't resist the joyous atmosphere and congratulated us as well.

My instincts worked for us again. Being already married, my mother wouldn't turn her back on us. When we first entered the house together and I introduced Mary as my wife, my mother was astonished and at the same time not unhappy to meet her. My mother's love for her child was genuine; she hugged and kissed me saying the Jewish blessing "Mazeltov." Though somewhat grudgingly, she welcomed Mary into our home, hugging and kissing her. They instantly liked each other. She told me that she liked Mary and would pray to God to ask for me to be forgiven. Mary's parents also gave us their blessing. Her sister, Anna, was also happy. She had never objected or tried to stop Mary from marrying me.

To our happiness was added another great event. At the end of the year 1950, the M.A.I. ordered a reorganization of the whole structure of the company on the military system. At the same time, it was announced that contracts for non-commissioned officers were void. We were told that we had to sign new contracts if we wanted to stay in the army, or else we could choose to become civilians. Indeed, it was a fortuitous event, and it happened just as I had told Eugen it would when we initially signed.

Our unanimous decision, Mary, our parents and I, was to not sign. The director of the company was shocked and disappointed over my decision. All the other non-commissioned officers in the company signed except Eugen and me. Then, after two days, the commander informed us that we would be hired back, as civilians.

Eugen was very happy that he had finally got rid of his military uniform and so were Mary and I. He got married in 1951 with a lovely girl, Clary from Timişoara. Mary and I, and Vesa Bujor, another friend of ours, were witnesses at their wedding. He past away in 2002 his wife and son Gaby still live in Romania, in Bucharest. They always welcome me warmly on my visits to Romania.

But the most important thing was that I was together with Mary. I was happy that my mother accepted Mary into our apartment. Mary respected all my mother's religious customs and never tried to influence her otherwise. My mother gradually felt very close to Mary. Her warm and genteel character convinced my mother that she was a wonderful person. Mary loved my mother dearly and hugged her every time when she left or returned home.

Every morning, it took us about thirty minutes to travel to the new location of the company in the district of the Linden-tree. The building was a former school. The stairs and the front entrance hall, constructed in white marble, were impressive. The ladies' dressing room and the office of the artistic director were on the first floor. All the administrative offices, including that of the commander, were on the second floor. The rooms for the choir, the orchestra, and additional administration offices were on the lower level. The entrance to the dance studio was from the first floor hall. The studio was a well-equipped, huge gym. The studio had a mini stage and the gentlemen's dressing room. On the east sidewall, there were rib bars, which we used for a ballet barre and other purposes. On top of the rib bars was the kind of basket used for basketball games. On the right side of the studio entrance in the corner was the shower room. The women and men alternated the order of who would be first to take showers. We always had to yell to each other, "Are you ready?" The west side of the studio's wall had big windows and doors. In summertime we enjoyed opening the doors and spending our breaks on a wide terrace, which led to a huge courtyard.

I was thankful for my destiny. I couldn't have asked for more happiness than a man can endure and yet I had it. I was getting more than my share, living with Mary. We never had a honeymoon, but all the days that followed after our marriage were like a never-ending honeymoon. We lived always in the present, and we enjoyed every moment as a new beginning.

We were not hiding our love any more. At every opportunity during rehearsals we hugged and kissed each other and held hands. The dancers became accustomed to it and nicknamed us "the doves." Not everybody, however, approved of our openness.

In one general meeting, the company's political deputy lectured us about the history of the Romanian Communist Party. We were tired from rehearsals and bored from the lecture. Mary leaned her head on my shoulder. Mary and I were sitting in the first row, directly in front of the lecturer, holding hands, a natural thing for us to do. The next day the company's communist organization secretary called me into his office. Angrily and with a harsh tone, he scolded me for so-called "immoral" behavior. I couldn't believe it. I was afraid to answer. Being a member of the communist party, I could not offer a contradictory opinion. Mary, who was not a member, and next day told the party secretary that we love each other and that this was a natural expression of our feeling. She didn't think that it was improper behavior.

"The doves"

At the next party meeting, the secretary presented my "wrong behavior" case and I was strongly criticized by some of the more zealous members of the organization. I wanted to express my opinion but I remained silent, frightened of the consequences that could follow. The communist organization expected a self-criticism from me for my so-called bad behavior, but I wouldn't do it. As a result I was given, a warning regarding my future conduct.

I left the meeting with a bitter taste in my mouth because of the organizations attempt to impose their power on my private life. Maria was outraged and told me to withdraw from the party. I told her that if I did, they would throw me out of the company.

After rehearsals, I would remain alone in the studio, perfecting my technique, practicing alone for hours, doing *chaines, a la seconds,* and jumps in a circle. My *pirouettes* improved in quality and quantity. I was able to do four *pirouettes* consistently and sometimes six or seven. Mary often joined me and we would observe and correct each other. We were always the last to leave the studio and we felt that we were improving every day. These extra rehearsals gave us so much satisfaction.

One day when Mary and I were alone in the studio, I showered first and waited for her in the marble hall. She came out of the dressing room carrying the bag with her rehearsal clothes. She came close to me, lowered her bag to the floor, and put her arms around my neck. Her eyes were gazing with love into my eyes like never before. I thought that I would melt with pleasure. She kissed me with passion and her singing voice touched my heart.

"Tati scump (Dear Tati) I am pregnant."

I covered Mary's face with kisses and picked her up in my arms as if she were in a basket and whirled around the hall with her. I had the feeling that I was flying, lost in a world of ecstasy. She held me tightly with her arms around my neck and her head on my chest; we both had a good, happy

57

laugh. We were so thrilled that we didn't notice that some people had crossed the hall and were watching us with curiosity. They couldn't possibly guess the reason for our sudden happiness. I lowered her from my arms; she took her bag, I put my right arm round her waist, she lowered her head onto my shoulder, and we left the building.

I had an unusual feeling. I don't know how to describe that feeling. My heart was throbbing with excitement as never before. Maybe the thought that the dearest person in my life was going to bear my child or the thought that I was going to be a father ignited that feeling. Her face was also radiant with joy. She was going to be a mother. At home, my parents were overwhelmed by the news. In her spare time, Mary began preparing things for the child. My mother took care of her and helped her have as comfortable a pregnancy as possible.

The next day at rehearsal, Mary shared the news with the women and with the ballet mistress; I passed the news to the men. They all congratulated us, but the ballet mistress was concerned that she would lose a good dancer for a while. I was proud, "too big for my britches." I shared our news with my brother. He seldom came to visit us, but, on this occasion, he came to congratulate her.

The company went on many tours in various cities, such as Timişoara, Craiova, Ploieşti, Braşov, Cluj, Satu-Mare, Sighetul Marmaţiei, Oradea, etc. Mary continued to dance into her seventh month of pregnancy. Then, during the summer of 1951, the company went on a four-week tour through the whole province of Moldova, and Mary stayed home expecting the baby. Lonely and home sick, I longed for Mary every minute, day and night. The boys played cards or chess or soccer; I joined them to pass the time.

In the middle of the tour, while playing soccer on a field near the awaiting train, I was summoned by the commander of the company who told me the wonderful news: I had a son. He congratulated me and informed me that Mary and the child were doing fine. The news spread fast and on my way back to my compartment I was stopped and congratulated by the members of the company including Eugen. I ran to the post office and sent a telegram to Mary.

Later, at lunchtime I went to the dining car. Cheers, applause, and ovations greeted me. The restaurant was already filled, but Eugen had reserved a place for me near him. I ordered beer for everybody and clinked glasses with each person. All the women and the men from the dance department formed a line. One by one, they came to my table. I stood up and welcomed each one. I had to take at least one sip with each person. Some of the men urged me to empty my glass. Without my knowledge, Eugen ordered rum and poured it in my glass with beer. I started to feel a little dizzy from sipping so much beer, so I sat down. But Eugen insisted on drinking with me, again. I drank it with pleasure, without knowing that in my glass was a dangerous mixture. The drink had a fast and powerful effect on me. I was not used to drinking so much and especially not beer mixed with rum. My eyes became blurred and my vision doubled then tripled and then many, many more images, and the images went wild around the dancers and the restaurant and me whirling faster and faster until I lost consciousness. I woke up the next day in my compartment, not understanding what had happened to me. My compartment mate informed me that I had collapsed in the dining car, and the dancers had picked me up and brought me to this compartment.

Finally home, Mary welcomed me at the railroad station with our son in her arms. He was beautiful and healthy. Mary told me that the delivery had gone well and she felt fine. However, when she elaborated, she admitted that she hadn't expected to have such a wrenching pain, and that a man could not imagine how much effort and sweat a woman goes through to deliver a child. I was impressed. Her description of the delivery created in me a feeling of great admiration for her and for all the women in the world who give birth. In spite of the pain of the childbirth, she was proud and happy with our son. I thanked her, admired her, and kissed her. We named our son Eugen after my brother who had died during the Second World War. Later, we nicknamed him Gene or Genuț.

Mary had plenty of milk to nurse him. From other people's experience and from my mother's advice, we knew that nursing a newborn child should go on as long as possible. Mary was concerned about when she would be able to return to dancing and worried about how to continue Gene's nursing at the same time. She missed the daily rehearsals and the performances. She loved Gene, but she was eager to resume her dance activity. She started to do some very easy *pliés* and *battement tendu* at home in the living room. Her desire to resume dancing was over-shadowed by her fear that she would never again be able to devote her entire time to dance. She was worried that the pregnancy and delivery had lessen her ability to recover her former technical proficiency, that she would never be able to catch up or to keep up with the technical level of her colleagues.

Soon Mary started dancing, but with a reduced schedule. She started the ballet classes with a slow, careful approach. Her calves, thighs, hamstrings and the rest of the body were stiff, and she had the feeling that her muscles just refused to work. I encouraged her and helped her restore her confidence, and soon her face reflected hope. She resumed her work habits with more and more passion.

Mary was a wonderful, caring mother. She devoted all her free time to ensure the healthy, steady growth of our child. I helped her with my limited skills, washing the swaddling clothes and doing exercises with Gene after his bath. I was worried that Mary would not be able to handle the duties of both dancing and nursing, but she was determined to do battle and not to quit. Gradually, renewed confidence in her gave her a healing sense of peace, and she understood that what she needed was to trust in her potential. No day went by without her feeling that she had conquered a new space in her limber body. Each day she acquired more confidence in herself. Our love for each other was greater than ever. Her love for Gene gave her endless energy and soon she was able to express real emotion in her dance technique--better than ever.

In spite of an abbreviated rehearsal schedule, Gene's nursing still became a problem. The doctor recommended buying a cupping glass and said that Mary should draw out the milk from her breast and pour it into a special sucking bottle before leaving for work. It was a slow and exhausting procedure. The extracted milk was then held in the refrigerator. Our refrigerator was not electric, and my father had to be sure to buy the necessary ice for it. My mother took care to nurse Genuţ with that bottle. On the night of a performance, Mary did this operation in her dressing room. All her colleagues admired her. This time my father acted as express courier transporting the bottle from the theatre to our home while my mother acted as Genuţ's nurse.

We bought a perambulator and my father was in charge of taking Gene for a walk in the nearby Cişmigiu Park. We bought a camera and took a lot of pictures of him. After the nursing period, my mother helped prepare the food as indicated by Mary. This was a great help, especially when we had to leave the city for our routine tours. My mother became Gene's second mother. He was visibly growing and had started to walk. Sometimes Mary took him to rehearsals; her colleagues adored him. We were happy that we had our wonderful child and that my parents could help us, but we realized how difficult it was to raise a child with our working conditions. We were concerned about our child's well being. The tours of the company, the rehearsals and the performances were more and more often as Mary resumed our everyday rehearsal routine. She took her place in the old choreographies and was assigned new ones. I was given the opportunity to conduct rehearsals when the ballet mistress had responsibilities elsewhere.

THE RUSSIAN COUNSELOR

In Romania, the USSR continued to have a strong grip on political and economic affairs as well as cultural and educational activities. They sent advisers for ballet and dance such as Ivan Vasilievich Kurilov from Moscow. His mission was to transfer to Romania the experience and traditions of the famous Russian ballet school.

He was asked to choreograph a ballet for the Teatru de Operă și Balet (Romanian Theatre of the Opera and Ballet). He proposed the ballet *Macul Roşu* (*The Red Poppy*) by the composer Reinhold Glière. This ballet required many male dancers and the ballet department from the opera didn't have enough. Kurilov proposed selecting male dancers by auditioning men from all the companies in Bucharest.

From our company another man and I were selected. I was glad that Kurilov selected me, because it was a chance to dance in a full-length ballet and later to become a member of the opera ballet. But it didn't happen as I had hoped. I waited to be called to the rehearsal for the *Red Poppy Ballet* but the call never came. I contacted the opera and they told me that the rehearsals were already in progress and that my name was on their list of selected dancers, but the M.A.I. Artistic Ensemble leadership had refused to release me.

Frustrated and disappointed, I related my case to the chief of the dance department, who brought it to the attention of the artistic director. The artistic director didn't know either and had to ask the commander of the company.

After many days of helpless waiting, I was finally told to report to the commander. He offered me a seat and told me that it had come to his attention that I was displeased with the company's decision not to release me to the opera.

"Yes, I am very disappointed and I want to find out the reason. I am asking to be released immediately."

"We decided not to release you because the artistic director and I think that you deserve more he said."

"I don't understand what you are saying? What can be better than to be a dancer at the opera? This is a unique lifetime opportunity, and I want to be a member of the opera ballet."

"We need you here, and we think that our idea regarding your future is better. We have decided to send you to study ballet in USSR, in Moscow or in Leningrad."

My mouth was agape with surprise because I didn't know what to say.

This is just a pretext to derail me from going to the opera, and, on the other hand, I am married. I have a beautiful wife and a child. How can I be apart from them? My instincts were telling me.

Then, aloud, I said, "Comrade commander, it is an exciting proposal, but I have to consult my wife. She was happy for me when I was selected for the *Red Poppy Ballet,* You shouldn't have made a decision before consulting me. If your proposal for any reason does not work out, I have been deprived of a lifetime opportunity to dance at the opera."

He reaffirmed that the proposal was very serious but he could not order me to accept it. He reminded me, however, that I was a member of the Communist Party and I should consider their proposal as an assignment from the party.

Mary was as surprised as I was and agreed with me that this was just a pretext to stop me from going to the opera. In addition, her analysis of that proposal was more accurate than mine. She put her arms around my neck and kissed me.

"You know very well how much I love you and that I will do anything for you," she said. "I will not stop you from going to the USSR, I would be happy for you. But I think that the commander lied to you. He wouldn't have called you in if you had not asked all those upper-echelon people for an explanation. I think this trip to Russia is a gimmick."

I agreed with Mary's assessment and realized that a refusal to follow the party's orders was a serious offence and could endanger my future career. By this time I had lost the opportunity to go to the opera anyway. We decided that I should accept the commander's proposal.

He was pleased and sent me to the personnel officer to make application. For us, the matter was closed, and we didn't pay attention to the gossip that surrounded us. Some of my colleagues even came to congratulate me and wished me good luck. I smiled at them and told them that it would never happen.

Mary and I were right. With the date to leave for USSR fast approaching, I was not informed about the departure. Two day's prior to the scheduled departure, I was called by the personnel office and told that I had been too late with my application. There were too many candidates who had submitted applications long before me and they had priority. The dancers from the company expressed their regrets. They never knew the truth.

Maestro Kurilov, simultaneous with his work at the opera, accepted the task of working with our company. He taught ballet and character classes and examined the dancers closely. He considered some of the dancers not up to his professional standard and asked the dance department chief to re-audition the dancers in order to weed out the non-qualified ones. As a result about five or six dancers were given other jobs and replaced by dancers who had been on the waiting list from prior auditions.

Satisfied with the new look of the department, Maestro Kurilov choreographed two dances, a Ukrainian and a character *Pas de Deux*. He created a solo part for me in the Ukrainian dance and selected me for the character *Pas de Deux*. Later he asked me to teach his classes when he was not available, and he made me his assistant.

My solo part in the Ukrainian dance was a combination of both high jumps, *pirouettes*, and a technical jump executed in a circle, called the

barrel. The last was very difficult for me, but when Kurilov demonstrated the movement, it looked easy. When I tried to do it, I couldn't. After many tries and his corrections, I finally succeeded in doing it once, but the movement required consecutive repetition in a circle. It was springtime and the premiere for the Ukrainian dance was

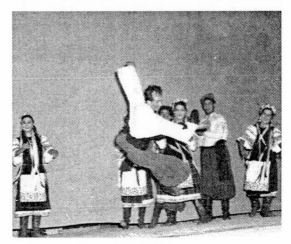

The barrel

scheduled for the fall season. Maestro Kurilov asked me every day how the barrel was going and I had to demonstrate it. He was pleased with my progress. He gave me the necessary corrections and encouraged me to continue practicing. I realized that I had to work very hard to master it, but I was not discouraged. I made a pledge to him that by the premiere, I would be able to do a perfect circle.

The cultural minister annually organized a nation-wide dance competition for amateur Romanian dance groups. Mary and I loved to go to watch the gala performance of the best groups selected. Two groups from Transylvania impressed me: one group presented a couple dance from the Someş region and another group presented a girls' dance from Căpîlna. I was enchanted by the girls' dance from Căpîlna and from the day that I saw the girls from Căpîlna on stage, their image was imprinted in my mind. It developed within me a desire that I had never felt before. Under the spur of the moment, I felt that I would like to choreograph a dance about the girls from Căpîlna. I felt that I had creative potential for choreography, but I had to postpone my desire. It was not possible at that time because I was just a rehearsal director's assistant and had not yet been promoted to choreographer. But I suggested to the chief of the dance department that she should choreograph a dance exploring the rich, original folklore material from these dances. The suggestion was accepted but the chief of the dance department chose only the dance from the Someş region.

For the dance from the Someş region, a group was formed to go to the village of Sălcuţa in order to collect information about the steps. One member of that group was a folklore specialist Ion Popescu Judeţ whose purpose in the group was to write down the dances, step by step. I was also included in that group because of my ability to learn dance steps very quickly.

We had to learn three dances, *Dea Lungul, Invîrtita,* both couple dances, and the *Bărbuncul,* a dance for men only. We started with the *Bărbuncul;* a very technical dance with twisting leg movements and palm hits on the boots. The dancer designated to teach us was Ion Cîmpeanu. He impressed me very much with his limber body incredible technique, fast rhythmical movements and perfect musicality. He was able to kick his leg as high as any classical dancer. He could sharply slap his boots with his palm while he danced a variety of steps. I asked him if he would like to come to Bucharest and become a member of the company. His answer was yes. He started to teach me the steps; I had good technique, too, and a keen kinetic memory. He was astonished to see how fast I caught on. Judeţ, the folklore specialist, was dismayed that he was not able to keep up with us with his dance notation.

After a while, we took a break. I excused myself, and when I returned to continue learning the other dances, I was surprised that Ion was unwilling to show me any more steps. I asked him why. He answered that he was tired, so I said that we should rest, and continue in the afternoon. But in the afternoon, he refused, again, on the grounds that he was not feeling well. I was disappointed that I couldn't learn more. We returned to Bucharest reporting what had happened and recommended that Ion Cîmpeanu be hired. Being permanently a member of the company, he would be at the disposal of the choreographer to teach the necessary steps for the dance. Ion Cîmpeanu was indeed hired and became a well-respected, professional dancer. Later, as Ion and I were drinking a glass of wine, Ion confessed to me the real reason why he had refused to show me more steps. According to Ion, Judeţ had told him that I was a clever Jew; and, if Ion taught me all the steps now, I would never invite him to Bucharest. Ironically, I did just the opposite.

The company asked Maestro Kurilov to choreograph a dance based on Ion Cîmpeanu's dance material. Ion was an inexhaustible supplier of dance steps for the choreographer. Maestro Kurilov, with his spontaneous sense of fantasy, created delightful moments, sometimes with comic inserts, which resulted in an excellent choreography. The dance entitled *Nunta de pe Someş (The Wedding from Someş)* was orchestrated by Viorel Doboş and well received.

Maestro Kurilov contributed greatly to the development of dance in Romania. The dancers enjoyed working with him because he was always in a good mood. He liked, from time to time, to take a sip of beer from the mug that was at his disposal on the piano. His influence on our dance department was felt many years after he left. We all missed him. After Maestro Kurilov's return to his homeland, however, the chief of the dance department took credit for Kurilov's dance. The dancers and I wondered how such a thing could be possible. It was a deliberate violation of the choreographer's copyrights. Ironically, I later experienced that kind of injustice myself.

DIFFICULT TIMES

The company's tours in Romania increased in number and length. We touched almost every major city. Each tour broke our hearts because it was impossible to take Gene with us. My dear parents took care of him, we worried about leaving him for long periods of time and we missed him more every time. Returning from a tour that lasted sometimes three or four weeks, we always found that he had changed. By the time he reached the age of three, we found that he had become a charming little boy.

Our happiness was also disturbed by my father's illness. He complained of severe pain in his stomach. The harsh life in the labor camp had taken its toll. The diagnosis was cancer and surgery was recommended. After surgery he recovered temporarily, but soon he was gone. He died on February 26, 1953 at the age of 59. He had changed a lot after coming to Bucharest. He had given up gambling and dedicated his life to his family. He loved Gene and had strolled with him every day in Cişmigiu Park. We missed him very much.

The success of the company's performances in Bucharest and throughout the country impressed the country's cultural leadership. As a result, the company was sent to perform in Bulgaria. Mary was in a difficult position; she was pregnant again because contraceptive pills were not available. The chief of the dance department told Mary that she could not miss the tour and advised her to have an abortion. We took her advice seriously.

We traveled to Bulgaria on November 15, 1953 and performed in almost all the major cities: Sofia, Vratsa, Plovdiv, Dimitrovgrad, Khaskovo, Stara-Zagora, Sliven, and Stalin (Varna today). We returned home on December 9, 1953. This was the first time Mary had traveled in Bulgaria. I had been there before in 1948 with the *Flacăra* Artistic Company. For us it was like another honeymoon. We were the only married couple in the company, so we had our own compartment in the train and a separate room in the hotel. That made us happy.

In Sofia, dancers from the Bulgarian Dance Company came back stage after the performance to congratulate me for my solo in the Ukrainian and Military dances. The Bulgarians gave us a lot of beautiful presents. We didn't have a lot of money, but together we had enough to buy Gene a sheepskin coat.

Genuţ in sheepskin

Bucharest received us dressed in

white with a cover of freshly fallen snow. The snow was glittering, reflecting the bright shining sun. We didn't have sunglasses, and it was difficult to view the sheer beauty of it. Genuţ was happy to see us and wanted us to play with him in the snow to make a beautiful snowman. We dressed Genuţ in the new sheepskin coat bought in Bulgaria and went out. We taught him how to make and throw a snowball, and, in no time, he bombarded us non-stop. How happy we all were.

■■■

It was in a Sunday morning when we were both at home. Mary was busy in the kitchen learning how to cook something special, from my mother and I was occupied with sweeping and dusting the rooms. Genuţ liked the snow very much and wanted to go outside and play with other children and we let him go outside alone. After a while we heard a knock on the door. We wondered who that could be because usually people who came to our apartment used the doorbell. I opened the door and saw Genuţ sobbing. I pick him up in my arms and asked him what happened? He continued to sob and didn't answer. I called Mary from the kitchen and she repeated the question. I saw on his face that he was scared to death. His sobbing became more and more intense. I put him down and Mary wiped his tears and his runny nose with a handkerchief. She told him, don't cry, everything will be fine; but his sobbing didn't stop. We continued to prod him.

"Did you have a fight with the other children?"

He answered no with his head movement.

"Did somebody else hit you?"

He gave the same negative response.

It took a while until he stopped sobbing and mumbled something that we couldn't understand.

"Dear Genuţ, my dearest, please speak louder."

"I fell in the basement," he finally blurted out.

We were perplexed and asked where and in what basement. Let's go; you show us the place. We took him by the hands and he led the way. Indeed, he led us to the basement of our apartment building and showed us the place. On the basement floor was the wet, bent pasteboard and snow. He had fallen through the skylight into the basement.

In the small courtyard of the apartment building was a flat skylight, which could be opened when it was necessary to throw fire logs into the basement. In the summer, when one of our neighbors threw their logs into the basement, the skylight had been broken and temporarily covered with a pasteboard. The landlord, who was in fact the Romanian state, neglected to replace the broken skylight. The snow covered the skylight and Genuţ couldn't see it. The snow soaked the pasteboard, and when Genuţ stepped on it, the pasteboard gave way and Genuţ fell through it into the basement.

We were stunned; we couldn't believe that he had fallen ten feet. I asked him if he was O.K., if he felt any pain. He pointed with his hand to his left hip. We understood that he had fallen on his buttocks and had hurt his hip. Probably the sheepskin coat softened the blow so we were lucky. It could have been worse or even fatal. We pledged never to let him play alone, again. In the following days, weeks and months, we watched him closely. He didn't complain any more about his hip and we didn't observe any other signs of damage from his accident.

In the summer of that same year, the kindergarten organized a one-month camp. My parents, Mary and I were reluctant to let him go. The teacher from the kindergarten convinced us that it would be to Gene's benefit to experience community life with other children. Indeed he enjoyed it very much. He learned new skills, and made friends. The day when he returned from camp we noticed that he had grown taller, but, at the same time, he was limping with his left leg. We asked the teacher who was in charge of the camp what had happened, why Gene was limping. The teacher informed us that she had noticed the limping during the last week of camp. He was fine until then and had played with energy and joy together with his friends. We asked Gene what had happened.

"Do you have pain when you limp?"

"Yes."

Our thoughts went back to his accident in the basement. Maybe the impact with the ground weakened his joint and as he grew, the ligaments or the hipbone from his left leg didn't developed as strongly as the right leg. We took him to the doctor right away. He examined Gene, but he couldn't establish a diagnosis until he saw the results of the x-rays. We were very anxious, and the hours and the days seemed to never pass. Our waiting ended and the ordeal started.

The doctor was right. The hipbone on the left side showed signs of decalcification, and for that reason it hadn't grown as strong as the right side. He suggested putting his left hip and leg into a gypsum cast to avoid further decalcification of the damaged hip and prescribed a calcium supplement. If it didn't heal, then it would be necessary to have surgery to insert a metal stem to equalize the other hip. We were totally devastated. We didn't know what to say and, at first, accepted his verdict. Then we decided to have a second opinion. The result was the same. Our little darling was put into a gypsum cast and, for three months, lost his freedom to walk, run and play with the neighborhood children. All he could do was lie on a blanket on the floor. My parents played with him and we bought different toys and sets of games.

After rehearsals, Mary and I, alternating, shared our free time with him. We bought a set of cards with the alphabet and numbers. The cards were colorful and had pictures showing animals or things that matched one of the letters or numbers. Giving him all that attention pleased him. We wondered and admired his patience. He never complained or

Mary on the floor with Gene

even asked when the cast would be taken off. He acted as if everything was as it should be. We, on the other hand, were very anxious to get rid of the cast and to find out the results.

The cast was taken off, and the new x-rays showed no changes in his left hip. The doctor repeated that it was necessary to proceed with the surgery, to insert a metal stem. This time we consulted many doctors, but the answer was always the same.

In the meantime, Gene had developed some kind of convulsion, often losing consciousness. We went to our regular doctor who concluded that Gene had epilepsy. We repeated our pilgrimage to other doctors and they all told us what we didn't want to hear. We were in a panic that he was really epileptic. I called my brother and asked him for help. I knew that as a high-level Communist Party activist, he and his family had access to the best doctors of the party's policlinic and hospital.

My brother highly recommended an internationally recognized doctor named Piți Vasiliu, who had treated my brother's son. He was a doctor who participated in international medical conferences and was familiar with the latest achievements in the medical field. My brother succeeded in arranging an appointment with the doctor.

Dr. Vasiliu examined Gene for more than an hour. Mary and I were sitting on pins, waiting in his living room, but it was worth the wait. Gene and the doctor made their appearance and it looked like they had become friends. The doctor's calm and smiling attitude inspired us with a sense of relief. Indeed, he told us that Gene did not have epilepsy. He thought that Gene had a vitamin and mineral deficiency. During the examination, he had taken blood from Gene, and he would take it to the policlinic laboratory. He told us that as soon as he got the results from the blood test, he would come

69

to our house and would prescribe a daily dietary program for Gene with some vitamin and mineral supplements.

We also showed him the x-rays of Gene's hip and asked him for his advice. Should we submit Gene to surgery or not? The doctor carefully examined the x-rays, and his response was that it was not necessary to have surgery at this point. We should await the results of his program. With our hopes uplifted, we spread the good news. The blood tests confirmed and reinforced the doctor's diagnosis; they also reaffirmed his position that surgery was not necessary at this time.

Dr. Vasiliu was always on time. His presence in our house radiated confidence and lifted our spirits, which were on the verge of despair. He was a tall, good-looking man with dark hair and pleasant manners. He always greeted Mary by kissing her hand, as was the custom in Romania. Gene liked him, too, and listened attentively to his explanations. He came every week and analyzed the results of his treatment and prescribed new dietary and supplement guidelines. He was satisfied with Gene's recovery and so were we. I thought that if I ever needed a doctor, I hoped that I could find one like him.

BEGINNINGS AND THE END

Major Nastovich Petru, a new commander, took over the reins of M.A.I. Artistic Ensemble and guided the company in a new direction. He improved the discipline in all the departments and ordered that annually, professional reexaminations should be held. The sort of dancing I was doing in the company started to annoy me. The majority of choreographies were Romanian dances based on original, gathered folk steps so, in my spare time, I took ballet classes from Floria Capsaly at her house. My everyday intense, personal physical training after the rehearsals molded my body for a different style of dance than that required by the company. I liked to perform and was not being cast in enough dances. I was dancing only in the choreography created by Maestro Kurilov, which was rarely included in the program. In this environment, my creative mind pined for an opportunity to choreograph.

The opportunity arrived with the approaching International Dance Festival and Competition in Warsaw, Poland in 1955. I was excited by the event because I thought that for the competition I would like to choreograph some miniature dances for Mary, myself, and for some of my colleagues who were interested. I came up with some new ideas, but I hesitated to start lest I might fail. My dear angel, Mary, encouraged me. Her words succeeded in fading away my doubts and giving me wings with which to fly into a new world of creativity.

I did a character *Pas de Deux* for Mary and myself, *Idila din Făgăraş (The Idyll from Făgăraş)* using folk steps from the Southern Transylvanian region, which was Mary's birthplace. Mary and I had never danced together before although I had wanted so much to dance with her. She had always been paired with a taller partner. She was as perfect a partner in the dance as she was in my life. Working on the choreography with her was exquisite. The dances had an elegant style with a lot of wheeling under the man's arm and with sudden changes of place. She was spinning around me like a whirlwind with an ease I had never encountered in another dance partner. She always felt and anticipated my movements in another direction; she helped me develop the right choreography to accomplish the desired effect. Rehearsing the dance with her gave me great confidence in my work and helped me find excitement in the process of choreography. I forgot that I was preparing for a competition and dancing with her was worth more than any prize or reward.

At the competition, we won the bronze medal for the performance as well as the choreography; but for us, we won the inestimable reward of inner pleasure. At the same competition, I danced with five other men in a

Romanian character dance called *Briul (The Belt)*. It was a very technically difficult dance executed in a presto rhythm with quick crossing and fluttering leg movements. For this dance, I was awarded the gold medal along with the other dancers. All those results validated Mary's unwavering confidence in my creative potential to choreograph. And so the time and energy spent on my creative work was not for naught. The outcome gave me confidence in the future.

The leadership of the company reacted positively to my outstanding achievement at the international competition. They were impressed by the miniature choreographies presented at the festival. The artistic director also asked me if I was interested in using more dancers to choreograph a dance for the company. I was excited.

In my mind, I envisioned the beautiful girls from Căpîlna. I asked him if I could choose the kind of dance I wanted to choreograph but they wanted me to choreograph a Moldavian region dance suite. "Moldavian dance suite? Hmm…I don't know. I have to give it some thought." I was alerted to the fact that I should first consult my source of inspiration, Mary. She was as excited as I was by the proposal, but she wondered, as did I, why a Moldavian dance suite. Why didn't they let me choose my own dance? Should I or should I not accept their proposal? I had mixed feelings about it. The miniature dances done for the festival were of my own choosing. The Moldavian suite was a request, not an inspiration. Again, Mary was the one that convinced me to accept it.

"I want you to remember that you have a natural feeling for dance called talent, and the miniature dances that you created prove that you also have a natural talent for choreography." Mary's words were encouraging, but I was still reluctant because I wanted to choreograph only what I chose for myself. She continued, "I have no doubt that you will create a good work. But, even if you fail, you can consider it good experience for the future."

Mary's trust in my creative potential thrilled me. She poured courage, confidence, and dedication that launched me into new horizons. Armed with such a valuable resource, I didn't wait for the week to pass. The next day after class, I told the artistic director that I would accept his proposal. My wife was again right about my creative potential. I succeeded, and as a result, I was promoted to the position of deputy to the head of the dance department.

I was obliged to create other dances as requested by the artistic director Viorel Doboş, who was also a composer and the conductor of the company. In this way, I choreographed *Suită Someşeană (The Dance Suite from Someş)* based on the music created by Viorel Doboş, the Russian dance based on the music by Nicolae Beloiu and a Hungarian dance. A modest beginning had opened up within me a strong permanent desire to express my creativity in dance. I especially wanted to choreograph the dance *Dansul Fetelor din Căpîlna (The Girls of Căpîlna)*.

■■■

Sports and culture were two of the main priorities of the Communist Party. Major funds were assigned for these purposes and were distributed to different ministers and organizations. In this way, the Communist Party ensured the continuation of high-level quality in sports and in cultural activities for the purpose of demonstrating to the capitalist world the superiority of the communist regime. Our artistic company was one of the institutions subsidized by that money. The company's members benefited by receiving good salaries and comprehensive fringe benefits, that far exceeded those of the general population. We also had, access to special stores that were not open to the public.

In the summer and in the winter, we got a well-deserved vacation too. The M.A.I. provided villas at the sea and at the mountains for us. The company's doctor advised the dancers to divide their vacation-time into two sessions: first, at the sea and second, in the mountains.

We followed his recommendation and took Gene with us to the sea.

Mary and Iacob vacationing at the Black Sea

There we had a good time and enjoyed being together with Gene. On the beach, every morning, my wife lay down on the towel and enjoyed the sun. Gene played in the sand, trying to build a castle. With his little buckets he would run back and forth to the sea to fill them with water in order to pour the water on the sand to solidify his construction. Everyday, I was reminded of the pledge I had given to Maestro Kurilov to perfect the barrel maneuver.

73

I practiced the barrel movement over and over. Not having a place for rehearsal I practiced on the sand, which was very difficult, so I decided to practice closer to the water where the sand was more solid. We spent two weeks at the sea and toward the end I asked Mary to watch me doing the barrel. I was excited. I felt that I was auditioning for a dance position. I knew that the judge was very critical, looking always for the best quality. I started the barrel and did a perfect circle. I impressed her, and I was rewarded with hugs and kisses.

In the winter, the second half of our vacation, we traveled to Sinaia, a very famous health resort for hiking and skiing. It was well known because

Mary and Iacob in Sinaia

there was the winter palace of the former kings of Romania, which was now a museum open to the public. We visited the royal palace and did a lot of hiking. I loved to ski and took my skies with me. It had been a long time since I had learned and practiced skiing on the Semenic Mountains near the city Reşita about 95 km. from Timişoara. I enjoyed it very much. At this time in Sinaia there were no cable cars, so I had to climb to the point from where I began my descent. Mary and Gene remained at the bottom of the ski track and watched me descent. One day, after I had skied down many times on the old track, I saw other people using another track. I was tempted to try it, however it was not my lucky day. The track was longer than the other one. The descending was exciting. As I reached the end of the track, I bumped into a hard obstacle, which was covered by snow. The impact was very strong and I felt a harsh pain in my right knee as I rolled down the hill. When I managed to stop, I saw Mary and Gene running toward me. Mary asked if I was OK and what had happened. I told her that I had had an unpleasant encounter with an unknown enemy. It was an evil hour. She helped me get up, and I was able to stand on my feet, there was a severe pain in my right knee. The enemy turned out to be a stump of a tree hidden under the snow. She found my skis but the right one had been broken.

The walk back to the villa was very difficult for me. There was no taxi available and it was a long walk. Mary tried to support me under my arm, but the pain in my knee became less and less endurable and we had to stop and rest. It took us more than an hour to get back to the villa. I dropped on the bed, and she undressed me. The sight of my knee horrified us. It was all black and blue, and swollen like a melon.

My wife cried out, "Oh my God! It looks so ugly. What shall I do?"

She wept bitterly. Gene was scared and didn't know what to do. Mary put a compress on my knee with a towel soaked in cold water. She was sobbing.

"You will not be able to dance any more, or at least not for a long time" she said.

"Don't worry I will be fine in no time," I said.

But I wasn't. The swelling and the bruise healed very slowly. Like Mary, I started becoming concerned that I would not be able to dance any more. The doctor told me to have patience and everything would be OK. After two weeks of rest and ultra-sound treatment, I was able to resume ballet classes, and in a week with the doctor's permission, I was able to perform again. Relieved, we forgot the evil hour from Sinaia and resumed our daily routine: classes, rehearsals and choreography.

■■■

In Romania, August 23, the day of the country's liberation from German occupation, was a great holiday. It was celebrated with a grandiose cultural performance. Tamara Cap, the head of the department, and I were called to a meeting where it was discussed what the contribution of our company should be for that great celebration. The artistic director asked us if the dance department would like to create a dance with the theme of the liberation of Romania. The commander's political deputy underlined that the dance had to project the Communist Party's and the Russian army's decisive roles in our country's liberation and in the happiness of the people. I couldn't commit myself because I was not the head of the department, but I emphasized that for creating such a dance, it was necessary to have a libretto. I should have kept my mouth shut. I got myself involved by talking about a libretto. I was asked if I had somebody in mind. I thought about Comrade Florin Raba who was a writer that had worked with a musical revue group, which also belonged to M.A.I. My proposal was unanimously accepted.

"Can you do the choreography?" the commander asked me. The head of the department probably felt that she was being left out and intervened, "I am sure he can do it and I will help him."

I was stunned by her intervention. She had the gift of gab. She was the one who always looked for help from the other dancers. I asked myself how could she help me? I was sure that it was a new trick of hers to get credit for nothing. "That is a good idea; two heads maybe will create something good," said the commander. I didn't dare say anything.

In the party, each member was given obligatory personal tasks. I couldn't find a good excuse to say that I would not do it. I knew from earlier experience that in a meeting of the Communist Party, I would still be assigned that task anyway. They would say that it was mandatory for a member of the party. *I lowered my head and swallowed my real desire to say no.* Aloud, I said, I would try.

I told Mary about the meeting and about the task given to me, and she also understood that I didn't have a choice. She was happy for me that finally the leadership of the company saw in me, as she had seen from the beginning, a potential choreographer. As always, her happiness gave me confidence and inspiration to work.

I was satisfied with the final outcome of the libretto, a copy of which was given to each one of the company's leadership for approval and for their political input. The final version was given to the composer Viorel Doboş who also was the artistic director. The dance was entitled *Eliberarea Patriei (The Country's Liberation)*.

The composer created a wonderful composition, which inspired me. The more I listened, the more interesting were the dance images that came into my mind, and I transposed them visually. I created new movements to express the ideas in the dance. Tamara just stood around and in time approved of my dance movements. I started working with the dancers with great enthusiasm as Tamara merely watched me creating the whole choreography. I cast myself as the leader of the communist underground fighters. It was the principal roll in the ballet, and I created an emotional character inspired by the memory of my brother as a communist underground fighter who was killed by the Germans.

The dance was received enthusiastically; it was a hit. The first and the most important appreciation and congratulations came from my dear wife. She kissed me and then hugged me for a long time. The dancers, who knew that I alone had done the choreography, surrounded me. They were excited by the success and showered me with their congratulations. I thanked each dancer for his or hers brilliant performance. The congratulations continued from the members of the choir, orchestra, and certainly from the commander and his political deputy. I thanked the composer for his wonderful, inspiring music, and we congratulated each other. In the dressing room I looked in the mirror before I removed my make-up and saw on my face the many imprints of the women's kisses.

I danced Eliberarea Patriei (*The Country's Liberation*) choreography many times. It was selected for the gala performance celebrating the day of liberation from the Nazis, which was again a stunning success. The dance was also introduced into the permanent repertory of the company. Sometimes in the same show, we did the Ukrainian dance. Both dances required a high level of technique, extreme effort and endurance from my body. In the mornings before each show, we rehearsed; I did my personal warm up before each performance. In spite of that, my muscles felt tense and gradually lost their elasticity. I forgot that in winter I had had a skiing accident. We needed a break, but we didn't get one.

The performances went well but my legs gave in. We had a performance in the *Grădina de vară Boema (The Summer Boheme Garden),* the permanent summer theatre of the company; and during my solo in the Ukrainian dance, I jumped higher then ever, but my landing was devastating. My right knee collapsed like a castle of playing cards. I couldn't stand up on my feet so the dancers had to help me off the stage. The curtain was closed and it was announced to the public that I was injured, but the rest of the program would go on. My right knee was swollen and I felt a horrible sharp pain in my left side. I was taken to the hospital's emergency room. The diagnosis was meniscus ligament ruptures.

After the performance, my wife came to the hospital where she learned of the diagnosis. I saw the sadness in her warm lovely eyes. She felt, as did I, that this was the end of my dancing career. The doctor suggested surgery. I was reluctant, but, in the end, I agreed. The surgery at that time was very long and unpleasant. I was depressed, discouraged, and blamed myself for the ski accident. Mary visited me every day after rehearsals and helped sustain my morale.

"Don't blame yourself. Skiing was your pleasure and the accident was your fate. There's nothing that you can do now. Look to the future; it is a bright one. You are a recognized choreographer. The company and the dancers are waiting for you."

"I am young and I don't want to give up dancing."

"Well, let's monitor your recovery, and we'll see what happens after."

The recovery progressed slowly and I was nervous and recalcitrant toward everyone. I blamed the doctors and complained every day about trifles. I had special exercise therapy but the flexibility of the knee was not the same any more. I took solace in the fact that, even though I would not be able to dance any more, I could look forward to dedicating myself to choreographing and eventually to teaching.

I returned to the company and was warmly received by the dancers, who wished me good luck in my creative work. I watched with sadness the dance rehearsals from which I was excluded since I could not be a dancer any more. My dream to dance at the opera vanished forever and I became a spectator a future teacher and choreographer.

THE FAR EAST

Rumors were spreading that our company was nominated to go on tour in the Far East. Therefore, we were being closely scrutinized. Everybody questioned, where in the Far East? Than the head of the department told me that the artistic director wanted me to choreograph a Chinese dance.

"Are we going to China?"

"We are nominated for going, but the minister of culture has not yet decided which of the companies will go. We have to prepare to be ready for many auditions to come."

I promised her that as soon as I finished my research on China I'd let her know if I could do it or not. She demanded an answer on the spot, but I needed time for research and confronted her.

"Why don't you do it?"

"I don't know anything about Chinese dance," she replied.

"Well, I am in the same situation."

I had cornered her. She didn't have a way out of this situation she accepted my conditions. Both Mary and I went to the main library and did a comprehensive documentation about Chinese folk art in general and particularly about folk dance. The scarf dance, which was the most popular folk dance all over China, appealed to us. As soon as I got the music, I planned the choreography and started the rehearsals with six couples. I enjoyed choreographing this number as the scarf gave me a variety of possibilities to create spectacular moments in the dance. After seeing the dance, the artistic director approved it.

Commander Petre Nastovich announced officially that the company would make a two-month tour in China. The news that everybody had anticipated was received with an explosion of shouts and general enthusiasm. Mary and I were also part of this explosion of enthusiasm, but, at the same time, ambiguous thoughts crept into our minds.

"I will not see Gene for two months," Mary said to me.

"I will see him, but I will not see you for two months. I don't think that they will take me on this tour; I am no longer a dancer."

"They should. You choreographed the Chinese dance and it needs to be rehearsed. You are the only one who knows it, and I need you; I don't want to be without you."

Not too long thereafter, the composition of the troupe going to the Far East was announced. Both Mary and I were included, Mary, as a dancer, and, I as the assistant of the department head. Mary and I were happy that we would be together. Gene would be in the care of my mother.

Sunday, May 20, 1956, was the day of the departure. The 125 artists of the M.A.I. Artistic Ensemble now named *Ciocîrlia (Skylark)* were on their way to represent the Romanian people's art in China. The departure was scheduled for noon but the majority had already gathered at the Mogoşoaia Railroad Station at ten o'clock in the morning. The platform was crowded with family members and friends who came to say goodbye. Gene and my mother came to say farewell to us. We hugged and kissed them and gave her the last instructions regarding Gene and the house. The locomotive whistle broke up this emotional farewell, and everybody boarded the train and ran to the windows to wave good-bye. The train departed on schedule. It moved slowly to give people the chance to follow us to the end of the platform. They waved their handkerchiefs with tears in their eyes. We watched Gene and my mother until the train made a curve and they disappeared from our view.

Mary and I were very emotional and hugged each other and shed tears. They were tears of happiness for being together and of regret that Gene was not with us. As the train reached a considerable speed, the houses and the trees slid by, and the departure from our loved ones was felt heavier. With jokes and a variety of amusements, however, the joy of the tour surrounded and conquered us. It was our first night in the sleeping car and we continued on with our endless honeymoon.

On the 23rd of May, we entered Moscow. We left Moscow with the Trans-Siberian train headed toward China. The Trans-Siberian connected the two continents, Europe and Asia. The dancers were busy every morning taking a mandatory classical ballet class taught by me. For two weeks, the corridor replaced the studio. It was not the ideal studio, but it served as a momentary vehicle for maintaining the best physical condition of our legs and bodies. An accordionist from the orchestra played the music for the class.

After the ballet class, the rest of the day was spent with all kinds of enjoyable activities. Mary and I learned a new card game called pinochle, a variant of rummy. Mary crocheted a sweater for me. We spent time just watching from the window the immense landscape of pine and birch trees in the Ural Mountains. Sometimes, I played chess, or read a book.

As we passed the Ural Mountains and left behind the European and Russian territory, we entered the vast land of Siberia. We looked forward to reaching Otpor the last city of the USSR, which connects this country with China. At that station, the wide wheels of the train's cars were changed with smaller ones. The Chinese rails were narrower than the Russian ones.

Curiosity and the anticipated pleasure of meeting people with an ancient culture were enormous. We arrived at the railroad station of Manchuria, the first Border City in China. It was a small city and so was the station, but it was so crowded that I had the impression that the whole city was there to welcome us. The atmosphere was like that of a holiday. The station was decorated with Chinese and Romanian flags, with an abundance of multicolor flowers and the portraits, of each country's leaders.

Like an avalanche an assembly of children pioneers welcomed us all dressed in their uniforms of white shirts, red scarves, and dark blue short pants for the boys. The girls wore short skirts. They offered us silk flowers hand-made with their distinctly scrupulous skill. They attached them to our clothes just above our hearts, which were beating vigorously, excited by such an emotional event.

At nightfall, with regret, we departed from that wonderful scene; and, as the train slowly moved away, we could hear from everywhere the word "zai-jian, zai-jian, zai-jian" which means so long or good-bye.

On our way to Beijing, (Peking) the Chinese organizers distributed tickets of different colors and as yet non-perforated numbers to be attached to our luggage. Each color represented a different floor in the hotel and we had to perforate the numbers of our designated rooms on that ticket. We were told that we had to leave our luggage in our train compartments and that we would later find our luggage in our rooms. I was skeptical of that arrangement and expressed my concern to our commander that our luggage would be lost or mistakenly directed to another room. He cautioned me that we had to trust their organizational skill.

The weather was gorgeous with a warm summer sun when the train stopped in Beijing, the capital of China. Peking was constructed in 1121 B.C.E. and since then has had several names; today it is Beijing. The station's platform was decorated with beautiful ornaments on a larger scale than in Manchuria. It looked liked a wonderful flower garden on a silk background.

The Romanian Embassy's attaché, the Chinese Cultural Ministry's representatives, artists, journalists, reporters, and the whole company of the artistic ensemble of the Popular Chinese Army were there to welcome us. They offered us magnificent bunches of flowers, and the Military Band played the anthems of the two countries.

Exiting the station, we were welcomed by a series of other hosts who formed a human corridor so we could hardly pass to the buses, which awaited us. It was a warm and impressive manifestation of friendship. Our arms couldn't hold the multitude of flowers given us all along the way. That overwhelmed me with a joyous thrill.

The buses took us to the hotel Sin Chen. The Chinese were amazing organizers and very punctual. I was astonished as I entered the room selected for my wife and me. All our luggage was there, lined up in perfect order. I was amazed and at the same time pleased that their organizing skill was indeed perfect.

The hotel was new, built in a gorgeous modern style and it had two restaurants on the first floor and one on the sixth floor especially for foreigners. In the hotel, there were shops with Chinese merchandise. I admired the fans and gewgaws made of ivory.

On the same day as our arrival, we had a social gathering in the evening with artists and members of the Chinese Cultural Ministry at the Beijing hotel. We entered into the big reception room of the hotel decorated as if for a holiday. All over were fresh flowers spreading their pleasant fragrance. The architecture was definitely Chinese, with multiple colored sculptures of dragons. On the ceiling and on the walls were painted phoenix birds. For me it was a new style I had never seen in person, just from pictures and books. It was magnificent and thrilling to be able to experience in person such a different environment.

Mary and I had the pleasure of sitting with four Chinese dancers from the Army's Dance Company and another six dancers from our own company. The conversation with the Chinese dancers was limited to gestures and mime. Mary was the first to try one of the Chinese dishes, but

Iacob at the Winter Palace

she didn't like it. The wine was very strong and served in small glasses, and, from time to time, we took a sip and said the Chinese gan-bei, which means cheer or good-luck. Finally the European food arrived: fish cooked in tomato sauce, aspic or marinade; roasted chicken; and pork loins on a tray. At the end of dinner was ice cream and fruit. It was a delicious fiesta.

The next morning we had our first rehearsal. That evening the audience was composed of writers, composers, actors, dancers and artists. Of course, the newspaper critics were also there. All of us had stage fright including myself. I wasn't performing, but my Chinese dance was at stake. The performance was a huge success and the Chinese dance had "iron" applause (everybody clapped at the same time in unison). All the newspapers published superlative reviews on the first page with many photos taken of our performance.

We woke up to a beautiful sunny day. Flowers were everywhere. On the morning's schedule was a visit to The Imperial Winter Palace. The entrance to the courtyard and the view of the palace was an unforgettable one. The first building was named The Quiet Temple where the emperor worked and welcomed foreign ambassadors. The next building was The Leisure Temple for the emperor, but at the time of our visit it had been transformed into an historical museum with items from 1200- 4000 years ago. The third building was named The Ceremonial Temple, in which different ceremonies, such as the emperor's weddings, receptions and feasts, were held. Continuing our visit we entered into the emperor's palace where he spent his private life, far from the everyday problems of state.

The Romanian ambassador, who attended the performance, informed us that to obtain a ticket for our performance, the people had been obliged to stand in line from 2:00 A.M. The next day, the orchestra attended a recording session at the Beijing radio station and the dancers were filmed at the TV station. In the afternoon, we spent our time shopping.

We had our first rehearsal and performance at the Summer Theatre of Beijing, which had a capacity of 5,000 people. After the rehearsal, we were invited to a special restaurant more than 200 years old. Only Chinese food was served at this restaurant. However, I liked the famous roasted Beijing duck and I tried to eat black egg but I didn't like it.

It was announced that we would have a gala performance for the government at the Governmental Council Theatre. As the curtain went up, I could see in the first row the Prime Minister Zhou Enlai (Ciu-En-Lai) and the members of the government. We were excited and eager to present our best performance. After the performance, the Prime Minister came on stage to congratulate the leaders and the members of our company. He and the members of the government liked it so much that in his speech he expressed his opinion that it was a shame that only a fraction of the Chinese people would be able to see such a wonderful performance in the two months. We were shocked when Zhou Enlai (Ciu-En-Lai) told us that his government would like to extend our tour for another two months, and he would contact our government to arrange the details.

The next day the commander of the company announced that the Romanian government indeed had accepted Zhou Enlai's (Ciu-En-Lai's) proposal and had approved the extension of the tour. To the commander I underlined the fact that we were equipped only with summer clothes as we had been instructed and as was appropriate for a two-month tour in June and July. The commander didn't like my intervention. I saw in his eyes the sparkle of his dictatorial attitude. He responded with a voice that signaled that he didn't like to be contradicted. He told us that we should write to our families requesting winter clothes and that the decision was final; we should not comment any further. He emphasized the importance of our mission, which was entrusted to us by the Communist Party. We should continue our tour with the same enthusiasm, and forget our personal feelings. Mary and I were disappointed by his answer, but we didn't have any choice and so we resigned ourselves.

My wife's birthday was approaching on June 15 and I wanted to buy her a surprise gift. Since we were together all the time, I had to find an excuse to be alone to buy her a gift. I lied to her that I had a very important meeting with the commander. She loved all kinds of broaches, and in the bazaar, I found a unique, beautiful ivory broach. She loved it and wore it throughout the tour and later at home. That evening all the leaders of the company congratulated her and gave her a combined present of a silk scarf and a box of Chinese chocolates. Members of the orchestra played, and everybody sang "Happy Birthday" to her.

Our visit to the Imperial Summer Garden was like a dream. It was indeed a palace of beauty, superb and grandiose, where the emperor spent his time during the summer.

In the evening, we got ourselves all rigged up and went to a banquet with the two major Chinese ballet companies from Beijing and the Cultural Minister. The generosity of the Chinese hosts dumbfounded us when each member of our company received a personal gift. The girls got a silk blouse and a fan, and the boys, a bottle of Chinese wine and Ginseng herbs. The reunion marked the end of our stay in Beijing.

Next, we found ourselves back in the Chinese train's sleeping car on our way toward Port Arthur. After the morning rehearsal, I was notified that our company received a gift from the Cultural Minister, new costumes for my Chinese dance. The costumes were splendid, made of natural silk and embroidered with Chinese motifs. I was deeply touched by their gift. Our former costumes had been made out of nylon. I felt exquisite pleasure, thinking that they really appreciated my choreography and wanted to see the dance in authentic silk costumes.

It was hard to believe that one-month had gone by since our departure. Melancholy gripped my heart, yearning for Gene. Mary sighed often and sometimes even cried, not knowing what was happening to him at home. We hadn't received any letters and we were very concerned. I approached the commander and asked him if it was possible to inquire about our family through the Romanian Embassy in Beijing. After a week, he told us that our family had been contacted; they were fine. It was only a momentary relief. We still had three months more to go. The activities of the troupe settled into a routine: visits, shopping, rehearsals, and performances.

In Shenyang we were informed that the tour was extended by another two months at the request of the North Korean, Vietnam, Mongolian and

Russian governments. Six months! We couldn't believe it: however; we had learned our lesson and didn't protest any more. I reminded my wife that we hadn't written home for the winter coats yet, and suggested that we should go shopping for coats. She agreed. We both liked the long leather coats, with the removable lamb fur lining, and we bought one for each of us. In Shenyang, we had the occasion to see traditional Chinese Opera for the first time. Here the dance department also started to learn a Mongolian dance. This city will forever be in my mind because at our performance, my Chinese dance earned a zai-yi-ge (encore). We continued our tour in China in the cities of Anyang, Shenyang, Fusein and Changchun. Welcomes, receptions, visits, shopping and successful performances were similar.

In Changchun, an unexpected and unpleasant thing happened. Some of the members of our company got sick after lunch. Some of the members of the orchestra were taken to the hospital. We went to the theatre but on our way more and more people got sick. We started the warm up, and every minute a dancer got sick. As a result the evening performance had to be canceled.

The Cultural Minister rushed up to Changchun to investigate the situation and expressed an apology in the name of the Chinese government. The result of the investigation determined that the sickness was a result of egg poisoning from the ice cream. Fortunately, I hadn't eaten any ice cream at lunch; but, unfortunately, my wife did, and she got sick, too. Our commander gave an order that nobody could write home about the food poisoning, so as not to scare the people back home.

After two days we resumed the rehearsal and the performance routine. The people who had been disappointed by the cancelled performances were able to attend a performance held in a huge outdoor theatre. I never saw such a big crowd; we were told that the attendance at that performance was over 24,000.

■■■

On the evening of July 8, 1956, the company was once again in train compartments, this time on our way to North Korea. Did I ever think that I would travel to this part of the world? No, but here I was, watching new faces and new sights through the window. We arrived in the evening in P'yongyang (Phenian), the capital of North Korea and had a pleasant welcome at a nice hotel, the only one in the city. In the morning, we visited the city. All over we saw ruins from the Korean War. The houses were rather shabby, and I saw a lot of women carrying their small children on their backs.

The performance was held in the Opera Theatre. On the program was included the Moldavian dance, another choreography of mine, instead of the Chinese dance. We were invited to see the Professional Ballet School from P'yongyang. We attended a class and a performance of the sixth grade.

We traveled by bus to P'anmunjŏm. I saw many American soldiers, a US Military Police border patrol and the helicopter-

American MP patrol

P'anmunjŏm – 38th parallel truce table

landing platform on the other side of the border. At that time, I never thought that one day I would become an American citizen. We entered the building where the armistice between the United States and North Korea was signed. In the middle of the room, the mark of the 38th parallel went exactly through the middle of the table on which the truce was signed. I couldn't believe that I was able to witness in person this historical site.

Back in P'yongyang in the evening, we gave a performance on an open-air stage at the foot of a hill. The audience, sitting on the hill without chairs, was estimated to have been more than 40,000. I wondered what these people could possibly see from such a distance.

In general, Korea was a poor country and the people were struggling to rebuild their country after the war. In P'yongyang, the non-married men from our company could very easily get a woman in bed for just a piece of soap. Cleanliness was a problem in Korea; there were no cleaning tools or cleaning substances. Flies were everywhere. On the Korean train, we suffered from hot weather, and the mosquitoes literally devoured us on our way to Namp'o. After the performance in Namp'o, we continued on our way toward the Korean border city of Sinuigu, than crossed into China to the city of Andun.

■■■

It was very good to be back in China and to get rid of the Korean flies. It was incredible to notice that in China we didn't encounter flies. The Chinese government had launched a campaign to exterminate the flies. The same Chinese train crew waited for us and welcomed us with the same friendly spirit.

We left behind the torrid weather as the train took us to west central China. We arrived in Taiyuan, a big city of 2,500,000 people with many children. The welcome was unusual. From the train to the hotel, people came out from their houses and applauded us with enthusiasm. They were curious to see the first non-Chinese company to visit their city. As a matter of fact they followed us everywhere and looked at us as if we were creatures from outer space. In stores, they surrounded us and talked to us, but we didn't understand and couldn't answer. One of our Chinese guides explained that the people had never seen a European face before.

We were impressed to find out that the outdoor theatre was actually built in three days especially for us by thousands of volunteers. The evening performance was held in that big outdoor theater, but, even so, the stage was equipped with all the necessary technical equipment. The dressing room was neatly arranged. They couldn't install a water supply, but we had plenty of water in buckets. As soon as we emptied the buckets, they were immediately replaced. More impressive was what happened during the performance when it started to rain. Our musical conductor stopped the performance, but the people didn't move from their places and asked us to continue the show. We resumed the performance, while they stood wet and clapped with an enthusiasm I had never encountered.

Our departure from the city was postponed because it was announced that a powerful typhoon was approaching the city. We were fortunate that the typhoon lost its power before it reached the city. We only saw how the sky darkened and a strong wind with rain stormed the city. After the typhoon passed we still couldn't leave the city because a bridge where our train was supposed to pass had been destroyed. We had three days of leisure with no rehearsals and no performances stuck in the city in a stand-by situation waiting for the news that the bridge had been restored.

We received another letter from home, saying that everything was fine. The news made us feel relieved for the moment. The many welcomes, the gifts, the performances, the visits in each city, all marked the passing of one day after another, bringing us closer to home. Our overwhelming success in all the cities, the opportunity to visit ancient cities, pagodas, museums, bazaars, restaurants, and the chance to attend various Chinese performances, all kept us in reasonably high spirits.

After the cities of Jinan and Tianjin, we were back again in Beijing. Mary and I went to visit the Go-Mo-Jo Historical Museum. I didn't take notes, so I only remember a few specific items. I remember that a lot of Go-Mo-Jo poems were displayed, and I will never forget Genghis Khan's warrior boots.

It was August 23, the day of the great holiday in Romania. It was the

Iacob on the Great Wall of China

liberation day of our country from fascist Germany. On that occasion, a visit to the Great Wall was organized on a voluntary basis. Only Mary and I joined the leaders of our company for that visit. The Great Wall had been a defensive fortification. Now it had been restored and had become a very popular tourist attraction.

It is the greatest walled frontier construction, the most wonderful piece of architecture ever undertaken by man. Watching it fascinated me; walking on the top of it and learning the history of its construction made me feel as if I were traveling back in history.

Iacob (left) and Maria (right) on the Yang-Tze

We continued our tour, this time in three airplanes. Before departure we were advised to take with us only things that were necessary for about eight or nine days and leave the rest of our belongings on the train. The planes were military ones and the journey was very rough.

We saw the Yang-zi Jiang (Yang-Tze River) winding through the land. After two hours in the air, we arrived in the city of Chongqing. The beauty of the hotel stunned me. It was a huge new building, constructed in the Chinese architectural style with beautifully colored pagodas.

On the Yang-Tze River we boarded a small passenger ship. There was a lot of commotion, people running with excitement from one place to another, exploring the ship. About 2:30 A.M. they calmed down, and the silence of the night settled in. I was lying on my bed thinking of Gene and my mother as the ship took off from the Chongqing port, and I fell asleep.

We were informed that the yellow color of the river was from the mud, which the river collects from the banks on its winding journey. The journey on the dangerous Yang-zi Jiang (Yang-Tze River) continued. Sometimes the river flow was narrow and sometimes so wide that I couldn't believe that it was a river. The landscape on both sides of the river was splendid with rocks of different forms and shapes. Between them there were holes in the side of the bank in which we saw people working. Our Chinese translator informed me that, unfortunately, they didn't have regular houses yet, and they live there; those were their houses. He continued to tell me that it was very risky to live there, that many people died because every year the raging Yang-zi Jiang (Yang-Tze River) grew and flooded the holes.

I enjoyed the ship because it gave me a sense of freedom. We could move freely from prow to stern. We could take off our outer clothes and remain only in our bathing suits. We could play music and dance any time. We conducted our ballet classes every day on the deck, enjoying the beautiful weather. Once in the afternoon, we organized an outdoor dancing fete, dancing until it grew dark. Later in the night, leaning on the bulwark, we admired the full moon reflected beautifully on the Yang-zi Jiang (Yang-Tze River). This reflection was off the stern one day while the day before it had appeared off the prow of the ship. Admiring the moon and the sky crowded with stars, I imagined myself flying together with Mary through that immense space toward Bucharest and beaming Gene up with us. Telepathy made my wife turn toward me and suddenly tell me, "I am thinking of Gene." I embraced her and told her, "me too" and with this melancholy beautiful image, we went to bed.

Solitary moment on the Yank-Tze

I considered that trip a mini-vacation, and our varied activities made us feel that the six days on the Yang-zi Jiang (Yang-Tze River) had passed quickly. It was a wonderful experience that I will never forget. I could honestly say that I regret it ended so quickly.

We were taken to the train, and Mary and I rushed to our compartment to see if our belongings were there. Our clothes were hanging just as we had left them in perfect order. I was deeply impressed. It amazed my wife and me and everybody in the company. I was really embarrassed that I hadn't had the confidence to leave our belongings on the train without mistrust.

The train made its way towards Shanghai, the city to which everybody had been looking forward. My curiosity grew with the speed of the train as we came closer to Shanghai. From the window, the view of the western-style skyscrapers, not in the Chinese style, made it obvious to me that indeed Shanghai was a modern city. A huge crowd welcomed us and the buses could barely make their way through the crowd. We arrived at the hotel, another skyscraper. The room designated for Mary and me was on the seventh floor, and at night the panoramic view of the city was beautiful.

In Shanghai, the Chinese authorities surprised us again with an extraordinary gesture. Every member of our company received a new long leather coat lined with lamb fur. That gift was welcomed with great joy, and

the sound of cheers resounded throughout the entire hotel. The Chinese government thought that with the extension of our tour, we would be unprepared for the cooler weather, since we hadn't planned our wardrobe for winter. As for ourselves, Mary and I were disappointed because we had already bought coats, but the gift was welcomed. This was our fortune and we were confident that we would find a use for them.

After lunch, Mary and I took a jinrikisha (rickshaw) and went shopping at an international store, especially for foreigners. It was a peculiar, awkward feeling to be pulled by a human being. The man was a

Shopping in Shanghai

short fellow who didn't wear a shirt, and I could see his very muscular upper body. He was running with us as if we were feathers instead of a burden of 250 pounds. The weather was hot but he didn't display the least effort in pulling us. As we passed a bridge and the road became gradually more up-hill, I finally saw the strain of his muscles along his spine and the flow of his sweat. Mary and I took pity on him and asked him to stop. He wondered why we had descended from the jinrikisha, and protested. We walked over the bridge ourselves, and, with my hand, I indicated to him to follow us. We resumed our place on the jinrikisha, and he continued to pull us with greater speed than ever. Obviously the short break at the bridge had restored his energy. We arrived at our destination and paid him more than what he asked for, but he refused it.

In the store, we looked for the fabric department. Mary liked a green gabardine material. She wanted to make an elegant winter coat of it to be lined with mink fur. We bought the mink fur to make a beautiful lining. Mary and I wandered through the store looking for other merchandise and we found nice silk shirts and silk underwear for both of us. The packages multiplied and became difficult to handle. A salesperson came to our rescue, suggesting that the store could take care of our packages by delivering them to the hotel. I didn't know what to do. Again, I was afraid to trust a stranger with our purchases, but Mary reminded me that the Chinese had proved to us many times that they could be trusted. We gave the salesperson the name of our hotel and our room number, and we left.

Mary and I looked for a jinrikisha, and to our surprise the former jinrikisha puller came running and stopped right in front of us. We never imagined that he would wait hours for us, but we were pleased by his action. Evidently, it was difficult for jinrikisha pullers to find new costumers, so for him it was worth waiting for us. Relieved of most of our money and satisfied with our shopping, we relaxed and enjoyed the ride back to the hotel. We thanked him and again tried to pay him more than the usual charge, but he rejected it as he had done before. We were delighted to find in our room all the merchandise we had bought. That was a fast delivery!

The whole company visited the musical and dance conservatory and admired their performance of classical dance and music. Later, back in Romania we learned about the horrible Chinese Cultural Revolution lunched by Mao Zedong (Mao-Tze-Dun) who ordered the destruction of everything classical. My thoughts returned to those young talented dancers and musicians, I was saddened by the thought that they could no longer dance and play the classics.

The director of the Shanghai Conservatory wanted his dancers to learn a Romanian dance. The commander of our company entrusted the assignment to me. I rehearsed with them in the mornings, and I was pleased by their enthusiasm and their ability to learn quickly. On the night of the good-bye reception an unexpected event happened. The choreographer of the Shanghai conservatory dance group came to congratulate and to thank me for the dance I had staged for them. I was happy that they liked my choreography, and I expressed my joy in having worked with them. He had a glass of wine in his hand. He clinked my glass and hooked my right arm; I was obliged to drink the whole glass of wine.

But this was not the end of that event. Behind the choreographer, there was a line formed by the Chinese dancers with whom I had worked. Each one of them toasted with me and insisted that I drink the entire contents of

the glass. Everybody enjoyed watching this except me who felt that my brain was losing control. I didn't know what I was really doing or what would be the end of this. The end was that I woke up with a terrific headache, still bewildered and intoxicated. My wife told me that I had gotten drunk to the amusement of all the others, and that she, helped by some dancers, had taken me to our room. It took me a whole day to recover, nourished only with hot tea.

Iacob staging a dance at the Shanghai Conservatory

Now the company was back on the train heading toward the beautiful city of Hangzhou. The Chinese people called it the city with the silk sky probably because the main industry was the production of natural silk. We were told that it was heaven on earth. The city was indeed magnificent. The hotel was nice, both outside and inside, and situated on the very edge of the lake. In the room, a mosquito netting covered the bed and the view of the lake from the window was breathtaking.

We had visited many sites in China by now but this trip on the boats across the lake was unforgettable. The lake was huge, surrounded on three sides by mountains and one side by the city. There were three islands spread out in the middle of the lake. We stopped on two islands and I felt as if I were in a fairy tale. The island was charming with many miniature pagodas, winding walls of rocks, and small bridges over streams with different colors of fish.

For Mary and me, the beauty of the city, as well as a sense of artistic successes couldn't dull our homesickness and the torment of loving and missing our son. We were not the only ones who had these thoughts, which were responsible for developing a strain of nervousness in the company. I sensed an increasingly restless behavior in the members of the company, a fatigue, and some illnesses. Many mistakes began to appear in the performances, and we had to replace some of the dancers who were ill. As a result, it was increasingly necessary to hold intensive rehearsals. Also, counseling with some of the members was necessary. Mary and I were lucky in a way that we shared a strong love that tied us together.

The train was heading with the members of the company toward the next city of Guangzhou (Canton). The city was famous for its leather goods; the shoes were beautiful and very cheap. Mary fell in love with all of them, and couldn't decide which one to buy. They were only models, if we wanted them we had to order them. We did and paid. The salesperson gave us a receipt, and promised us that in two days the shoes would be ready. The weather had become very hot, so we took a jinrikisha back to the hotel.

The next day was the 1st of October, a big holiday in China, the celebration of the Chinese Communist Revolution. The city organized a celebration in their stadium. Our company was invited to watch the parade.

The next day we tried again; likewise, all the stores were closed. The Chinese crew informed me that victory day was celebrated in China for three days in a row. Mary and I were in a tangled and desperate situation because we would be traveling to Nanning city and lose the ordered shoes. I explained the matter to the Chinese leader.

"I don't know how to help you, but give me the receipt and I will see what I can do. This is the situation," and he advised me to have patience. He promised me that he would do his best to solve the problem.

I told Mary of my conversation with the leader of our Chinese crew and we both understood that we had lost the shoes, forever. I was mad, but my wife, like always, calmed me down and said, "I lost some shoes but we have our love for each other and for our family. This is the more important to me."

The train headed south and the weather became unbearably warm. The landscape changed also and we could see more tropical plants. Members of our company used their fans to ventilate their hot faces. In the hotel, we found electrical fans, but they didn't help. After rehearsals, we escaped to a swimming pool to cool down. At the performance, the dancers sweated as never before. In the dressing room, they found all kinds of tropical fruit. After each dance, they gobbled them up. The Chinese designated some of their people to help us. These people took the oranges and grapefruits and squeezed them into glasses for the dancers. In that way, the dancers survived the unbearable heat during the performances.

We were approaching the end of the Chinese tour. We found out that we had done sixty-four performances in China and thirteen in North Korea with about 500,000 people attending the performances.

October 12, 1956 was the day that we left China for Vietnam. In the evening we had the farewell dinner and we received the usual gifts. It was our leader's turn to hand out gifts to all the members of the Chinese crew who accompanied us during our tour. It was an unforgettable emotional farewell. Spontaneous hugs and kisses could be seen all over as tears flooded everyone's faces. Each of us went to the Chinese crew and thanked them for the magnificent care and attention given us during the tour. At the railroad station, a huge crowd of people and several Chinese orchestras with noisy percussion instruments made the farewell electrifying. The train started to move and the Chinese crew was still hanging on the steps of the train shaking hands, hugging their favorites and kissing their darlings.

■■■

We were advised to take with us no more than what was necessary; the rest would remain on the Chinese train. We had learned from past experience that when we returned, everything would be just as we had left it. The Vietnam train had two dining cars but no sleeping compartments. Tropical fruits were served in excessive abundance, mangos, papayas, kiwi fruits and coconut. For some of us who remembered what we had learned in the French language class in school, communication with the Vietnamese people was a little bit easier. In the room, netting was used against small lizards and mosquitoes to protect the bed.

During the first day in Hanoi, we took a tour of the city with buses. It was a city with beautiful buildings, influenced by French architecture. The tropical vegetation enchanted me; palms and coconut trees were everywhere. In the town, the common form of transportation was the bicycle or motorcycle. The Vietnamese girls were charming and beautiful, and some of them found temporary sweethearts in our company.

It was announced that we would have the honor of being invited to meet the president of Vietnam, Ho Chi Minh. We stopped at his residency. I found him nice with a modest attitude, very communicative and approachable. He welcomed us. We gathered around him, and everybody wanted a picture with him; some even succeeded in getting an autograph. He wished us success and a good time in Hanoi and promised to attend our performance. Indeed, he came to the gala performance. At the end, he came on stage and personally offered flowers to many women and hugged and kissed them.

My wife liked lizard and snakeskin shoes and handbags. We didn't have as much money as we had had in China, so she only bought two pairs of shoes with handbags to match them. She was happy to have at least these two pairs; having given up hope that the shoes ordered and paid for in Guangzhou (Canton) would ever be recovered.

It was fascinating walking in the jungle, a mysterious form of nature, which was so new for us. I loved the coconut trees and I was tempted to climb them to get a coconut so I did. The accompanying Vietnamese showed me how to crack-open the coconut and drink the contents of it. Mary and I loved it. We received hats made from the bamboo trees and many other gifts. The time spent in Hanoi extended our tour and made us feel farther from home, but I never regretted that I had been on that side of the world.

Going back to China we passed the border, and I saw the Chinese train. My wife entered the train compartment first and shouted with joy. I then saw the reason for her incredible excitement. All the eight pairs of shoes ordered in Guangzhou (Canton) were lined up on her bed. She hugged me and flooded my face with her kisses.

Maria with jungle friend

We found the receipt and also a note from the chief wishing that my wife should wear the shoes in health and happiness. He also wished me great success in my career. Mary tried them on and they all fit her like a glove. We were so overwhelmed by this event that we didn't even notice when the train pulled out of the station when somebody called us to the restaurant for lunch, the train was already in full speed toward Mongolia. We traveled four days, crossing China from south to north, taking us a bit closer to home. We stopped in the city of Nan-Po and were asked to descend from the cars because the train had to be carried across the Yang-Tze River by a ferryboat and we had to go in another boat. On the other side of the river, I was pleasantly surprised to see once again the Chinese Chief Tong-zhi "U" (Comrade "U") the name that everybody called him. There was an explosion of cheers and cries by the whole company. Mary and I were particularly glad to see him, as it gave us a chance to thank him for resolving our shoe crisis. For Mary and me, the opportunity to visit China was one of the greatest events in our lives. It was a revelation. It left a profound emotional impression on us, which we would carry with us forever.

■■■

The weather in Mongolia was very cold, and the leather coats came in handy. The brandy served at mealtime also warmed us up. We were speeding along on the train while our minds were racing like the speed of light towards home. Out of the windows I saw an endless, uninhabited land covered by a coat of snow with the bright sun radiating off the surface; but the beams couldn't warm us up.

As we came closer to the capital of Mongolia, the scenery changed. Mountains appeared on the horizon. We had a warm welcome in Ulan Bator in spite of the harsh chilly weather. In the evening, we presented a gala performance.

The snowflakes spread their white crystals over Ulan Bator and the surroundings as if the world was at peace. On the outskirts of the city, we visited a village where people lived in yurts (Mongolian tents), which were easily folded and transported to another location. Near the yurts were horses and camels used for transportation over the vast steppes of their country. In movies and in schoolbooks I saw camels; but now for the first time I

Iacob and Maria on camels in Mongolia

witnessed live camels carrying merchandise and people. I asked one of the owners of the camels if I could mount one. First, he helped me to mount while Mary took a photo. Then it was her turn and I took the photo. While I was on the back of the camel between the humps, I imagined that I was an explorer crossing the vast steppes.

The days in Mongolia weren't easy, and the performances were not up to our usual high standard. The concentration of the performers was poor because their minds were already traveling home faster than the Trans Siberian train.

Compared to the perfect organization and warm hospitality of the Chinese people, the Moscow welcome was a disappointment. Except for a few officials, nobody came to welcome us. We had to carry our own luggage to the bus. In the lobby of the Moscow hotel, we had to wait to be allocated to our rooms. As we waited, the Russians stared at us and some even approached us and asked where we had bought our leather coats. One of them asked if I wanted to sell my leather coat to him. I told him that I would have to consult with my wife, and I asked him to come back the next day.

The next day we rehearsed at the Tchaikovsky Concert Hall, and afterwards, we went to the stores to get an idea of what we could buy if we sold our leather coats to the Russian guy. He gave us a good price, and with the money we bought a refrigerator and a tape recorder, items not available in Romania.

HOME

The closer we got to Bucharest, the more impatient we became. For six months, half of a year, the company members hadn't seen their children, wives, husbands, parents, brothers, sisters, relatives and their friends. I wondered if my son would recognize his mother and me. How had he changed? Had he grown? Was he pleased with his grandmother? Did his hip joint heal? Would we recognize him? All these anxious questions couldn't dull our ardent love for him and our boiling desire to see him.

The day of November 24, 1956 is still vivid in my memory. The station was the arrival point into our heaven, called home. The station was not decorated with flags or welcome slogans like they were in China but the people who came to welcome us were packed like sardines. The sight from the window as the train slowly rolled into the station was incredible; it was a sea of heads. I couldn't locate Gene or my mother. The first head I could distinguish was that of my brother because he was taller than the rest. Near him were Gene and my mother.

My brother's presence was a surprise and so was that tremendous crowd of people who hadn't come to our departure. Probably, they learned from the press about our great success and came to congratulate us. Anyway, whatever the reason, I was glad that my brother was among them. The train had just stopped and everybody began to bustle around. The crowd moved in an uncontrolled direction, nudging each other, looking to find their loved ones. People shouted the names of their families. Mary and I descended from the car and became part of this spontaneous hubbub. With difficulty we directed ourselves through the crowd toward the spot were I had beheld my brother. As we came closer, they also spotted us.

Mary lifted Gene in her arms and held him tightly to her body; he embraced her with his arms around her neck. They stood in that motionless grip like a statue for a long time. It seemed as if my wife wanted to recoup the many daily hugs she had lost during those six months away. I waited with patience for my turn to hug my son. He had grown. His face was very charming, and I could foresee a handsome man in the future. I took him by the waist and lifted him above my head and spun with him as I had done before so many times. After we all greeted each other unexpectedly, my brother who was carrying some of the luggage directed us to his car and offered to take us home. I was surprised that he had a car. He told us that since he had been promoted in his political job, he now had the privilege of a personal car at his disposal. I congratulated him. His chauffeur put the luggage in the trunk and drove us home.

Arriving at our lovely home, we unpacked hastily and handed out the gifts for everybody present. Gene loved the mechanical toys, especially the tumbling acrobat on the crossbeam and immersed himself in playing with them. We kneeled down near him and played for hours. The following days we met with our best friends, handed them their gifts, and recounted the stories from our tour.

My mother informed us that the doctor had visited our home once a week to take care of Gene. We were happy that Gene recovered and that the doctor was optimistic regarding his future development.

We bought a Bechstein grand piano and he started to take piano lessons. He made significant progress and played with much success at the music school concerts. Later, however, he lost his desire to play, preferring to play with other children. So we sold the piano.

■■■

After a short vacation the company resumed its normal activity. Now there arrived in Romania the second Russian Consultant Igor Smirnov, Ballet Master at The Bolshoi. For our company, he staged a sailor dance. For the Romanian opera, he staged the *Călăreţul de Aramă (The Bronze Horse),* music by Reinhold M. Glière. He invited me to teach character classes at the opera to prepare the dancers for his ballet. I was glad that he had asked me, but the leadership of my company was not pleased. Unfortunately, I had to postpone the realization of my dream for a later date.

After completion of their study, the students who were sent to the USSR returned. One of them, Vasile Marcu, who initially was sent from the city of Cluj, got the job as ballet master at the opera in Bucharest. He was asked to choreograph an original full-length ballet. The subject he chose was from Romanian history, *Haiducii (The Outlaws).* Hilda Jerea, a composer, created the libretto together with the ballet master, Gelu Matei. Hilda Jerea composed a wonderful score dominated by Romanian folk tunes. Vasile Marcu wanted to choreograph the ballet also based on Romanian folk elements, especially to delineate the character of the outlaws. But he was not familiar with the folk dances and looked for an expert in the field.

Marcu asked me if I would like to be his assistant ballet master and folk consultant to the ballet. I accepted his invitation with the hope that again this would lead to a permanent position at the opera. The ballet was well received and the choreographer was pleased with my contribution. As a result, he proposed that I become a permanent member of the opera ballet. Once again the door to the opera was opened for me. Thrilled by his proposal I accepted it. Mary was happy for me, but the *Ciocîrlia* Company was not. The *Ciocîrlia* wanted me to continue working with them. Finally, in 1958, *Ciocîrlia* reluctantly released me with strings attached. I had to continue working part-time with them, to teach classes and choreograph two ballets a year. Later, Vasile selected me once again to be his assistant for the ballet *Tricornul (The Three-Cornered Hat)*, with music by Manuel de Falla, and for the ballet *Romeo and Juliet*.

Ciocîrlia continued to demand more and more choreography from me. So, in collaboration with Floria Capsali Dumitrescu, I choreographed the ballet *Toamnă Bogată (The Rich Autumn)* to music by Mircea Chiriac. *Marea Sărbătoare (The Big Fete)* to music by Viorel Doboş, *Jocuri Populare De Pe Intinsul Patriei (Dances From All Over the Country)* to music by Viorel Doboş, *Harta Patriei (The Homeland Map)* music by Viorel Doboş and *Obiceiurile de Iarnă (Winter Customs of Moldova)* in collaboration with Tamara Cap, to music by Constantin Arvinte. In addition, I did the work and they took the credit because they were famous.

The dance *The Homeland Map*

I was not pleased about being pushed into those collaborations. I liked, however, to be alone with my thoughts when I created. I liked to work by myself, trying different ideas, changing them until I found the ones that best appealed to me. I couldn't imagine what it would be like to choreograph a dance with someone else. My creative process is an individual one. The dances that I choreographed for the Youth Festival in Warsaw and for the tour in China proved that I, working alone, possessed a great talent for the art of dance.

The department head always pulled the strings in her favor. Refusing to "collaborate," I would have created an enemy. I didn't want to antagonize anyone at that time, being afraid that I would jeopardize my position at the opera. Also, I thought that it would be a good professional learning experience for me. In conclusion, after many days of debating the subject with my dear wife, I accepted the inevitable. It was a good decision because all these dances were presented to the public-at-large and at the gala performances for the party and government leadership. That created the venue to make my name known to the public, the cultural minister and the leaders of the Communist Party.

Since I had choreographed the dance *Eliberarea Patriei (The Country's Liberation)*, my reputation as a choreographer spread all over the country. To that recognition was added the success of my other dances performed both at home and in China.

The Pioneer Palace, the center of the Pioneer Organization (similar to our girl or boy scouts), offered me a part-time job in their dance department, and I accepted it. Teaching children was new to me, but it was a delight to work with them. I was impressed by their desire to learn. They were like a sponge, absorbing quickly the material I taught.

CĂPÎLNA

From the day that I saw the girls from Căpîlna on stage at the Romanian competition for amateur groups, their dance had positively enchanted me. They didn't have any orchestral accompaniment. As they danced they had sung the melody, which was based on a syncopated polyrhythmic sound of their steps constantly changing the cadence of the song and the steps. I liked the manner of their continuously changing cadence of song and steps. Since that time, images of their dance swirled in my mind, like beautiful picture-slides. At home, in the streetcar, or at work, I enjoyed this imaginary show, which became an obsession. I looked forward to the day when I could project these images from my mind into reality on stage. I discovered a desire that I hadn't felt before, to use these images for choreography. On the spur of the moment, I felt that I would like to choreograph a dance about the girls from Căpîlna, to bring my images alive.

I spoke to the department head many times, requesting the opportunity to choreograph that dance. Permission was always diplomatically postponed because we were supposedly busy with other projects. I couldn't stand it any longer, so my wife and I had a brainstorming session about what to do. She thought that it would be wise if I would voice my request at the monthly meeting of Ciocîrlia, with all the leaders of the company. That way, I would find out the truth. At the next meeting, I presented my proposal, and the artistic director enthusiastically accepted it. He than asked the opinion of Tamara Cap, the department head, who stood stone still. She barely nodded her head and quietly muttered, "sure."

Constantin Arvinte and Iacob

At that moment in my life, the hypocritical character of my department head was revealed. A bell tolled in my head, warning me to be more careful in the future. I was naïve in thinking that I could overcome all the double-faced people. Throughout the years of my life, I have encountered many double tongued, hypocritical people, and I wasn't able to discover them in time. I recognized them only after they took advantage of me.

The artistic director of Ciocîrlia gave me a free hand to start the process of research and rehearsal, to bring my mental images to the reality of the public stage. With the composer Constantin Arvinte, and costume designer Ion David, I traveled to the village Căpîlna in Transylvania. I spent two weeks in that village learning the song and the intricate syncopated steps. I interviewed many villagers about their heritage and about the customs practiced in their village and the province of Transylvania. The accumulated information made my mind feel like the scattered pieces of a jigsaw puzzle. When I started putting the pieces in place, I discovered that this was an exercise requiring deep concentration. I had to block out all thoughts except those related to my project. The puzzle quickly began to take form and I felt as if I were putting together a work of art.

I liked in particular one of Căpîlna's wedding customs, and I based my choreography on it. I concluded my preparation by creating a short libretto. The girl who is to get married prepares a gift for her future bridegroom. For that purpose during the winter nights, she invites her girlfriends from the village to an evening sewing-bee. The gift for the bridegroom will be a rustic shirt, ornamented with traditional folk designs using small beads, spangles and multicolored thread. At the sewing-bee, each girl embroiders a different design on a piece of the shirt, and then the future bride sews the shirt together. At the wedding, she will

The Girls of Căpîlna

give him the gift. I created that libretto with my wife and myself in mind, as the bride and bridegroom.

I planned the choreography for twenty girls plus the bride and bridegroom. For the first cast, I chose for Mary to be the bride. Since I couldn't dance any more, I selected a good dancer to play my role as bridegroom. I dedicated all my creative talent and effort toward the successful outcome of that dance. In rehearsal, I realized that my image of

Mary as the bride was fortuitous; she and her partner responded quickly to my directions for both the steps and the emotional interpretation of the dance. I never told my wife that the dance was to be dedicated to her.

Fetele din Căpîlna (*The Girls of Căpîlna*) was enormously successful. On the opening night, my wife danced the role of the bride exquisitely. She expressed a genuine feeling of love, offering the shirt to the bridegroom. The majestic carriage of her body gave the dance a regal presentation. Her steps floated as if she were ready to leave the ground. Supported by the boy's arm, she turned with an incredible whirlwind, which nobody else in the company could match. Watching her, she thrilled my heart. I felt as if I had been hit by Cupid's shaft, just as I had when we first met.

Mary as the bride in *The Girls of Căpîlna*

After Mary took her bow, we met in the wings of the stage; we hugged each other and stood close together in silence for a long time. We both shed a few tears of happiness and confessed to each other. She told me that she had danced the role for me, imagining that I was the bridegroom, and I told her that I had dedicated the dance to her as an expression of my eternal love for her.

My choreography was a hit and was selected to be a part of the gala performances for the party and government. The cultural minister congratulated me and finally I was recognized as a very talented choreographer. The Ciocîrlia Company was proud of my creation and included the dance in all their performances in the country and abroad. The dance was part of the company's tour in the United States in 1966 but Mary and I weren't permitted to go on that tour because my wife's brother lived in Detroit. The Romanian government was taking no chances that we might defect or exchange information.

This dance was also presented during the company's tour of France. In Paris the famous French choreographer Maurice Bejart who attended the performance wrote a review in *Le Figaro* newspaper about the performance.

His review was reproduced in the Romanian weekly newspaper *Contemporanul.* His opinion of the *Dansul Fetelor din Căpîlna* (*The Girls of Căpîlna)* thrilled me:

"Scriind aceste rînduri îmi revine mereu in faţă *Dansul Fetelor din Căpîlna.* Este perfecţiunea in artă. Nu i se poate adăuga nimic. (Writing those lines, the dance of the *The Girls of Căpîlna* continually appears in front of me. It is the perfection in art. Nothing can be added to it)."

■■■

The leadership of the Ciocîrlia Company finally understood that I was capable of choreographing by myself without any collaboration, and they gave me the opportunity. There followed a series of creations: *Apărarea Patriei (Defense of the Homeland)* to music by Constantin Arvinte, *Brîul Cosînzenei (Cosinzeana's Belt),* on a libretto by Eugen Gal, to music by Constantin Arvinte, the *Omagiul Statuii (The Homage to the Statue)* to music by Viorel Doboş.

Brîul Cosînzenei

Hidden beneath the increased opportunity to choreograph, for the company, was a well-developed plan to take me out of the opera dance department, to again resume full time work at the Ciocîrlia. The leadership of Ciocîrlia had very good relationships with high-level persons from the party who were actually able to dismiss or transfer anybody they wanted.

One day after a rehearsal of *Romeo and Juliet,* Vasile Marcu, expressing his regret, informed me that I was fired. He avoided giving me any reason, except to say that he was sorry that he was losing me. I insisted on an explanation, but he shrugged his shoulders and told me there was nothing he could do. It was beyond his authority. It was an order. I asked him to tell me who had ordered it. He explained that if he divulged the source he would lose his job. I, therefore, resumed my full-time job at the Ciocîrlia as if nothing had happened.

I had liked the work at the opera, and I was disappointed and angry about what happened. I realized that talent was not enough to achieve my goals; I needed a high-level political relation. My brother was one of the deputy general managers of *Agerpres,* the Romanian Press Agency, so I asked him to help me regain my job at the opera. For the first time, I experienced real bitterness in my relations with my brother. Under the influence of his wife, who secluded herself from our family, he told me that he could or would do nothing. Feeling pressured by me to look into the matter, he told me that my situation had been decided on at a very high level, and it would be inappropriate for him to discuss it.

Echoes of the success of *The Girls of Capîlna* were heard all over Romania, and, as a result, I was invited to choreograph for other companies. I worked out a mutually acceptable schedule with the Ciocîrlia Company so that I was able to accept the invitation to the Ansamblul Secuiesc de Stat (Szekler State Ensemble) from Tîrgu Mures, the capital of the Regiunea Autonomă Maghiară (Hungarian Autonomy Region). I became resident choreographer with their company for three years. It was a young and very enthusiastic ensemble, eager to learn new choreography. It was a great experience and a fruitful collaboration.

Also, the Ciocîrlia Company nominated me for several governmental awards which were given to me on different holiday occasions: Romanian Cultural Medal in 1950, A second Romanian Cultural Medal in 1955, an Order of the Third Degree in 1959, and an Order of the Second Degree in 1960.

The opportunity to collaborate with the opera opened up once again when Oleg Danovsky, the principal choreographer of the opera, selected me to be his assistant for *Iancu Jianu* a famous outlaw like *(Robin Hood), Priculiciul (The Wolf Man)*, and *Întoarcerea din Adîncuri (The Return from The Deep)*, all full-length ballets. Also, on his recommendation, the choreography school of Bucharest offered me a teaching chair for character dance. I accepted it and loved working with talented children from all over the country.

■■■

The Ciocîrlia leadership announced that everybody should complete their high school diploma as a condition of continued employment in the company but that put us in a tangled position and we had to enroll in special night courses. For both of us, it was a real challenge to successfully combine work and study. I graduated the high school in 1957 and Mary graduated in 1960. For my position as the assistant to the department head, however, I needed a Bachelor's degree, also.

No university in Romania offered a degree in dance, so I had to choose between the "Music Conservatory" and the "Physical Institute." I opted and enrolled in the Institutul de Pedagogie din Bucuresti Facultatea de Educatie Fizica (The Pedagogical Institute in Bucharest Physical Education Department). The institute didn't have night courses, so I had to take courses by correspondence. It took me four years to finish my degree. I was on the run from one place of work to another and all the free time I had on Sundays or afternoons were gone. The practical exam for each sport was difficult, but the boxing exam was disastrous for me. I knew nothing about the technique of boxing, and my challenger was a professional boxer. We were supposed to fight, but I never even had a chance to reach him. He cuffed me bitterly and broke my nose. The end was bloody, but, happily, I passed the exam. Since then, every time I touch my nose, I feel the place where it was broken, reminding me of that cruel event. I did finally graduate.

The stress of the studying combined with the stress from my work ruined my health. Unendurable cramps in my stomach woke me up during the nights, forcing me to run to the toilet. After perspiring heavily, I usually fainted but I was determined not to upset Mary, so I didn't tell her. One morning, however, traveling on the streetcar with Mary on our way to rehearsal, the excruciating pains in my stomach hit me. There was no toilet to run to, so I had to hold myself and the pains became more intense. Mary immediately noticed my crisis.

"What's going on with you? You are so pale and you..." Everything was silent; I couldn't hear her voice anymore. I was unconscious for a while. The feeling was euphoric, like floating through yellow clouds, and the cramps disappeared. When I regained consciousness, Mary was patting my head with a handkerchief to wipe off the perspiration. Curious people from the streetcar surrounded us, offering to help.

"I don't know; he fainted, and I don't know the reason" Mary responded addressing to the crowd.

Later, I told her about the cramps and confessed that it had happened many times before; I had thought that the cramping was something temporary and it would go away.

When the company doctor took me to the hospital the diagnosis was a nervous crisis in my stomach as the result of exhaustion and frustration at work.

WARNING SIGNS

Communist methods began to frighten me. Anytime they pleased, people in authority could intimidate me or warn me of possible actions against me. I had to be careful of what I said or did; I had to be careful not to go against the party's severe rules or against a party member on a higher-level. The promises the Communist Party made of liberty and freedom were empty promises. While living in a supposed utopian society, I realized that the exploitation of a human being was greater and crueler than that of a capitalist society. The fact that I couldn't choose to work at the opera, where I wanted to work and where I was accepted, indeed, frustrated me.

During one of the rehearsals at the opera house, for a gala performance of the dance *Omagiul Statuii (The Homage to the Statue)* a frightening incident of intimidation happened. The statue that inspired me to create the choreography represented a triplet of laborers. At the beginning of the dance, three dancers, standing still and symbolizing the original statue, were carried from the wings onto the stage on a 4 by 4-foot platform held by four other dancers. The four dancers' steps were synchronized to assure the stability of the three dancers on the platform. During their walk onto the stage, one of the dancers who carried the platform slipped, and the three dancers on the platform momentarily lost their balance. The four dancers carrying the platform continued their walk to the center of the stage and lowered the platform onto the floor. The rehearsal continued very well but afterward, the special security officer called me over to him. His mission was to remain vigilant so that no one violated the party's line and prestige. I was surprised. I couldn't recall doing anything wrong but none of us knew when we might be accused. He accused me of purposely directing the dancer to slip, in order to symbolize the fall of the Communist Party. I was shocked and angered by the accusation.

"Are you looking for a pretext to frame me? What are you aiming for?" Without waiting for his answer, I continued, "It appears that you have no knowledge about dance. During any rehearsal, a dancer can slip or even fall, unintentionally. Before accusing me, why don't you ask the dancer, if I directed him to purposely slip?" He didn't listen to what I said. With his mean-spirited attitude and raised voice, he warned me that such slights against the party should never happen again. This episode shocked me, and I began to panic about my future. To me, this was a sign that I was in their field of vision and in danger of being kicked out of the company.

The following episode added to my suspicions even more: Hero Lupescu, a director from the opera, was assigned to put together a grandiose show for the liberation celebration in the biggest stadium in Bucharest. He asked me to be the choreographer for that show. I accepted because it was a unique challenge for me. I had to work with about four hundred dancers. He was pleased with my choreography and the dancers' performance.

The dancers used the Romanian and Russian party flags in the finale to create a variety of highly visual patterns. At the end of the finale during the first rehearsal, the dancers were instructed to place all the flags on the ground, exactly at the same spot from where they had taken them. This same security officer accused me of purposely directing the dancers to put the flags on the ground as a sign that the Russian and Romanian parties were going to collapse. This time, he shouted at me in front of all 400 dancers.

"How dare you put the flags on the ground. They are symbols of the eternal strength of our party!" This time I was more composed when I answered, "These flags are theatrical props and the prop man will take care of them" and I left him standing there, stunned.

The harassment continued, taking different forms. In a meeting with the leaders of the company, the folk dance specialist Gheorghe Popescu Judeţ was also invited. He accused me of distorting the choreography of the Romanian folk-dances with the material from my classical background. I responded that I create dances; I don't reproduce them. His negative opinion of my work actually reflected his own inability to create dances. He just copied the folk-steps as they already were. I created dances based on the folk-steps. I reminded him about the most eloquent example of my creations, *The Girls of Capîlna*, which continued to be very successful in Romania and abroad. I replied to Comrade Judeţ's accusation with a copy of the Bejart review about *The Girls of Capîlna*:

"Scriind aceste rînduri îmi revine mereu in faţă *Dansul Fetelor din Căpîlna*. Este perfecţiunea in artă. Nu i se poate adăuga nimic. (Writing those lines, the dance of the *The Girls of Căpîlna* continually appears in front of me. It is the perfection in art. Nothing can be added to it)."

He was irritated by my reply to his accusation. He concluded that the guidelines of the company, as specified by the communist party, include preserving the folk-dances exactly as the peasants danced them. I wanted to reply, but my wife nudged me advising me to stay silent. Certainly I couldn't agree with that policy, but I felt that she was right; it could be dangerous to argue against his remarks. It might be considered criticism against the communist party itself. Mary later told me at home that she guessed that Judet had been given the assignment to speak out against my creative work. Future events would confirm that her intuition was right, as always.

This realization created for me severe anxiety. I felt trapped in a situation out of which there was no escape. Voluntary exit from the party was suicidal. All I could do was to carry on under severe mental strain and fight as best I could against further intrusions of the Communist Party into my life. I also opposed my wife's entry into the Communist Party when she was solicited to do so. Being a party member was more significant to the communists than one's artistic ability and the consequences of her refusal were felt immediately. She was not taken with the ensemble on its Western tour, ostensibly because she had a brother living in America. Other members of the company who had relatives in the West were taken along, but they were members of the Communist Party. Even though I was a member of the Communist Party I was not taken either, Instead, Comrade Județ was taken. Obviously they planned to get rid of me. They were just waiting for the right moment and the most convenient pretext.

The Artistic Director asked me to choreograph a dance with military content. During my usual research, I didn't find anything exciting to inspire me. Close to our apartment was a beautiful park called Cişmigiu Park, where my parents often took my son Gene for a walk. One Sunday, as Mary, Gene and I were having our usual outing in that park and I was surprised to see so many soldiers from different branches of the armed services. Some of them were walking with girls, others were rowing on the lake, and others were in groups looking to find some girls. I told Mary that this could be the subject for my dance, and I even suggested the name *Întîlnirea (The Date)*. Because my wife loved the idea, confidently I started working on it. I spent many Sundays in the park observing the behavior of the soldiers and their relationships more closely. There were more soldiers than girls, and sometimes several soldiers dated the same girl without knowing it. This then became the subject on which I embroidered my choreography.

I selected the five-army branches that belonged to the Ministry of Internal Affairs (Militia, Border Guard, Security, Marines and Firemen). In the dance, the girl had separate dates with each one. The ballet includes many comic moments and at the end the soldiers find out that they have been cheated. It passed the company artistic director's censorship; but that didn't mean that it passed all the political tests.

Publicly the dance was very successful, and it was selected for the Government and Central Communist Party Committee gala performance. It was always considered an honor and a privilege to be selected for the party's gala performance and so far, during my ascending career, my choreographies had been presented several times at these performances. This time the selection of my dance would entirely change my career. Present at that gala performance was Ion Draghici, the Minister of Internal Affairs and member of the Communist Party Secretariat. He ordered his political subordinate to convene a special meeting to discuss the Communist Party guidelines as they related to my works. At that meeting was of course,

Comrade Judeţ the main critic of my creative work for the company was also there.

The minister considered *Întîlnirea (The Date)* dance an offense to the soldiers representing the five branches of the army who had separate dates with the same girl. This was considered immoral. He also felt that my dance was too much of a departure from the Communist guidelines regarding folk-dances. I was reminded that the principal guidelines of the Communist Party should reflect Socialism's reality. I was angry again and responded to these accusations, saying that my work reflected Socialism's reality, and I invited them to the park to see "reality" as I had witnessed it. My invitation and my request to be allowed to create freely without political pressures and directives not only fell on deaf ears, but also brought about unsympathetic and hostile reactions from my political superiors.

At that time, Khrushchev came to power in the U.S.S.R. and launched his campaign against the Jews, and the subservient regime in Romania followed suit launching its own campaign to eliminate Jews from important positions in public life. The fact that I was highly recognized professionally as a dancer, teacher and choreographer, and that my creations had received national and international attention did not exempt me when the anti-Semitic campaign began.

Major Nastovich, the commander of the company, called me to his office and informed me that I was laid off, on the pretext of needing to reduce personnel. Another colleague from the ensemble, the conductor Alois Honig, also a Jew, was laid off under the same pretext. No one else was laid off except for us. Comrade Judeţ was hired in my position. The commander advised me to contact the personnel officer, Comrade Khira, who eventually would contact the workers' employment to place me in a huge factory as an ordinary worker. Certainly, I was offended and refused to accept such a humiliating offer.

Fortunately, I found people who ignored the racial campaign launched by the Communist Party against the Jews. Fica Ion, the chairman of the artistic activity of the Pioneer Palace, generously offered me a full-time job. He would support me and create a pleasant working environment. Corpade, the director of the Choreography School, didn't fire me from my part-time teaching job and had the same friendly attitude as Ion, who condemned the racially motivated action by the Ciocîrlia Company. Neither job was as prestigious as the Ciocîrlia position, but they were good places to work with very nice people.

■■■

After my departure, the Ciocîrlia Artistic Company continued to perform my choreographies nationally and internationally, but my name was dropped from the billboards and programs because Brümmer was a Jewish name. Mary, who was not Jewish, was not laid off, but she began to feel the racial prejudice indirectly because she was carrying my name. Being a soloist, her name had to appear on the billboards and in the program. So they arbitrarily used her maiden name, Lascu, instead. When she requested that her married name be used, they circumvented the whole issue by no longer assigning the principal roles to her. Wanting to help my wife, I appealed to the Ministry of Internal Affairs to have my last name changed. I explained about the prejudice that my non-Jewish wife had to endure. My request was denied, as the clerk informed me that the Communist Party doesn't have a policy of racial or religious discrimination.

At this point a friend of ours came up with a helpful idea. We could change our names by divorcing and remarrying. Reflecting on our friend's advice, we decided to go through a formal divorce and then immediately remarry. The process of divorce was very difficult and painful. The court required solid evidence before granting a divorce. We didn't have any reason for the divorce, other than to change our name, and for the court that was not an acceptable reason. The same good friend volunteered to testify that I had been unfaithful and assaulted my wife many times. My dear son was instructed also to testify that I came home every night drunk and beat them both. Mary however, faced an awkward situation at work, when she announced our divorce plans.

Later in my life, I received a letter from Emilia Ocico, one of the dancers and my wife's dear friend, recalling the day that Mary announced that we were divorcing.

> "One day during a rehearsal break, Mary gathered all the girls in the dressing room and, without introduction, said:
>
> 'I have applied for a formal divorce from Jacky [my nickname as my colleagues called me]. We are divorcing! Don't be astonished; that's it!'
>
> In the dressing room, silence descended for a moment, and then came an explosion of questions, exclamations, and vehement arguments. The dressing room was transformed into Hiroshima. We knew that couples quarrel and people divorce, but Mary and Jacky? It is impossible! This model wedlock breaks up? Is it possible that two such people, so different from the rest of the chaff, with such a wonderful child as Genuţ, are going to tear apart? Is that possible? We girls from the dressing room couldn't conceive of it; we couldn't find any reason, absolutely nothing. Mary and Jacky represented for us the inseparable. But now what?

111

Jacky, when you two remarried, everybody from the company realized how much you loved each other and how determined both of you were to survive in these difficult days."

I thanked Emilia for her wonderful letter and for her friendship and admiration for both Mary and our marriage.

The divorce decree was granted on January 24, 1964 and we remarried on November 2, 1964. The 9-month delay was because of the endless paper work and medical examinations required. This unpleasant journey in a complicated labyrinth, forced upon us by the dictatorial communist rules, couldn't break our strong belief in a brighter future. With our love for each other and our strength toughened, we felt ready to face any future discrimination.

I put the trauma of the last year behind me and dedicated my energy and talent to my new full-time job at the dance department at the Pioneer Palace. The dance department flourished under my leadership, and in no time, I had incorporated an ensemble called Romanaşul (The Diminutive of Romanian). The children were selected from the city of Bucharest, and in one year, the Romanaşul presented fifty successful performances in Romania, in France, Yugoslavia and USSR. The ensemble was also invited to dance at the prestigious gala performance. The success of this ensemble went beyond my expectations, and the children were invited to other gala performances.

UNEXPECTED EVENTS

As I continued my story for my wife's brother Traian I reminded him of his trip in Europe and of course in Romania in 1965 when we met for the first time. The joy of his coming was over-shadowed by the fear that his visit would endanger Mary's position in the company. His visit was a revelation for us when he shared his experience in the United States.

Traian invited us to visit him in America to get a better idea of their lives. We told him that the company refused to take Mary on their tour to America and Western Europe because of him, and we thought that the Romanian authorities would refuse to issue us passports. He informed us that the press in America was talking about an eventual visit of President Richard Nixon to Romania and in his opinion; this would create a favorable political climate between the two countries. Romania had requested favored nation status, which would be an item on the agenda of the American president's visit. Traian suggested that we try to apply for passports at this one-time opportunity.

Soon after Traian's departure, we applied for three passports and waited anxiously to see the results. To our surprise after three months, the Romanian authorities gave my wife and me the passports but they refused to give our son Gene a passport. The Romanian government wanted to be sure that we would not defect. We didn't know what to do? Should we go without Gene? People advised us to go; it was a unique opportunity to get passports to visit a western country. We decided to go without Gene who remained with my mother.

Our visit to America changed our way of thinking about this country. We realized how we had been brainwashed by the communists. The standard of living in America and the abundance of food was beyond our imagination. We had a chance to visit many Romanians; with homes that reflected the American dream.

The Romanian people whom we visited in America told us to defect, to ask for political asylum. The suggestion was very tempting but we decided not to defect. We had a dear son back home and we didn't want to be separated from him.

The economic situation was getting worse in Romania, so the Communist Party ordered various mergers of factories, ministries and institutions. This merger campaign swallowed the Ciocîrlia Artistic Company, merging it with the Army Ensemble. Dancers were dismissed or selected based on an audition in front of a combined panel of judges from both companies. One of the judges was my friend Vasile Marcu from the opera who later told me that Mary had gotten the highest marks from the judges. But she had not been selected to the newly formed company because she had a brother in America!

Mary was devastated. I tried to comfort her but without much success. She cried all day not able to believe that this was happening to her. Gradually she realized that she had fallen into the same political trap as I was in, from which there was no escape. They had gotten rid of her, because she had a brother in America and because she was my wife. What had happened was not totally unexpected, but she was bitterly hurt.

■■■

When the campaign of racial persecution was launched, a wave of Jewish immigration to Israel began as well I thought at that point that it would be a good move for us to also emigrate. I was not sure that Mary would agree to be separated from her big sister who was like a mother to her. I always shared my thoughts with my wife, good or bad, and explained why I arrived at that idea.

"I was thrown out because I am a Jew and because I fought for free expression of my art. You are not a Jew, and they kicked you out because they consider you a danger to the country and party, and because you have a brother in America. My dear, the dictatorial regime will continue to hang over our heads and we never know when it will strike again. We never know with whom we can talk, if he is our friend or a spy working for the party. The telephones are bugged. Nobody dares to criticize the actions or the policy of the party. The only way to escape from this terror is to leave Romania. We have a chance now to apply for immigration to Israel. If you agree, you would have to convert to the Jewish religion."

"I don't mind as long we are together."

We applied for immigration and forward to freedom, but our ordeal was far from over. Our application was denied. My brother Zolty opposed our desire for emigration, afraid that it would trigger his expulsion from his high level position with Communist Party. Our application triggered my immediate expulsion from the party who classified me as a traitor to my country and to the Communist Party.

Our struggle for emigration had just begun. We knocked on the doors of many officials, and after many refusals, we decided to apply for help from the Israeli Embassy. Unfortunately, they couldn't help us, either. The last chance was the Central Committee of the Communist Party, but the result was the same: a post card was of denial. Everybody told us that we would never leave this country.

"You are young and we need you here" we were told.

"Hypocrites!" I said to my wife. We were desperate and we tried again with a new application, but this time to the United States but again we were stymied in our struggle to reach freedom. What could we do? My wife came up with the idea of writing Traian. Maybe he could help us from America. He was prompt in his letter promising to do everything possible to help us. He wrote that immigration to the United States had increased because of a new American policy. This policy allowed American citizens to unite with other family members from outside of the country creating, a new hope for us, again.

Indeed Traian kept his promise and succeeded. He asked Congresswoman Martha W. Griffiths of Michigan and Senator "Scoop" Jackson, chairman of the Senate's Foreign Relations Committee, to help him bring us to the United States under the Family Integration Policy. They intervened with the American Department of State and the American Embassy in Bucharest, requesting that assistance be given to us in our efforts to immigrate to the United States. Soon the United States ambassador in Romania informed us that we had been granted entry visas to the United States. However, he advised us to have patience in waiting for our release by the Romanian officials. The sunshine of new hope penetrated our hearts. Patience was our enemy and everyday we checked the mail for the approval card, but nothing came.

Then the Romanian press, radio and television announced that America's President Nixon would be visiting Romania and he arrived with his wife. The Gala performance in his honor was held at the opera house and I was proud that my dance group from the Pioneer Palace was selected to be part of the performance. The next day Mrs. Patricia Nixon accompanied by Mrs. Shirley Black (Shirley Temple) visited the Pioneer Palace and stopped in my class. I presented a short dance program for our guests and I vividly recollect that very emotional moment when the president's wife personally congratulated me. At that instant, I couldn't imagine that one day her husband would be my president, too and the very next day after President Nixon left Romania, I received a postcard directing Mary and me to appear before Romanian officials with our identification documents. We didn't know the purpose of the summons, but we were optimistic because the post card was not another rejection.

It was a nice day with bright sunshine, gleaming with hope. A major from the Minister of Internal Affairs welcomed us. With his unusual cordiality and politeness he got right to the point and told us that our emigration request had been approved. My heart began to pound with joy and I felt as if it were going to jump out of my body. Mary told me that she felt the same way, but we both restrained ourselves.

115

The major woke us up from our restrained ecstasy by telling us that we had a problem to resolve. "What problem?" I asked. The major saw my scared face and told me to relax. Very calmly he said that we must decide where we wanted to immigrate? I told him that I didn't understand what he was asking for. "You have requested," he said, "to immigrate to two countries, Israel and the United States of America. Both of your requests have been approved. Now you have to decide where you want to go."

Both Mary and I were dumbfounded. We looked at each other, lifted our shoulders and said to the major, "Anyplace, just let us go." "My duty," he said, "is to make you understand that you can choose either one." I asked him politely for his opinion, where he thought we should go. He glanced at his watch. It was a Friday afternoon and he was in a hurry to get to a soccer game. Hastily, he answered.

"I am not authorized to advise people what to do; but knowing that your wife has a brother in the United States it seems more appropriate to choose that direction." We agreed and signed the paper that he then pushed in front of us. After that, he told us what we had to do next.

We left the major's office with a feeling of uncontrollable excitement. In the street, we got carried away and started dancing. People who didn't know the cause of our ecstasy just stared at us. Maybe they assumed that we had just been released from a lunatic asylum! In part, that assumption was real. We were being released from a country oppressed by a "lunatic" Party.

Our son welcomed the news with great joy. Within two weeks, we had run all over the city to comply with the particular instructions given by the major. Then we performed our last duty to the state. We had to present receipts that proved that we didn't have any debts, either to the state or to any other institution or organization. With all those receipts and our identification papers, the three of us went to the emigration office of the Ministry of Internal Affairs. We had succeeded in selling our car, furniture, and all our belongings. Each of us was allowed to take with us only one set of clothes and a valise weighing no more than forty pounds.

We were eager to have the passports in our hands. The moment arrived. They handed us the passports but not before we surrendered all the awards received from the government. Who cared? We just wanted to leave as quickly as possible. We were victims of the communist ideological nightmare as were so many others. We were afraid that they would change their minds as they had done so many times with others. With the passports in our possession, we were able to purchase tickets at the Romanian Tarom Agency for our flight to Detroit.

When my brother found out that we had been approved to immigrate to America, he called me and requested a meeting. Glad that he had called, I invited him to our house. Surprisingly, he asked that our meeting be kept secret and take place somewhere secluded. He apologized for his former opposition to our emigration, and he expressed the hope that I would understand and sympathize with his awkward situation. He told me that he was happy for us and that he agreed with our decision. Before he departed, he asked me for a favor. With an emotional voice he said, "Dear brother, I have a son as you do, and I am asking you to do everything possible to get him out of this country."

I was touched by his plea and promised him that I would do everything possible for his son, Saşa. He hugged me and wished me good luck. My brother finally realized the hoax behind the ideology of communism. He finally understood that to maintain your job in the communist society, you have to humiliate yourself, compromise yourself, and obey their every request. He finally understood that the Communist Party's promise of a free, sincere society, different from the dictatorial fascist one and the capitalist one, was a lie. After our departure, my brother was demoted to a lower position. I kept my promise though and his son is now living in New Jersey.

Later my brother Zolty visited his son Saşa in New York. At that time my relationship with my brother was not the best because we had strong disagreements about our mother's well being in Romania. I had many discussions with Maria, whether or not I should put the matter behind me and meet my brother in New York.

I hadn't seen him since my departure from Romania, fifteen years earlier. I always loved my brother and admired him for his brilliance. He had been a role model for me when we were growing up because of his dedication, strength and perseverance. In school, he had graduated *magna cum laude*. He had started his career as a journalist after the Second World War, at *Scinteia*, the Communist Party's official newspaper under the name Zamfir Brumaru. He was first a feature writer, soon rising to become one of the editors. Because he could speak several foreign languages fluently, he soon specialized in writing and editing foreign policy speeches, and later was promoted to the *Agerpres* National Wire and News Service, (The Romanian Press Agency). In the early 1960's he was promoted again, becoming one of the deputy general managers at the *Agerpres*. He also became the equivalent of a press secretary for the Romanian Council of Ministers.

Zolty loved his job, and spent many nights working over time. He really believed the communist message. Only relatively late did he realize the hoax of communism. Most of the change in his attitude came after 1964, when he and his wife went on a vacation in Western Europe. His attitude became clearer in 1968 after Russia's invasion of Czechoslovakia.

In 1972, he was demoted to deputy chief editor of the *Munca (The Work)* newspaper because I immigrated to the United States. Because the work was much less challenging and because his salary was substantially reduced, he became depressed. Soon after, he suffered his first heart attack. After a few weeks in the hospital, he was retired on disability and placed under permanent medical treatment with various drugs. My heart wanted to see and meet him. Maria totally agreed with me.

It was an emotional reunion and during our two days together I convinced my brother to come home with us. He accepted our invitation, and we drove home together. During his stay with us, he was overwhelmed by everything: our beautiful house; the high standard of living; my ballet studio; the studio at the university; the way Maria took care of him; and, most of all, by our grandchildren.

My brother took great pleasure in playing with the children and they loved him. The horse-mounting game was the children's favorite. They didn't know about his heart condition so one of us took over the role of the horse, giving him a chance to rest. Zolty was my only close relative; my mother had died, and I wanted him to be with us. I told him that he was welcome to stay as long as he wished and not to return to Romania. He was always a proud man and didn't want to depend on others. His judgment was that in Romania, he and his wife had good pensions. If he came to the United States at his advanced age, he would not be able to find work and sustain himself. He didn't want to be a burden to us. This was another great mind wasted by the communist regime.

Unfortunately, his visa was soon to expire, and he had to return to New York in order to fly back to Romania. He was very happy and proud to see me, to see that I had succeeded in the United States in my profession. He enjoyed Gene, my son, and his family, and thanked me for bringing his son to the United States. He departed, and we never saw him again.

Later I received the bad news that my brother in Romania had died in a tragic way at the age of 68. This was a terrible loss for me; he was my only close relative still in Romania. We remembered vividly the days he had spent with us during his visit to the United States. My brother's wife was leaving on vacation for a treatment of mineral waters and he had accompanied her to the train station. The police had blocked traffic to allow the motorcade of the Communist Party's secretary Ceausescu to pass, and they arrived at the station late. To catch the train, my brother and his wife started to run. She jumped on the train, and he put her valises on the train. The train departed. My brother waved his hand toward his departing wife till the train disappeared from his view, but the effort of running with the heavy valises in his hands had increased his blood pressure and he collapsed. By the time the ambulance arrived, it was too late; he was dead.

"Here I am Traian. That was my story that you asked for. I don't now if this is what you wanted." Anyway I thanked him for his patience and for the dinner and the pleasant evening and especially everything he had done for us. We were indeed a happy family.

MY FIRST DANCE TEACHING

Traian is a unique individual; His love for his sister Mary and her family was genuine. He devoted his time, wisdom, and energy, to helping us in all matters. I can never thank him enough. He always encouraged me and told me that I could accomplish a lot with hard work, dedication and will. To uphold and underscore his words, he told me the following story.

"Jacky, look around you. On the ground you'll see lots of dollars. To get them, you'll have to bend down to pick them up. The more quickly and efficiently you bend down, the more dollars you will get." I understood his analogy and have remembered it always.

Traian was familiar with the Detroit Folkdance Club through his Romanian friends who were members. Traian contacted Ben Chang, the coordinator of the club, and told him about me. Ben invited me to teach some Romanian dances. Ben suggested that I make a recording of the music and write down the steps of the dances that I intended to teach so I could sell them at the workshop. The workshop went over well, and I was asked to repeat it. He also invited me to teach at the Detroit Folkdance Club's Annual Fall Camp. Mary and I presented new Romanian couple dances. The wonderful outdoor experience included a party, singing, and a campfire. Ben and the participants particularly enjoyed the Romanian dances.

One day Traian suggested that we contact the *Detroit News* Drama and Music Critic Jay Carr, who might give us some advice on whom to contact for a job-teaching dance. I agreed and so Traian wrote him a letter. On March 22, 1973, Mr. Carr responded very kindly to that letter. He welcomed me to the free world and suggested contacting Mrs. Harriet Berg at the Jewish Community Center. We called her and she agreed to meet with us there as soon as she found time in the schedule for the class.

My first ballet class, however, was not to be at the Jewish Community Center. One night Traian asked me to come over. He had some letters for me to read.

"What letters? From whom are these letters?"

"The letters are from four dance schools."

"What?" I exclaimed. "I didn't write to anybody."

Traian with his never-ending calm answered, "I did and I am sorry that I didn't inform you about this. Remember, the night when you told me about your life and work in Romania? I wrote a résumé based on your story. I opened the Yellow Pages and sent about fifty-resumes to all the dance schools, companies, colleges, and universities in the Metropolitan area. I wasn't sure of my initiative. So, I waited for the results to tell you, Jacky."

Jumping into my Nova, I drove to his house, so eager to read those letters. There were four of them; generally all the letters said that they were impressed with my résumé and wanted me to call them for an appointment. Traian had done all this on my behalf.

I was so eager to teach that in my excitement I didn't realize that I had major time conflicts with my boss, Mr. Guttman, the tailor. He was understanding and wished me good luck. My first class was at Mrs. Summers' Dance School located on Woodward Avenue in Detroit. I was disappointed in the studio, which was neglected with a leaky ceiling, and too small for any series of high jumps. Finding the situation impossible for me to teach in, I suggested we leave immediately. But, the always-wise Traian said, "Stai," in Romanian. Frustrated, I obeyed. I had four beginning level students. I wanted them to enjoy my class but how could they in such a dreadful environment? Thinking this was a waste of time; desperately I looked at Traian. He was smiling and inclined his head as encouragement that I was to continue. For me, this was an hour of torture that ended surprisingly. Mrs. Summers was very satisfied with the manner in which I had conducted the class and paid me $8. I couldn't believe it. I had earned $8 for only one hour's work! Wow! It was far more than I expected. It was the first payment I received for a ballet class and I have superstitiously preserved those dollars over all these years.

Traian contacted Mrs. Wise and Mary Lazar accompanied me to those classes to help with the translation. Mrs. Wise's studio was located in Birmingham in a bright second floor studio with large windows and a high ceiling. But the floor space was small and not good for jumping. Mrs. Wise had good intermediate level students and she advertised my classes in the newspapers. A reporter interviewed me for a feature story in the newspaper.

Mrs. Berg kept her promise and called me for a trial class at the Jewish Community Center. My class there was in the morning and included ladies only. These ladies liked my class and Mrs. Berg hired me for one class a week. She also offered me a character master class and a summer workshop. She invited a reporter from the *Detroit Jewish News* to interview me.

Mrs. Berg staged a play entitled *The Little Lady Who Couldn't Learn,* a renaissance dance drama performed by the Young Dancers Guild and Festival Dancers at the Aaron Deroy Theatre at the Jewish Community Center. She asked me to take part in it, playing the role of the ballet master William of Pesaro, a renaissance Italian ballet teacher. It was a combined role of dancing and speaking. The dancing part was easy but speaking English was very difficult.

"Perfect," Mrs. Berg said, very satisfied. "Your Romanian accent matches the character."

Harriet Berg later asked me if I wanted to choreograph a dance by Bela Bartok based on Romanian folk motives. In Romania, I had primarily worked with professional dancers not amateurs so I wasn't sure what the outcome of this choreography would be. The twelve girls in the dance were not all at the same level technically so I created solo parts for the best dancers. At the completion of the dance, I was satisfied. On January 27, 1974. The dance, presented by the Young Dancers Guild proved a great success. The audience applauded many times during the performance and cheered when the dance ended.

Iacob as
William of Pesaro

Meanwhile, I started to teach at the Tayntons' dance studio located in their house, in Detroit. Indeed, this was the smallest studio so far. Actually, it was a dining room transformed into a dance studio. After my trial class, they offered me two classes a week and paid me more than all the other studios. My schedule became hectic: English study at home, teaching and choreography and work as a tailor. Consulting with Traian about whether I should quit the tailor shop and dedicate myself to just teaching, he shared more wisdom.

"No. You have to be patient and wait until you have consolidated all your teaching positions into a permanent secure job. Wait for the good results and opinions of your classes to bear fruit in the long run."

In the meantime I was called to teach by other studios and conventions, such as the Lois Meissner Studio, the 1973 Convention of Dance Masters of Michigan, Inc., and the Anida Sedala School of Dance from Chicago. For the Chicago engagement, I had to ask Mr. Guttman's permission to leave work for two days in order to fly to Chicago. This time he was reluctant.

"You are abusing my patience and my goodness. You are missing too much. I understand your legitimate desire to find a future in the United States with your real profession, but from my business point of view, it is not convenient and I will have to hire somebody else."

I was shocked and at the same time embarrassed. I didn't know what to do or what to say. I started to perspire. I stood in silence and dropped my head, staring at the pants on which I was working at that time. Gradually I relaxed, and I dared to answer him. "Mr. Guttman, you are right, but this is a unique opportunity for me to be known in another city. Please let me go. I promise that this is the last time I will miss work."

I couldn't believe that I dared to answer him, but my survival instincts signaled me that I was doing the right thing. I expected that he would yell at me or fire me on the spot, but he didn't. He moved around, continuing his work, looking now and then at me. Finally he stopped working, faced me, and kindly, speaking with a controlled voice.

"Permission granted, but I will ask you to work overtime without paying you an overtime fee."

The next day I flew to Chicago to teach ballet classes and do some choreography for the Anita Sedala School of Dance. During the flight, I remembered that refills of juice and soft drinks were free, so I didn't have to endure any thirst.

The classes went well. I was pleased with the dancers and, with confidence; I started to choreograph the *Romanian Rhapsody* based on George Enescu's music. I adapted this choreography to the number and ability of the dancers. The Anida Sedala School of Dance presented the dance on May 31, 1973 at the Drake Theatre of Barat College. It was a big hit.

Back in Detroit I again choreographed *The Romanian Rhapsody* for the Taynton Studio. It was presented in June 1973 at their Out-Door Studio Theater, and it was a great success. The Tayntons named me Associate Artistic Director for their company. I continued teaching and choreographing for the Tayntons many years thereafter.

Mrs. Lois Meissner, president of the Dance Masters of America, invited me to be a judge at their pageant. The convention of Dance Masters of Michigan, Inc. in October 1973 was another opportunity to meet other dancers, teachers, and choreographers from all over the country. It was the first time that I actually signed a contract. I was asked to teach character dances and *Pas de Deux* (partnering) classes for an hourly fee of $65.00. The fee impressed me, but it was only for two hours of teaching.

Even though the classes were crowded, I enjoyed the teaching. For the first time, it wasn't necessary to bring my heavy tape recorder; I had a pianist. A pianist is always a relief for both teachers and students. Live music, if played well, makes the student feel more connected with the content and the rhythm of music. I continued to teach in all the studios where I was hired.

TURNING POINT

Mrs. Nowak offered me one class per week for the Harbinger Dance Company, which was located at the Detroit Community Music School in Detroit. The class was a mixture of intermediate and advanced students and after a few weeks, the students were so pleased with their progress that they asked Mrs. Nowak to offer me more classes.

At that time, Harbinger was preparing for its annual concert at the Detroit Institute of Arts Theatre. The Company's performance brought about the turning point of my career in the United States. Mr. Dominic Missimi, coordinator of the program for the consolidated arts department the University of Detroit and Marygrove College (U of D/ MC) was in the audience on opening night. Afterwards, I was told that Mr. Missimi jumped up excitedly and wanted to meet the man who taught the ballet classes. He congratulated me on my achievement and expressed an interest to meet me for a job interview. I happily accepted.

Our meeting was held across the street from the Marygrove campus, at Simon's Deli. We chatted about many things and he asked a lot of questions: about my family, my country, and my professional background, about my teachers, and my arrival in the United States. Etc. The meeting lasted about an hour, but for me it was an eternity. I answered all of his questions. For him, apparently, I appeared calm; but he didn't know what was going on in my brain and my whole body. This was my first interview and I was frustrated by all the questions but I wanted a quick answer. Was he willing to hire me or not?

That hour, which changed my future, was torture. Finally, he proposed to hire me for two-week long workshop classes. I was confused and frustrated. I had expected a full-time job and I didn't understand why I had to go through another trial period after he had seen my results at the Harbinger Dance Company. Reluctantly, I told him that I needed to consult with my wife and brother-in-law Traian before I could give him my answer.

Traian explained to me that at the college level and some institutions in the United States it is a regular custom to have a trial period, and that for Mr. Missimi, the upcoming workshop would be a good opportunity to see me at work. I also called my friend Gaby in New York. She was the well-known teacher and choreographer Madame Darvash who had studied classical ballet in Russia and immigrated before us to the United States. She had opened her own ballet school in New York where she soon became successful a well-deserved positive reputation. She encouraged me to take the job, as did my wife and brother in law. So I accepted Missimi's proposal. The contract for the workshop, stipulated that the classes would be cancelled if there were less than twelve students enrolled. I was scared because I didn't know that I would attract the required number of students for each class. Traian encouraged me to have more confidence in myself and I signed the contract in April 1973. I was delighted when students came from all over Michigan and I ended up with a large enrollment.

Mr. Missimi offered me another contract, but still not full-time, which made me angry, and I wanted to quit. Mr. Missimi explained that he appreciated my work very much, but that at this point he did not have the necessary budget to offer me a full-time job and he promised me that in the following year he would have the necessary budget. I signed the contract covering the period from September 4, 1973 until April 28, 1974 with the academic rank of Lecturer.

It was obvious now that I had to quit the tailoring job so I thanked Mr. Guttman for his generous understanding of my situation and for his help during the time I had worked for him.

Iacob in class

In the classes were about twenty girls and six boys majoring in dance, plus other non-matriculated students, over the age of eighteen. Some of the girls and the boys had good technique and the potential to develop further in a dance career, but most of them were just average dancers, looking for a degree.

Preparing meticulously for my classes, I achieved my goals. I emphasized the importance of the arms, feelings, expressions of their faces, and projection to the audience. I also encouraged them to pay attention to their academic disciplines. From experience, I concluded that the better the student was in academics, the better the results were in dancing.

For a student, the learning process never ends and the same is true for the teacher. I had to prove that my teaching was forever being updated in order to maintain my leading role in front of the class. For that purpose, I went to the Jacob's Pillow Festival in Massachusetts, the Mid East Regional Festival, in Toronto; and the Midwest Regional Festival, in Indianapolis, over a span of several years. This non-ending learning process has guided me throughout my entire teaching career.

One day, Mr. Missimi told me that he planned to add a performing company to the dance department at Marygrove, and he asked me to choreograph a dance for the upcoming concert of this company. He explained to me that this concert would mark the debut of Dance Detroit as a resident company of the University of Detroit and Marygrove College. He suggested César Franck's music, *The Symphonic Variations for piano and orchestra*. He handed me the record on the spot. At home I listened to the music many times but I was uninspired. I found another piece of music, Sergei Rachmaninoff's *Rhapsody on a Theme of Paganini,* which suggested to me the possibility of creating beautiful dance patterns or images. Luckily, Mr. Missimi accepted my selection.

The music has an introduction and twenty-four variations. In the introduction, I presented the entire company, twelve girls and boys in a motionless pose, and then I divided the rest of the score into five sections. The first section was for four boys. The second was for a girl and four boys. The third was for seven girls and a *Pas de Deux*. Section four was a *Pas de Huit*, and section five was the finale.

The debut of Dance Detroit was held at Music Hall Center, in downtown Detroit on May 12, 1973 and in her review, Debra Cash of *Dance Magazine* wrote:

"The school is on the right track to becoming a local cultural institution."

As a choreographer, I had learned to combine my classical training with my gift for the folk dance, acquired during my work with the *Ciocîrlia Dance Company* and I had developed my own style. I learned to combine or melt a subtle folk-dance or a waltz movement with beautiful classical ballet virtuosity and I was happy to be part of the first Dance Detroit concert. And finally, I earned a full-time contract with the academic rank of Instructor for the 1974/75 school years. I signed the contract without hesitation. Another dream came true. One of the most satisfying experiences of a new immigrant is signing the first contract. However, one of the biggest mistakes of a new immigrant is neglecting to thoroughly examine the contents of that contract. I didn't know about the different academic ranks, and I found out later that I was hired at the lowest full-time rank and not at the rank comparable to my schooling, training and skills.

The following summer, I received an invitation to go to Lansing and meet with the director of the Lansing Ballet Association Mr. Tom O. Thompson. He asked me if I wanted to be the artistic director of their companies. I accepted this new challenge, and rearranged my schedule so as not to interfere with my work at the college. Soon I started to work on a new choreography, *Classical Symphony* on Prokofiev's Symphony in C for eight girls and one boy. In May 1974 the nine dancers presented my choreography during the Mid-States Regional at their annual festival in Detroit. My collaboration with the Lansing Ballet Companies was another success and lasted many years until my workload became too hectic.

Dance Detroit was now a new dance company, well received by the public and critics. Mr. Missimi asked me to be the ballet master and associate director of the company. Simultaneous with these rehearsals, I had to stage the dances from the third act of the opera *La Traviata* by Giuseppe Verdi for The Michigan Opera Theatre, and prepare for the upcoming production of the full ballet *Coppélia,* by Léo Delibes.

To make the *Coppélia* production possible, it needed the combined efforts from many cultural and educational institutions. In addition to the Detroit Institute of Arts and the University of Detroit/Marygrove College, the production of *Coppélia* had been assisted by a grant from the Michigan

Council for the Arts. Fortunately the Boston Ballet Company was very generous in lending us their *Coppélia* sets designed by Robert De Mora. The ballet's rich fantasy practically dictated its own delicate Eastern European costumes, and Nancy Missimi created the kind of dresses that every ballet dancer dreams of.

Outdoor performance of *Coppélia* at Heart Plaza in downtown Detroit

Coppélia at the Detroit Institute of Arts Auditorium marked the third appearance of Dance Detroit in concert. Dance Detroit succeeded in arranging a wonderful collaboration with the Detroit Women's Chamber Orchestra under the direction of guest conductor Carlos Rausch. I was proud of the Marygrove dancers who really gave a stunning performance and I still treasure the letter given to me, by the artistic director and the whole cast. I also treasure the document of "SPECIAL TRIBUTE" issued by the STATE OF MICHIGAN, referring specifically to the *Coppélia* performance and my choreography.

What a wonderful way to end a year! Eugen, my son, was a full-time student at Wayne State University. Maria, my wife, was still working at the factory. She wouldn't consider my request to give up that job. We all celebrated New Year's Eve together with Traian and his family.

"I can't believe that everything has happened so fast, I told Traian, I remember how impatient I was; and now, there are these sudden successes and invitations to teach and choreograph in different places."

"Jacky, your talent, dedication and hard work made this happen."

Michigan Opera Theatre again applied to Dance Detroit to perform the ballet in their production of the operetta *Die Fledermaus*, with music by Johann Strauss. The operetta was to be performed at the end of February and I was very busy preparing and choreographing a new ballet so I suggested that I create a suite with excerpts from the character dances of *Coppélia*. The director of the opera liked my idea and the ballet was a huge success with positive reviews from Jay Carr of the *Detroit News* and Clarence E. Persinger of the *South End*.

At the Jewish Community Center I met a very talented dancer and choreographer, Denise Szykula who liked my classes and my choreography. In April, she called to inform me that she had her own company, and that she would like me to choreograph a solo piece for her. Thrilled about her offer I selected for the piece three parts from Stravinsky's music: Eccentric, Andante, and Madrid. I named the dance *Stravinsky Suite*. It was a joy to work with Denise. Her body molded with ease, responsive to my every technical demand. Her movements were dynamic and expressive and well projected. Her company, Nonce Dance Ensemble, presented a performance in April 1975 at the Rackham Memorial Auditorium, and she included my piece in the program.

Detroit's Bicentennial Dance Festival during the last week of May 1975 came to a climax in a public concert at the Music Hall Center. There were ten companies from the Detroit area and The *Free Press* Music Critic Mr. Collins George reviewed it on June 2.

"All of the dances were interesting. One does remember with special pleasure, however, the high level performance of the *Coppélia* suite by Dance Detroit."

With so many new collaborations I was very busy that summer. The University of Michigan Department of Dance organized a workshop and invited me to be part of it. Also the Toronto Summer School in Dance under the direction of Diana Jablokova-Vorps, artistic director of the Toronto Regional Ballet Company invited me to teach at their workshop. On that occasion, I choreographed the *Romanian Rhapsody* by George Enescu for the third time since I had arrived in the United States.

A GENUINE ADMIRER

The classes at Marygrove were open to everybody. There were a number of students who were not dance majors but took classes to achieve grace, good placement, or good technique. Among these non-matriculated students, I had one who distinguished herself from the others her name was Joan Solaka. Joan was tall, and beautiful, with a white complexion, brown hair and long leg. She was a commercial model, so her purpose for taking classes was obvious. I knew nothing about her except that she never missed a class and she was a beautiful lady. At the end of the term, she approached me to thank me for my teaching, and offered me a cheesecake.

"Iacob, I love you." Jokingly, I answered, "Joan, I am married." She replied, "I know, I am married too; but I love you because you are a very good teacher and choreographer. I will invite you and your wife for dinner at my house in the summer. I want you to be known in the Detroit Metropolitan area."

"Thank you, I am looking forward to it," I replied.

Sometimes in life we come upon things we can't predict and even understand it because it never happen to you anything similar. It was in May that Joan Solaka kept her promise; she invited us for a Friday night dinner at her downtown apartment. Greeting us in her usual friendly manner, she hugged Mary and me and introduced us to her husband Tom. It was a stroke of good luck to meet Joan Solaka who obviously recognized my creative talent. Joan called my attention to one particular gentleman. She pulled me toward the table where he was playing poker and told the gentleman to take a break from the game. His name was Marshall Turkin, and he was the executive director of the Detroit Symphony Orchestra. Addressing him, Joan presented me, "This is the man you need. He is the choreographer and ballet master at Marygrove. You gentlemen have a lot to talk about."

Mr. Turkin came right to the point, asking me if I would like to choreograph a full-length ballet, *The Nutcracker* for the Detroit Symphony Orchestra.

"Why do you need a new *Nutcracker* ballet?"

He invited me to sit down on the couch near him, and told me the real situation. Benson Ford had donated a grant of $25,000. With that money, the DSO had purchased new sets and costumes from the former Washington National Ballet, which was now dissolved. The correct process is to create sets and costumes that evolve from the choreographer's ideas, not vice versa. But I was a newcomer to the United States, and if I wanted to prove my talent I had to take advantage of all opportunities.

129

I paused before answering. Mr. Turkin sensed my hesitation and said, "I see that you are not so pleased with my offer."

"No, no, I am honored and pleased with your offer; but I have one condition. If possible, I would like to see all the sets hung on the stage, each act separately, in addition to the inventory of the costumes, arranged in the order in which they were used by the Washington National Ballet. Then I will give you my answer."

"That is a fair request, and I will let you know when and where we will be able to do it."

In the meantime, Joan finished with the preparations for dinner and called us to the table. Sitting near Mary, I took her hand and told her the incredible news. I was bewildered and couldn't yet believe it. She took the news calmly and kissed me. Then, she looked deeply into my eyes and told me that her brother Traian was right. He always said that, according to a Romanian proverb, "One never knows when and from where the rabbit will bounce up," which means that we never know when good things will happen. I kissed her again, feeling her calmness taking over my body. I was back in the relaxed atmosphere of the evening.

Joan was not just a beautiful lady; she was also a fine cook. The dinner was excellent with good wine delicious, a variety of desserts, and my favorite, chocolate mousse. Joan was naturally curious about my conversation with Mr. Turkin, and she was glad to hear that we had made progress. She had confidence in my talent and wished me luck. I can say that I never experienced an evening more exciting like that.

After a week, Mr. Turkin called to invite Mary and me to the Ford Auditorium. We went the next day to the auditorium and found a beautiful display of the sets and costumes on stage. Following the inventory, we counted the number of costumes to determine the possible size of the cast but we both liked the colors of the exquisitely well-designed sets and costumes.

"Marshall, I need more time to think about it. I need to adjust my ideas about this ballet with the immense amount of visual information collected today. I ask you to give me a fair amount of time for that."

"What is a fair time for you?" "About a month." "Good enough," he said.

And the month passed very quickly. Mary and I worked on the ballet day and night. We listened to the music, and analyzed each dance separately. How many dancers we needed all together, girls, boys, children, acrobats and professional dancers? Exhausted, we looked at each other, and our eyes said the same thing: Yes! We can do it!

I called Marshall and told him the good news, and he was glad to hear it. He invited me to discuss the details of the contract and at the same time, I

proposed to invite two well-known principal dancers for the roles of Sugarplum Fairy and the Cavalier.

"I propose the principal dancers from the National Ballet of Canada, Veronica Tennant and Sergiu Stefanschi." Mr. Marshall was delighted.

Sergiu and Veronica accepted my invitation and again, Marshall was pleased by the wonderful news. For me, it was to be a reunion with Sergiu, because we had worked together at the Romanian Opera.

After Labor Day 1975, I resumed my dance activities at Marygrove College and I told the chairman of the dance department the good news about my negotiations with the DSO. He was overwhelmed and made it

Iacob with Veronica Tennant and Sergiu Stefanschi

known to the president and dean of the college. I was shocked, however, when he told me that he would take over negotiations with the DSO. I protested angrily.

"This is my private connection with the DSO; even though I proposed to do *The Nutcracker* with Dance Detroit, I will not let you interfere with my private enterprise."

He was surprised at my strong opposition and didn't say a word, but I found out later from Joan that, behind my back, he had several discussions with the symphony, and made decisions, without consulting me, regarding the contract. I confronted him about it.

"I am sorry, and it will not happen in the future," he apologized.

However he continued to interfere without consulting me. I was so concerned about the quality of my work that I neglected to contact the DSO. I, therefore, suffered the consequences. On December 8, 1975, Mr. Missimi handed me a contract in the form of a letter as an agreement between Dance Detroit and me. This was another shock to me. I realized at that point that there was nothing that I could do. I consulted with Maria, Traian, and Joan. We all arrived at the same conclusion, that we should wait until after the performances and then immediately contact Marshall, the director of the symphony. So I signed the letter begrudgingly. I found out on the night of the first performance that Mr. Missimi had already signed the contract between Dance Detroit and the symphony on July 25, 1975. My signature on the letter was superfluous.

For a moment, I thought that I was still in Romania where the authorities disposed of you however they wanted. I thought that in the free world such a thing couldn't happen. I learned in time that in the free world everything has to be written and supervised by a lawyer. Certainly it hurt and disappointed me, but I learned my lesson.

In the meantime, Maria, Eugen, and I realized another part of the American dream. We moved into our first new house, in Redford. At the same time, Maria quit the assembly line job and started teaching ballet for Marygrove's Continuing Education Department.

THE FIRST NUTCRACKER

For my wife and me *The Nutcracker* ballet was an enormous undertaking.

Dance Detroit had well-trained dancers, but I didn't have the necessary children and the acrobats. I didn't yet have my own ballet school, so I asked

Mr. Missimi to organize an audition for the needed parts. I don't remember the exact number of the participants in the audition, but the dance studio at Marygrove was packed. It was very exciting, I put the youngsters through exercises and I looked for very musical children. Two children impressed me. I chose Anne Murray for the role of Clara and Anthony Randazzo for the role of Fritz. Anne continued to perform Clara until 1977,

Tony Randazzo as Fritz and
Ann Murray as Clara (left)

and then we lost touch until the twentieth anniversary of *The Nutcracker* when she came with her husband and two children to celebrate with us. Anthony only danced with us for that year because he was accepted into The National Ballet of Canada School and pursued a professional career. He became a successful principal dancer with the San Francisco Ballet and after thirteen years, he returned to perform the principal role of Cavalier partnering with Evelyn Cisneros, also of the San Francisco Ballet.

Since we had to perform at a high enough level to complement the world renowned Detroit Symphony Orchestra, it was always mandatory for month of rehearsal.

I used an analogy to make them better understand the importance of rehearsal.

"This is a cruise on a huge ship called *The Nutcracker,* It is making a long trip and you are surrounded by water. If you jump off the ship a shark will eat you, and I am that shark so you mustn't miss rehearsals.

Most of the parents were very supportive. They helped with costume fittings, and they organized props and parties. There was a sense of general enthusiasm and pride to be part of this performance with Dance Detroit and DSO. On December 20, 1975, we had the first rehearsal on stage at the

Ford Auditorium with the orchestra. The floor was not smooth enough for dancing so we literally rolled up the 48 by 32-foot vinyl floor from Marygrove's dance studio and moved it. We had approximately one hundred members in the cast and we did a run-through with the orchestra. But when we arrived at the finale of the ballet the conductor suddenly stopped the music. I hadn't noticed any mistakes on stage or any need to adjust the tempo, so I asked the conductor why he had stopped. He calmly pointed to the huge clock in the pit and told me:

"The time of rehearsal is over." I couldn't believe what he had said, so I asked him, "Are you serious?"

He stepped out of the orchestra pit as the members of the orchestra packed up their instruments and started leaving. The friendly conductor, Mr. Theo Alcantara, explained to me that there was nothing he could do about it. It was a union rule. Disappointed, sad, discouraged and angry, I told him, how I felt.

"It's a shame that two minutes from the finale they have to stop, and at the same time it is an unfriendly gesture by the orchestra toward an artist who is just making his debut." "Don't take it personally. It happens to everyone, and we have learned to comply with it," he said.

The "two minutes" obsessed me all night. I asked myself if the orchestra union was right. *Maybe, yes,* I answered in my mind. But again "two minutes." Even if they were right, as a courtesy to a newcomer, somebody should have warned me of that particular union rule. I still expected them to grant me those "two minutes."

The next day was the dress rehearsal. I was still boiling mad over the two minutes, thinking that I might have to work a long time in the future with this orchestra. I decided to use this rehearsal to make them understand how I felt. Two minutes before the end of the finale, I stopped the conductor.

Surprised, he asked me, "What happened?" "Nothing happened; I just donated two minutes from my allotted time to the orchestra."

The orchestra was furious, and somebody from among them shouted at me, "You are smart; you want to become president of the United States?"

"I would like to, but I can't because I was not born in the United States."

Anyway, I learned my lesson and it never happened again; I never tried to extend the rehearsal time.

Opening night was, a joyous moment for Mary and myself. It was, a hit and this great success continued for twenty-three years. The audience welcomed me not just as a resident of their city but also as a choreographer and it was a wonderful feeling. The headline of Mr. Jim Gallagher's review, from the Detroit *Free Press*, December 20, 1975 read, "Dance Detroit's *Nutcracker* has style, precision." The article continued, "*The Nutcracker*

The Nutcracker – Dance of the Flowers

comes like a dessert on this year's pre-Christmas menu of cultural events. The symphony management hopes this year's four performances will be the beginning of a tradition. While this *Nutcracker* is only the second full-length ballet in Dance Detroit's repertoire, it was performed with a style and precision worthy of a much more experienced company. Those who attended the initial performance also shared that hope."

And Susan Slobojan's review in the *Detroit News* read:

"Choreographer Iacob Lascu, who is also an associate director and ballet master of the company, has tailored it well, and *The Nutcracker* provided proof that there is talent enough in Detroit to make importing *Nutcrackers* from other cities unnecessary."

So on April 27, 1976, I received a new contract with the rank of Special Instructor III, which in the Marygrove College Faculty Handbook is equivalent to the rank of associate professor. For me, it was a long overdue victory, but not fully satisfactory, because their decision was not retroactive to the first contract. In conclusion, Mr. Missimi's mistake was never totally corrected but we all moved forward anyway.

■■■

I had in my class a student, Timothy R. Dewart who was a beginner ballet student and a professional designer. He had designed the growing tree for *The Nutcracker* production. One day he invited me to lunch at a place across the street from Marygrove College.

"I have been appointed Artistic Director and Production Designer for the Bicentennial Committee of the Episcopal Diocese of Michigan. I hope that you will be part of my team."

"In what capacity?" I asked him. "As director and choreographer for a musical drama." he replied.

He gave me the score and his plans for the scenery, the duration of the drama, and information about the orchestra and the choir.

"Where will this musical drama be performed?" I asked him. His answer shocked me: "At the Cathedral Church of St. Paul."

"You are joking. How do you plan to do this?" "I am not joking. I will build a huge stage in front of the altar," he replied. "Give me some time to ruminate on this. I want to share this information with my wife."

Mary was as excited by the offer as I was. He didn't wait for my answer. The next day he handed me a formal invitation from the Bicentennial Committee of the Episcopal Diocese. I was surprised by his hasty move, but I was thrilled that he had so much confidence in me.

I accepted the invitation to stage and choreograph *The Pilgrimage*, a musical drama. It was a liturgical lyric drama in celebration of every man's journey from bondage toward freedom under God. The drama was based on the story of Moses and the Exodus. Participating in the program was the Cathedral Chamber Orchestra & Episcopal Diocesan Singers and the dance students from U of D/MC. One of the dancers was Madonna Ciccone. She became "Madonna," the famous singer, dancer and movie actress, but, to my knowledge, in her many interviews she has never referred to this interlude in her career.

The Pilgrimage production with singers and dancers and the children's movement through the church with candles in their hands, climbing up the mountain, was truly impressive and had a great visual effect upon the audience. On June 4, 1976, I received a tribute signed by the Bishop of Michigan H. Coleman McGehee Jr.

"The Bicentennial Committee of The Diocese of Michigan presents to IACOB LASCU this expression of profound and heartfelt gratitude, for your skill as DIRECTOR OF PILGRIMAGE."

This was a new level of achievement in the New World. The requests for new choreography never stopped. Ms. Denise Szykula applied for a grant from the Michigan Council of the Arts to have me choreograph a new piece for her company, Nonce Dance Ensemble. I named the piece

Concentric/Eccentric and it was performed at concerts in the spring at Birmingham Groves High School.

The late summer 1976, Oakland University hired me for a part-time job. Later the head of the dance department Carol Halstad, asked me to do some choreography. My first choreography for Oakland University was a modern dance entitled *Unforeseen* based on Harold Farberman's music *Classical Percussion*. I also staged the *Piano Concerto No. 1* based on the music by Emerson, which was previously performed by Dance Detroit.

Then the University of Michigan School of Music invited me to do the choreography for a dance number in their production of *Die Fledermaus* by Johann Strauss. For this production, I selected the music *The Emperor's Waltz*, also by Strauss. I worked with three couples from the Marygrove dance department. They danced beautifully in all four performances at the Power Center for the Performing Arts in Ann Arbor. In his review in the *Ann Arbor News*, *Freedom* Mr. Norman Gibson wrote.

"The magnificent choreography of Iacob Lascu was enhanced by the talented dancers in the royal ballet."

CELEBRATION AND MY MOTHER'S VISIT

The source for all these accomplishments was at home. Maria, my wife, was my inspiration, my friend, and my critic. She created an ideal atmosphere for me to work and frequently came to the rehearsals to observe the progress of my choreography. She always found time to listen to my ideas or the music that I selected and give her opinion, which I trusted implicitly because it came from her devoted loving heart. She wanted me to do the best job, so she didn't hide her views and she didn't flatter me. We would discuss in detail my choreography and sometimes she was critical in her remarks, and I would have to defend myself, but regardless of the opinion, her spirit gave me extra enthusiasm for my rehearsals.

We often celebrated our accomplishments in the New World, thinking with gratitude of all the wonderful people who had helped us. On our 25th wedding anniversary we held a celebration at our house. Friends, colleagues, and the directors of the private ballet schools where I taught came to celebrate with us. Traian and Olga, our sponsors; Walter Lazar, the Chevrolet dealer, and his wife Mary who had helped me translate in my ballet classes; and someone dear to us who was instrumental in determining my destiny, *The Nutcracker* Fairy Godmother Joan and her husband Tom were there too. We received lots of precious gifts including a little silver bell that Mary used to call guests to dinner.

Mary and Joan Solaka,
our Fairy Godmother

We were a happy family; our love for each other and the unforgettable help from our friends, and family gave us the strength, will and dedication to gradually rebuild our disrupted lives. After just four years, we had accomplished the dreams that we had shared during our flight to the New World. Our task now was to consolidate what we had accomplished and set new goals.

Gene, my son had become a full-time student at Wayne State University. Mary's classes with the children at Marygrove's Continuing Education division were tremendously successful and she was asked to teach at the summer workshop. The enrollment grew, and the children and their parents adored her. *The Nutcracker* received enthusiastic recognition by the general public, the dance organizations from the Detroit Metropolitan area, and the Detroit Symphony Orchestra.

During those four years, I often had an ardent desire to see my mother who still lived in Romania. I shared my feelings with Mary, and she suggested inviting my mother for a visit. I sent my mother a round trip ticket and a formal invitation the necessary affidavit to obtain a visa from the American Embassy in Romania. She stayed with us a month.

We took my mother to Farmer Jacks supermarket. The abundance and variety of products stunned her. In Romania, she had to stand in line for meat, fruit, oil, and other products just to find out if the items were even available. To have a chance to even get meat, she had to be among the first in line at 5:00 A.M. Still brainwashed by the communist regime, she voiced her opinion to us in Romanian.

"This is propaganda; you have taken me to a special market arranged by your government to make people from a foreign country believe that in the United States there is such abundance."

She said this because when foreigners would come to Romania, they would be taken to a special market where they could find anything. I didn't argue with her about Farmer Jacks. Instead, each day we drove her to another supermarket in a different suburb, so she would realize that we were not trying to trick her.

"You convinced me that the United States is like the Promised Land as described in the Bible, milk and honey in abundance. I am happy for you that you are here." So I asked her to stay and she began to cry.

"What's wrong, mom?"

Continuing to cry, she said, "I have another son in Romania as you know. He asked me not to remain, because he will be thrown out of his job and his family will be persecuted if I stay."

We tried to convince her that it was just a matter of time and they would get rid of him anyway but she would not be swayed.

My mother was very religious and very strict about the Jewish Orthodox rules. I couldn't take her to the synagogue on Saturday morning with the car because of her religious belief so we had to walk quite a long distance, but it was good exercise. My mother was also a fantastic cook she was a specialist in chicken soup, gefilte fish and desserts. Maria did everything possible to make her feel at home and prepared our house so that my mother would be able to live according to her religious beliefs. We bought an additional freezer, so she could store her kosher food separately. We also bought brand new dishes, knifes, spoons, forks, etc. At the end of her visit, at the airport my mother hugged me and said.

"Dear Iancala, your wife Mary is a wonderful person and you made a good choice. She proved to me that you couldn't have found a better Jewish wife. I consider her the best Jewish wife that I have ever met," she whispered.

I was thrilled. It proved to me that with all the impediments to our relationship, my decision to choose Mary as my wife was justified. I was thrilled that fate had been so good to me and dedicated the rest of my life to Mary. She left us heartbroken and I never saw her again. She died four years later at the age of eighty-two.

PERU

I always liked to read or watch documentaries about the discovery of ancient places, and the stories surrounding them. I hoped that some day I could afford to travel to Peru to visit Machu Picchu. The opportunity came unexpectedly when the college dance department invited Mrs. Anna Sokolow, acknowledged teacher and choreographer from New York. Mrs. Vera Stastny, director of the Ballet San Marcos from Lima, Peru, who had come to the United States on an exchange, accompanied her. At Marygrove, I presented some of my work for them, and they also observed some of my classes. Mrs. Stastny told me that in her company in Lima, Peru there were nine girls and five boys, and she asked me if I could come to work with them and choreograph *The Rhapsody on a Theme of Paganini by Rachmaninoff.*

"Yes, if you can accommodate your needs to my schedule. I have to be back for the fall term, which begins right after Labor Day."

She checked her calendar carefully; finally, she raised her smiling face from her calendar and asked me if I could come for two weeks between August 14 and 28,1976.

The schedule was a bit tight for me, and I hadn't had a chance to talk with Maria. Knowing her, I was sure that she would be happy for me, and I answered, "yes."

I applied immediately for a passport and I received a white one, which allowed me to have just one reentry into the United States. I called Peru's Embassy in Washington for a visa, and they told me I didn't need one. I was so excited when I spoke to them that I didn't mention that I was not yet a U.S. citizen. Here started my trouble.

As I arrived in Peru and proceeded through immigration and customs, I was arrested for not having an entry visa for Peru. I told them that I had requested a visa from the Peruvian Embassy in Washington, and had been told that I didn't need one. Unfortunately, on my white American passport, it was written that I was born in Romania, which was still a communist country at that time. The Peruvian immigration officers told me that I was not welcome in their country. I protested and told them that I had been invited to come to Peru by the Ballet San Marcos Company. My protest was in vain. They pushed me into a small office and gave me a form on which I had to write in detail who I was, what my profession was, what my "real" purpose was in coming to Peru, etc. Their attitude frightened me. I wanted to protest again, but I thought that it would only make the situation worse. I begged them to allow me to make a phone call to the U.S. Embassy, or let me go and meet Mrs. Stastny, the director of the Ballet San Marcos, who was waiting for me. Reluctantly, they granted me the phone call.

I called the embassy. The secretary connected me with the ambassador, who told me that I should wait with patience, and he would speak with the chief officer of security in Peru. Frightened, I awaited the outcome of the conversation. After a while which seemed like an eternity for me, their conversation ended and the officer, smiling, apologized as he guided me to the exit where Mrs. Stastny was waiting. What a happy ending! I finally could relax and hug my hostess. She asked me why it had taken so long to pass through customs. I told her the whole story.

I expected to be taken to a hotel; instead, I found myself in front of a private house. I realized that they had money problems, too. It was her friend's house, where I would reside during my stay. Exhausted from my trip and the misadventure at customs my face revealed my fatigue. Stastny suggested that I take a nap and her friend showed me to my room. Left alone, I dropped on the bed, and I fell asleep "stone dead."

The rehearsals were held at the dance studio of the Ballet San Marcos, a resident company of the Universidad Nacional Mayor de San Marcos, which is largest national university in Lima, Peru. The daily schedule was tight, starting with a one and a half-hour ballet class taught by me, than a fifteen-minute break, and a rehearsal for the *Rhapsody*. Next, came lunch and another rehearsal.

I had to finish the *Rhapsody* in the two weeks of my residency in Lima. I had the full support of the dancers; they enjoyed my classes and my choreography. Sometimes they were exhausted during the rehearsals, but they never complained. Vera, the director of the company, attended all my rehearsals; she would have to rehearse the *Rhapsody* after my departure. The premiere of their performance was planned for October 4, 1976.

The last day of rehearsal was August 28, but the starting day of my fall term at Marygrove was not until after Labor Day. This was the right moment to fulfill my dream of seeing one of these ancient places that excited me most, Machu Picchu the 15th century Inca city was at the top of my list. I told Vera of my desire, so she helped me with plane ticket, map and hotel reservation. I arrived at Cuzco and I visited the city and the beautiful church.

The hotel organized group trips to Machu Picchu, and I joined one of them. They advised us to take chewing lozenges, especially for endurance at high altitudes, and I did. We took a train to the mountains, toward the valley of the great original Inca Empire. There a bus waited to take us up to Machu Picchu. When we arrived on the plateau of the mountain, the panoramic view was incredible emphasizing the unique beauty of this renowned site. The majesty and indescribable enormity, the exuberant vegetation, and the precipitous mountains that rise at 7,897 feet above the sea level created a scene that I will never forget. This marvel of Incan architecture was the second revelation in my life of a man-made wonder (the first was the Great Wall of China).

Returning to Lima, I made the final touches on the choreography. My departure was very emotional. I received presents from everybody. Hugging, kissing, and tears were mixed with persistent requests for a return trip.

It was a great experience for me and I enjoyed it tremendously, but I was home sick. I was happy to see my family waiting for me at the airport. I had bought them all presents and I shared with them my experiences with the company and recounted my adventures and impressions of Lima, Cuzco and of Machu Picchu.

I couldn't attend their opening night because of my duties at Marygrove. Later Mrs. Stastny sent me a printed program and a letter in which she told me that they had performed the *Rhapsody* eight times in their own concerts and three times together with the famous Russian ballerina Maya Plisetskaya. The audiences had reacted marvelously. I received a Christmas card signed by the dancers saying that my presence had been an important turning point in their careers as well the reputation of the company, *The Rhapsody* was immensely successful, and they all wanted me to return.

We moved to another new house in Southfield. It was very comfortable with three bedrooms, a library, a dining room living room, and a huge, finished paneled basement. We were fortunate that the former owner left us all the beautiful draperies and chandeliers as well. My son Eugen constructed a dark room in part of the basement to work on the photographs required for his degree in photography and the garden was filled with flowers and blooming trees. Mary spent hours and hours in that garden adding lots of carnations and roses. We all loved our house and garden and named it "The Lascu's Paradise."

THE INJURY

I wanted to have my own copyright over *The Nutcracker* production and I needed to fight to have direct negotiations with the Detroit Symphony Orchestra. My dear fairy Joan talked with Marshall, the director of the Symphony, to explain my point of view. As a result of our meeting, the contract for the 1976 season was signed only between the symphony and me. I was relieved of the mental strain, the fear of being defrauded of my work. Now I could concentrate on future activities.

But something always unexpected happened with the DSO. Marshall Turkin, the executive director of the symphony, called me to discuss the principal dancers for that year's *Nutcracker*. I reminded him that we had already asked Sergiu Stefanschi and Veronica Tennant the previous Christmas, to return this year. Marshall told me that he had already made arrangements with Jacques d'Amboise and Kyra Nichols from the New York City Ballet. I was pleased to have these two great dancers, but, at the same time, I was very disappointed by his unilateral decision, made without consulting me. I expressed to him my concern that in the future he simply couldn't make decisions like this regarding artistic matters. I was the artistic director of *The Nutcracker* and responsible for selecting the dancers for the show, including the principal dancers.

Iacob with Jacques d'Amboise and Kyra Nichols

He told me that it had been a sudden opportunity. The symphony's influential and political supporters had suggested those dancers and he could not refuse. He said that he had forgotten to call me. Shocked to find out that the influential and political power could make artistic decisions without consulting the choreographer I suddenly drew a very scary parallel with the political power of communist Romania. Marshall promised me that it would never happen again and, it didn't happen during his administration, but future DSO administrators would make decisions without consulting me.

We never knew what our daily life would bring us. There were ups and downs, sunshine and rain, good feelings and pain, health and illness. My life was no exception. In one of the rehearsals for the Chinese dance, two boys had to execute aerials in a circle. I was not satisfied with their execution and demonstrated it myself. This is a difficult movement and I didn't warm up enough, so during the execution I felt a pain in my lower back. For the moment I didn't pay attention to the pain, continuing the rehearsal with the same energy and enthusiasm. At home the situation changed for the worse. The pain in my back was excruciating I couldn't bend forward to untie my shoelaces. I felt numbness in my entire right leg. I couldn't sit in a chair for any length of time; I had to lie down on the floor on my back. I was scared that my spine and leg would be paralyzed. My wife tried to comfort me with all her love. She massaged my back and legs and helped me to undress but the pain didn't pass. I took some Bayer aspirin to kill my pain.

In the morning, I continued my classes with the help of painkillers. I had to do my job and there was no time to think of my pain. In the afternoon, Mary took me to the doctor. His diagnosis was that I pinched the sciatic nerve in my back, and he recommended surgery. I went to different doctors for a second, third, fourth and fifth opinion. All recommended surgery-- the knife. To all the doctors I answered, "No! Only over my dead body!" I didn't want surgery; my inner feelings told me that I could get well without cutting my precious body. I continued my daily work with painkillers and with the hope that slowly and with patience I would get well. In the meantime I couldn't even go to a movie because I couldn't sit that long in a chair.

One day a student of mine invited Mary and me to dinner at her parents' home. After we were served the soup, I asked permission to lie down on the floor on my back. Her mother asked me what was wrong. I told her the whole story. She picked up the phone and called a friend of hers, a doctor at Ford Hospital. He examined me and told me that I didn't need surgery. He said my muscles were having spasm and gave me some muscle relaxants. Also, he gave me some special exercises for strengthening the abdomen, stomach and back muscles. He also gave me a piece of advice: "Do the exercises every day!" Since then, I have done them every day faithfully.

The rehearsals for *The Nutcracker* never ceased. Despite my injury, I was present every day. Following the previous year's success, this year's production was given more attention by the press and radio. The famous late-show host J. P. McCarthy interviewed the New York City Ballet Principal Dancer Jacques d'Amboise and myself. I was thrilled to be interviewed beside Jacques. It was my first interview on a Detroit radio station. Many others would follow.

At one of the rehearsals on stage, during his variation, Jacques also injured himself, and couldn't continue the variation. I was very concerned about the situation, and I asked Jacques if he would be able to dance.

"Yes, I can do the *Grand Pas de Deux*, but I will not be able to do the variation and we should eliminate it."

I disagreed "We have to find another solution. Could we call somebody from the New York City Ballet to replace you."

My suggestion was welcomed and Dan Duel, another principal dancer from NYC Ballet, arrived on the day of the performance. He managed however, to rehearse on stage before the show. For the first time in my experience, the *Grand Pas de Deux* was changed into a *Pas de Trois*: Jacques did the *Pas de Deux* with Kyra, and Dan did the variation and the coda. It was not the real thing, but it was an interesting experiment.

The symphony was overwhelmed with *The Nutcracker* success. I received a letter, on January 11, 1976 in which Marshal congratulated me and asked me if it were possible to add a performance for the following year. I agreed to add one performance, to make a total of six.

Time passed by and here we were again rehearsing and performing at the Ford Auditorium. I was glad that my friend Sergiu Stefanschi was able to return. Since Miss Veronica Tennant was not available he danced with another wonderful partner, Vanessa Harwood. The eighth summer school of the Marygrove dance department also invited Sergiu to teach. On this occasion he stayed in our house, and we had more time to chat and reminisce about our work in Romania.

For the future *Nutcracker's* performances, I contacted Peter Diggins, a freelance agent for principal dancers. For the 1978 season I selected two wonderful principal stars from the Joffrey Ballet, Denise Jackson and Gregory Huffman. The performances went very well as usual. Susan Slobojan's review in the *Detroit News*, dated December 29,1978, recognized the quality of my choreography technical accomplishment of the company Dance Detroit:

"Dance Detroit brought Tchaikovsky's *Nutcracker* to Ford Auditorium last night that was easily the freshest the area has seen this holiday season. Best of all, it served as a stellar example of how far Marygrove College's young resident company has progressed in a mere year's time. In general, it's an extremely pleasant surprise how much the entire company has improved."

MY OWN BALLET SCHOOL

During my dance career in Romania, I had not been accustomed to receiving letters from students, so here in the New World I was surprised to get them. One letter in particular impressed me very much; it was from Debbie Chase, a Marygrove graduate.

> "Dear Mr. Lascu.
>
> What can I possibly say to you, as my teacher that can convey all the love & respect that I have for you? You have made a deep impression on my life, the things I have learned from you I will carry with me throughout my life. Your devotion to dance has instilled in me a great love for the art. I think what sets you apart from other teachers are your constant searches for a new & better way to convey an idea to your students. You are constantly bringing fresh new thoughts to the class without abandoning the tried & proved methods, so your classes never should become routine. You have always been very good to me & treated me so well. I will miss you a great deal. You are the greatest. Someday I hope to be a good teacher. I am grateful for having had you as my teacher. Thank you!
>
> Love, Debbie."

This letter reflects the purpose in my teaching. I am a firm believer in a never-ending learning process, so as a teacher, I never stopped learning and searching to improve my skills and methods of transferring my knowledge to the students. This letter gave me more trust in myself and encouragement in my work. This letter and the actual requests of parents encouraged me to open my own school.

At that time, our income was insufficient, to save the necessary to open a ballet school. The opportunity finally arrived in 1978. Again a good fairy came my way a student by the name of Maggie Citrin. She liked my classes, and many time after the class asked me why I hadn't opened my own ballet school.

"With my financial resources, I can't put into practice such a desire." She asked me if her husband Tobi could observe one of my classes at Marygrove.

"Anytime." I said.

He showed up in one of my advanced classes and commended me afterward.

"My wife told me that you couldn't open your own school because of financial difficulties."

"Yes", I answered.

"How much do you think it would cost to open the school?" I gave him a substantial ballpark figure, and he generously handed me a check for that amount. I didn't know what to say, I just shook his hand and hugged Maggie. They expressed the desire to meet Maria, my wife, and invited us for dinner at their house. Our gratitude to them was great. Without them The Lascu School of Ballet would not have been born.

At first, I was daunted by the prospect of being a director and running my own business. I wasn't sure I could do it, but I couldn't turn away the opportunity offered by Maggie and Toby. In communist Romania, I could never have had my own ballet school. Before we opened the school, I consulted many teachers and owners about their studios to learn how to handle this business. They all said that success depends on your passion and dedication to your work. They were right. Our passionate and dedicated hard work paid off, and the snowball in the form of the Lascu School of Ballet became bigger and bigger. The school became a landmark of excellent teaching, and its reputation became well known throughout the whole country.

We rented a small space in Southfield. We made a deposit of two months rent and we started to prepare for the opening. First, we constructed a resilient floor. We then put up the exercise bars and mirrors. Finally we raised the ceiling to the height necessary for partnering classes. For the time being we bought a record player with pitch control and many records of special music for ballet classes. Unfortunately, we couldn't afford to buy a piano or to pay a pianist at that time. We advertised the opening of the studio in all the major newspapers and just eight years after leaving Romania we opened our own school in October 1978. Our own ballet school, this was beyond our original American dream.

■■■

Lisa Pelio from Flint attended my summer workshop classes. She told her mother that she should hire me for their company. She took her daughter's advice and after the workshop, Mrs. Lena Pelio, expressing her daughter's high appreciation of my classes, informed me that she runs her own ballet school in Flint. She was the Artistic Director of the Flint Ballet Theatre and she asked me if I would like to be their company's resident ballet master and choreographer.

Mrs. Pelio suggested her plan to me that I could teach the classes every Monday. In the summer, I could choreograph a ballet for their annual fall concert that she would rehearse herself until the concert. I didn't know for the moment what answer to give her.

I had to think about it: I had arrived at the crossroads of my wonderful artistic achievements in the New World. This was a crucial moment; I had to make a firm decision about what I would do in the future. What should I give up to accept this appealing offer from the Flint Ballet Theatre? After many debates pro and con with my dear Mary, we arrived at a conclusion. I would give up the individual private schools and Oakland University so I could accept the Flint offer. I started my job in Flint on January 8, 1979. For The Flint Ballet Theatre, I choreographed the full-length ballet Coppélia. The principal male role Franz was Leif Lorenz from Dance Detroit and Lisa Pelio, a wonderful dancer with great sensibility, danced the role of Swanilda. The performance was held at the Whiting Auditorium on October 14, 1979. The audience enthusiastically received the ballet and the director of the company hired me for the next year, and so I continued working with them until 1987 and choreographed many ballets: *Rossini Suite, Graduation Ball, Mozartiana, Gershwin Concerto in F, Sleeping Beauty, La Fille Mal Gardee, Cinderella, Swan Lake* and in 1986 *Coppélia once again.*

The requests for collaboration continued. I signed a contract with the Michigan Chamber Orchestra to choreograph and direct three works by Stravinsky: *Concerto in Eb Dumbarton Oaks, Duo Concertant,* and *L'Histoire du Soldat.* It was a new challenge for the dancers and for me. Our collaboration resulted in a beautiful performance. My favorite piece was *The Duo Concertant,* which I repeated in April at the Dance Detroit annual spring concert. The *Oakland Press* Special Writer Michael Margolin wrote.

"First performed with the Michigan Chamber Orchestra, *Duo Concertant* was filled with sturdy, attractive partnering and fresh combinations of steps."

CITIZENS OF THE USA AND THE 10,000 MILES

By 1978 we all became citizens of the United States of America. It was a glorious moment in our lives. When the immigration officer interviewed us--a step in the process of becoming Unites States citizens--we presented him with a comprehensive autobiography. He was amazed and impressed by the events of our lives. We were now really part of this free world and I would not be detained if I didn't have a visa, as in Peru when I was not yet a citizen.

It was a time for us to celebrate. We decided to take a trip throughout the United States to get to know this nation better and at the same time visit our neighboring Canada. We named this trip "10,000 miles in five weeks." The trip was phenomenal, unbelievable.

We couldn't afford the luxury of a hotel or motel, for an extended time. We bought a Ford Econoline Van, and "handyman" Gene and "handy lady" Maria transformed it into a recreational vehicle fully equipped with a folding table/bed combination, carpeting, sink, insulation and electrical gadgetry. I provided the materials, and they did all the work.

Our mobile "house" in the Rockies

Driving north on I-75 our first stop was a campground near St. Ignace in Mackinaw City. Mackinac Island can only be reached by ship, and no motorized vehicles are allowed on the island. Travel on the island is done only by bicycle or horse drawn carriage.

Next we camped near the Mount Rushmore National Monument. We were very impressed to see the faces of former presidents Washington, Jefferson, Roosevelt and Lincoln carved into the granite wall of the mountain. We also visited the Crazy Horse Monument, which was not yet complete. The emerging shape of the horse and rider at the top of the mountain was impressive. We met the artist who was working on the Crazy Horse sculpture at that time and he showed us other works of his. To our surprise, we found a bust of the Romanian composer George Enescu.

We visited Yellowstone National Park with the amazing 10,000 hot

springs and geysers and the churning water with numerous thundering waterfalls carving the canyon. Our favorite was Old Faithful the most famous geyser of all, which shoots its plume of steam skyward approximately every hour. In Canada we camped at the magnificent Lake

Maria (at right) and "Old Faithful"

Louise resort. For Maria and me this place was the most beautiful site in the world, and, for me, it still is. The Chateau Lake Louise overlooking Victoria Glacier is a view that I will never forget. In front of the chateau were big flowerbeds of various colors and plenty of benches so the visitors could catch their breath and enjoy the all-around breathtaking views. We stood still for hours contemplating this marvel of nature. We then ventured into the village of Banff a lovely village surrounded by magnificent natural beauty and an ideal place to shop for Canadian crafts.

From Banff, we headed west on Highway 1 toward Vancouver. It is a beautiful city and we did lot of sightseeing visiting Stanley Park with its famous totem pole displays. We entered Washington State and camped in Seattle. There we visited Seattle's Space Needle and the former grounds of the International Exposition. We were fortunate that Seattle's Art Museum was displaying the Egyptian treasures of Tutankhamen, so we stood in line for tickets. We then headed south on the ocean coast.

We passed through the state of Oregon, entered California, visited the Redwood National Park, after which we continued going south and arrived in San Francisco. We began a beautiful drive through the city following the scenic drive signs. I liked the district with the Spanish style houses and the streets with cable cars. We crossed many bridges until we found a good spot for a great view of the Golden Gate Bridge.

Leaving San Francisco and going south on the coastal highway, we stopped in Carmel, with its picturesque homes, galleries and shops. The beach, of fine white sand and warm water, tempted us to take a dip in the ocean. We then took a walk into the city and stared at the attractive windows of the boutiques, filled with glamorous dresses and other chic merchandise. Everything was so expensive that we left with broken hearts because we could not afford to buy any of it.

151

Visiting Yosemite National Park, our hearts rejoiced again as we explored the unequaled splendor of the mile-thick mountain granite, the marvel of the beauty of the Yosemite Falls, the Glacier Point and El Capitan.

Maria and Iacob (in the background)
with Sequoia trees

Next, we drove to the Sequoia National Park and its Giant Forest. The trees were gigantic in diameter and one of them actually had an opening in its trunk, large enough for our van to pass through.

In LA, we spent a whole day in the famous Disneyland Magic Kingdom, this amazing and colorful display of fantasy and technical ingenuities. Maria was overwhelmed by the children's wonderland pavilion and bought the recording of the children's song.

Universal Studios in Hollywood, we were told, was the largest motion picture and television studio complex in the world, and we were able to see the studio's giant stages and its indoor and outdoor sets. We also saw more behind-the-scenes magic secrets and clusters of replicated street locations. Around LA, we toured Beverly Hills, walked the famous Sunset Boulevard and stopped at the renown Chinese Theater in Hollywood where we admired the feet and handprints made by the stars.

In San Diego, we took a tour of the harbor. It is a busy bay with commercial and imposing naval carriers, atomic submarines, destroyers and cruisers. We also visited the San Diego Zoo.

Being close to the Mexican border, we couldn't resist the temptation to visit Tijuana. It was not so much our curiosity to see the city as our desire to feel the freedom of passing unrestricted to another country as citizens of the United States. I can't express enough the immense excitement and thrill of this moment. It was our dream, our hope, while inside socialist Romania to be able to visit a foreign country without restrictions. Now the dream had come true.

After Tijuana we headed northeast into the state of Nevada. The glittering lights of Las Vegas fascinated us. We entered one of the many casinos, and gambled a few dollars. In the evening, we attended a performance by Tom Jones, our favorite British singer, known to us from recordings found in Romania. In Utah, we visited the picturesque Zion National Park and drove closer and closer to the most anticipated point of our journey, the Grand Canyon. We approached the canyon by the north rim from where the view reflected the spectrum of colors spread in front of us. It was a silent beauty, which could only inspire and capture our imagination. It was easy to be hypnotized by the canyon's grandeur, by its many colors, by its vastness as an incredible example of the spectacle of nature. In fact, it was gorgeous!

Our tour was nearing the end and we finished with the Painted Desert and Petrified Forest. We had discovered a portion of the beauty of this great nation, the United State of America. The feeling that we were citizens of this nation overwhelmed us, and we promised ourselves that we would continue to explore more of our country's beauty in the future.

■■■

I resumed my regular activities at Marygrove. In assuming the position as the new president of Marygrove, John E. Shay, Jr., took time to attend one of *The Nutcracker* performances with his family and he wrote me a letter on January 12, 1981:

"This is a much belated yet nevertheless sincere expression of admiration for your superb work in choreographing *The Nutcracker* with the Detroit Symphony Orchestra. The variety of dances and the spark of the performance were enthralling, and this was accomplished without sacrificing quality. It was the freshest, most dynamic performance of *Nutcracker* I have ever seen."

From left to right:
Sean Lavery, Maria, Iacob, Pat and Jack
Shay, Kyra Nichols

When Marygrove College formally installed its sixth president, Dr. John E. Shay, Jr., with ceremonies, performances and parties. A dinner was given in his honor, and Dance Detroit presented a small dance concert. He and his family also attended the spring concert at the theater of Marygrove College, which was also part of the Inaugural Celebration for Marygrove's sixth president. For that concert, I invited the wonderful couple from The New York City

Ballet, Kyra Nichols and Sean Lavery. The president held a reception following the performance. Later, I received another letter from him:

"The Spring Dance Program was a stunning success. The grace, beauty, and creativity of your choreography thrilled me. With this caliber of performance and, of course, the help of some generous benefactors, Dance Detroit is bound to be a huge success in the future."

The New Year in 1980 brought me a great sense of personal achievement. Marygrove's academic vice president sent me a letter: "At its meeting of April 22, 1980 the Academic Affairs Committee of the Governing Board approved your

Maria with Cynthia Harvey and
Ross Stretton at our home

Ross Stretton, Iacob and
Cynthia Harvey

promotion to the rank of Special Instructor IV, the equivalent of full professor. At the full board meeting on the same day you were granted job security [tenure] at Marygrove."

In the meantime Michael Krajewski, conductor and musical director of the St. Clair Shores Symphony and DSO invited me to do a full-length ballet with that orchestra at the Macomb Community Cultural Center. I proposed *Swan Lake*, music by Peter Ilyich Tchaikovsky, and he gladly agreed. I told Rose De Sloover, the new head of the Dance department, about the collaboration with the St. Clair Symphony and suggested to her that we should substitute Dance Detroit's spring concert with the full-length ballet *Swan Lake* in collaboration with my private school. This was the third full-length ballet for Dance Detroit and everybody was excited. I asked my agent from New York, Peter Diggins, if Miss Cynthia Harvey from

American Ballet Theatre (ABT) was available. Cynthia responded affirmatively and came with Ross Stretton as her partner, also from ABT (Cynthia and Ross also honored us with their artistry in many *Nutcracker* performances).

In the *Adviser Newspaper* review, Miss Toni Simonetti wrote, "Ballet master and choreographer Iacob Lascu was greeted with a standing ovation following the Saturday performance for doing wonders with the amateurs. Dance Detroit's finest talent was appropriately showcased. Two dancers showed particular promise: Maria Aversa and Meredith Dincolo."

A YEAR OF MANY EVENTS

Nineteen eighty-three was a year of many events regarding my job, school, collaboration, house, *Nutcracker* and family.

The enrollment in my school had increased considerably and the present location was not big enough to accommodate everyone. In Birmingham, Maria and I found a spacious 3500 square foot area with a high ceiling ideal for partnering classes. This time, we were able to buy a piano from a discount piano store and hire a pianist for the classes.

I reorganized the program and the schedule of the school. We offered pre-dance classes for ages 3-5 and 6-7, and organized six levels of ballet classes. Each class had a mandatory dress color. Maria was the secretary of the school, and taught the younger children. The most difficult ballet classes were always the children's ones. They demanded patience, perseverance, finesse, and most importantly a gift of capturing their attention. Maria had to bring the children closer to her soul and keep them with her during a complex set of exercises making them useful, pleasant and attractive. She had all the skills; she was a wonderful teacher and the children loved her dearly.

My classes also proved attractive to the students. I used alternate movements that involved the whole body, so the head, neck, shoulders, torso, hands and legs became a whole unit, creating a perfect, integrated, coordinated movement from the top of the body to the bottom. I avoided stereotypical repetitions of the exercises.

Simultaneous with teaching the technique of classical ballet, I tried to persuade my students to believe in their inner potential, which is infinite. Back in Romania, my teacher Floria Capsali Dumitrescu taught me that I had to trust myself, believe in my abilities, in my potential and in my talent. To be more convincing to my students, I made up a story, an analogy based on reality.

I liked western movies, and the subject of the gold rush inspired me. Those who worked harder and with more dedication extracted more gold than the people who took it easy. Not all the people who extracted a lot of gold were able to keep it. Some of them were unfortunate victims of hold-ups; then they lost everything and sometimes their lives. Now, here is my analogy. I told my students.

"All of you have a gold mine in yourself, called potential. To extract the gold from your gold mine you will have to work for it. The more concentration, and dedication you put into your hard work, the more wisely you use your skills, the more gold you will extract from your body. The results that you extract from your body are beautiful and are yours forever.

Nobody can take them away from you. Somebody can hold you up and take your money or your belongings, as they did with the gold miners, but nobody can ever take your talent and the wonderful results you have extracted from your minds and bodies by hard work. These are yours forever; work for them."

In the meantime Marshall Turkin, the director of the Detroit Symphony Orchestra, handed in his resignation and left for the Pittsburgh Symphony. But with or without him, *The Nutcracker* was still serious business for the Detroit Symphony Orchestra. All the performances that year sold out and again they added two more performances.

I was concerned about my working relationship with Oleg Labanov, the new Executive Vice President and Managing Director of the DSO, and his opinion of our performances. A letter received from him pleasantly surprised me: "Just a note to tell you how much I enjoyed your production of *The Nutcracker*. My wife and I had the pleasure of attending on Thursday, December 23, 1982. We had a wonderful evening. I look forward to meeting you."

In early September, I was pre-occupied by *The Nutcracker,* for this Yuletide production. I selected the dancers from my school as well as from dance schools throughout the Metropolitan area. Every year my demand for quality increased. I preferred to have children who had already performed a year, and could perfect the steps in a shorter time. I selected the acrobats based on their ability to do a headstand and also, I looked for particularly talented acrobats for solo movements.

The auditions for major dances were much more intensive. The dancers had thirty minutes to study a sequence of steps from a major dance, like the Flower dance or Snowflakes finale. If they couldn't learn the steps in the thirty minutes, then I couldn't use them. A trained body, a quick mind, a high degree of self-discipline, and a firm commitment are absolutely essential to achieve a high quality performance. This discipline and dedication to quality were the reasons why the audience and the critics alike called the Dance Detroit Company "Professional Amateurs." The dancers always fulfilled my expectations and made my performances look professional.

The symphony was pleased that the performances had sold out the year before, so they now presented me with a contract for twelve *Nutcracker* performances. My prediction that *The Nutcracker* would become an annual tradition well appreciated by the public had been confirmed. However, I hadn't expected such a dramatic increase in the number of performances, and I didn't know what to do. Did we all have the stamina and financial resources to uphold such a long performance schedule? I had to consult the dancers, children, parents and myself. The results of my query were an enthusiastic "yes."

For twelve performances, two guest artists would not be sufficient. Besides the well-known and admired couple Merrill Ashley and Sean Lavery from the NYCB I invited two other couples: Cynthia Harvey and Kevin McKenzie, principals from the American Ballet Theater, and Melinda Roy and Sean Lavery, once again from NYCB.

That year, one beautiful student from my school, Meredith Dincolo captivated my attention. She auditioned for the role of Clara.

My wife Maria and I saw every performance, and we were thrilled every time. We enjoyed the positive reaction by the public, even their laughter at the comic moments in the show. Michael Margolin in the *Oakland Press* remarked, "I can report this immense undertaking came off with swiftness and flair. Iacob Lascu has again managed to take a wide group of active dancers, talented amateurs, children, acrobats and two stars of the New York City Ballet and squeeze them into a wondrous, intensely theatrical two hours."

The success of *The Nutcracker* was not just in Detroit and its Metropolitan area; people from all over Michigan came to see it. The artistic director of the Children Ballet Theatre in Lansing, Mrs. Jeanne Mallchok, was one of them and she expressed her admiration of my highly trained dancers. She also invited me to teach master classes for her company. She asked me if she could borrow some of my dancers to be the principals in their Lansing *Nutcracker* production. In particular, she very much liked Margaret Shallcross and her partner, Norman Stalzer, in the Snow *Pas de Deux*. I heartily approved her request. That gave my students another professional opportunity to dance.

In the summer of 1983, Maria and I moved into a new house in West Bloomfield; an English Tudor built on a hillside with a sloping driveway. The house had four bedrooms and two and one-half baths. The master bedroom was big and the bathroom was just beautiful! Maria liked it very much which I must admit was the main reason that we bought the house. Maria kept the house immaculate. The backyard was big and surrounded by towering trees and nice bushes. Our son Eugen nicknamed Genuț had recently married Mihaela, a former classmate from Romania; they resided with us for a while.

Genuț graduated from Wayne State University, and decided to take his master's degree in Hospital Administration in Minnesota. Mihaela was pregnant, and when Genuț and Mihaela took their winter vacation with us in West Bloomfield, she gave birth. It was on December 21, 1983 on the opening night of *The Nutcracker,* and the stage manager announced to the audience that Maria and I had become grandparents that morning. Maria and I were at Beaumont Hospital in the waiting room eager to find out if it was a boy or a girl when finally Genuț showed up from the delivery room. To our unbelievable surprise he said, "We have twins, a girl and a boy Marie Constance and James Alexander." Mihaela and Genuț didn't know that she had twins in her womb. Modern medical technology with its sophisticated ultrasound apparatus hadn't shown that she was carrying twins.

After the eventful vacation, Eugen and his wife returned to Minnesota where Eugen graduated the following summer. After attending his graduation we flew back to Detroit taking the twins with us. Maria held one and I the other; I don't remember which one. It was fun; they behaved wonderfully. Eugen and Mihaela drove their car and arrived in West Bloomfield two days later. They continued to reside with us for a while until they moved into their own house.

Maria adored her grandchildren; she devoted all her time caring for them. One of her favorite moments was bathing them and I had the pleasure of assisting her; one time I videotaped the entire spectacle.

Every day, she strolled with the children in their perambulator around the neighborhood and to the nearby park, just as my parents had strolled Genuț in the Cișmigiu Park in Bucharest. She played with them in the garden, and in the house. Their favorite spot was the master bedroom because they could jump on and off the king-size bed. Marie and James adored her. She took a lot of photos and put them in albums according to their ages. Some of the photos were framed and spread all over our house. I was a stranger to them because I worked all day and when I came home in the evening they were already sleeping. Maria would let me quietly open the door, and I was happy just to take a glimpse of them.

10 YEARS OF TRADITION

Maria was always with me, near me, encouraging me, correcting me, promoting me, and admiring my work. I didn't notice how fast time was passing and how soon I was again rehearsing *The Nutcracker*. Even though it had been ten years since my first *Nutcracker*, the production remained as fresh as a newly minted coin. The press, radio and television were now all covering the event more extensively than usual.

The *Free Press* weekly magazine published a story about me, entitled "Iacob Lascu's Gift to Detroit." I never thought that my performance would be held in such high esteem as to be considered a gift. It was a poignant irony that the same passion and ability for dance that had led me to an illustrious career in my native country of Romania, was now being appreciated ten years later in the United States. It had taken ten years for me to prove myself in the United States having to start again from the beginning, as a newcomer and an unknown. My experience showed me that as with everything else in life, you have to have quality to succeed, but, certainly, you also have to have luck.

In the *Free Press*, Mrs. Lessem wrote: "Dancers from some of the best ballet companies in North America have come to a city not known for a dance audience, all because of Lascu. They were drawn by his reputation and his insistence on excellence."

She also interviewed Cynthia Harvey, principal dancer from the ABT, and Sean Lavery from the New York City Ballet. Ms. Harvey told her, "For a group of people who aren't considered professional, I don't think he's capable of putting on anything less than highly professional."

Mr. Lavery echoed her: "I adore him. He's wonderful! His dancers do everything 100 percent, full out. They are very serious, very professional. Lascu gets the best from his dancers. He knows the way to use them and what they can do."

In the *Detroit News*, Mrs. Susan Isaacs Nisbett also considered *The Nutcracker* as a present for Detroit:

"Not all Christmas presents come under the trees. One of the season's best opened last night in Ford Auditorium, where the Dance Detroit joined forces with the Detroit Symphony Orchestra. Lascu's company is thoroughly professional. The ten-page cast list Seven Claras, four Fritzes etc. is a proud, if lengthy reflection of the talent on which Lascu draws. Moreover, the company reflects Detroit's ethnic diversity in a way that few outside companies could ever touch. Particularly impressive was the excellent ensemble dancing. As Clara and Fritz, Meredith Dincolo and Dmitry Mikheyenko could hardly have been improved upon. Mikheyenko is a young dancer of extraordinary promise, and Ms. Dincolo, a slightly more finished dancer, has lovely feet and elegant point work."

Everybody came up with ideas of how to celebrate the achievement of this tenth year anniversary. The parents formed special committees for different objectives: posters, a cast party, T-shirts and a special commemorative program for the audience. This program included photos of all guest artists for the past ten years, conductors who had performed during the ten years, photos of Dance Detroit dancers, photos from past performances, articles about the anniversary celebration, and letters of congratulations.

Before opening night on December 20, 1984, Maria and I went to a dinner at the riverboat restaurant. We were seated at a round table for ten persons: my wife and I were seated across from Governor James Blanchard and his wife Paula. On our right were seated Mr. Gunther Herbig, musical director of the DSO, and Mrs. Herbig; on our left, were seated the President of Marygrove College, Dr. Jack Shay, and his wife Pat. Also present were Michael A. Smith, vice president and general manager of the DSO, and his wife. Gunther Herbig was the first and the last music director of DSO who ever came to see *The Nutcracker*. At the fifteenth anniversary of *The Nutcracker*, however, Governor Engler and his wife honored us again backstage on behalf of the State of Michigan.

At left: Iacob with Governor and Mrs. Engler
At right: Conductor Leslie Dunner

The performance was one of the best. The cast was outstanding, with the Sugarplum Fairy danced by Kyra Nichols, and the Prince danced by Sean Lavery, both from the New York City Ballet. Meredith Dincolo also known as Kissy danced the role of Clara, Maria Aversa the Snow Queen; and, Waverly Lucas, the Snow Prince. I chose Dmitry Mikheyenko and Conrad Belknap to play the role of Fritz that year, and were selected both by Baryshnikov for the ABT school. There were too many to enumerate them all, but they were all wonderful and after the final bow of the last performance of this tenth year, the curtain slowly came down with the cast cheering and hugging each other. Some burst into tears while others were laughing with joy at the satisfaction of their ten years of success.

After the performance the dancers were able to mingle backstage with Governor Blanchard and his wife Paula as well as with Maestro Herbig and

his wife, President Shay and his wife, Maria and myself. Some of the children and dancers were too shy to get near the governor. Others were too bold and asked for an autograph from the governor. He was very friendly with everybody and signed as many autographs as was possible till he departed.

In front: Iacob, Governor and Mrs. Blanchard and Maestro Herbig - Right behind them: Mr. and Mrs. Shay and Mrs. Herbig

That year the Senate of Michigan issued Resolution No. 653 honoring me. Letters and resolutions from many prominent people followed: Mr. Walter J. McCarthy, Chairman of the Detroit Symphony Orchestra; Mayor Coleman A. Young, City of Detroit; James J. Blanchard, Governor's Office, Lansing, State of Michigan; from the United States Senate in Washington, D.C., Senator Carl Levin; and Office of the President, Board of Trustees and Faculty of Marygrove College, Executive Office. They all congratulated us and thanked us for the wonderful cultural gift we provided yearly for Michigan's citizens.

Ten years had passed since the first *Nutcracker*, and twelve years since our arrival in the United States. What a change in our lives! Joan Solaka, my good fairy, hugged and kissed us; and smiling at my wife and me, she said, "I congratulate you; I was right; you are talented. I trusted my feelings and recommended you to the symphony. You proved that I have good artistic judgment. You established a tradition in Detroit."

I was aghast when I found out that the DSO wanted eighteen performances for the 1986 season. In my professional career, I danced almost daily in a performance, so I knew how difficult this would be. Now, with eighteen performances of *The Nutcracker*, I was deeply concerned about the technical endurance over the months of rehearsals and performances of the children and teenagers in the cast, which had now grown to 130. When I presented the parents and the dancers with the possibility that there would be eighteen performances and two dress rehearsals with the orchestra, I expected, an outcry. I was stunned to discover that the out crying was not in opposition but an enthusiastic approval accompanied with cheers.

I was fortunate to work with such talented, energetic, enthusiastic and devoted people. The audience never really knew what tremendous preparations were necessary nor were they aware of the nervous excitement that was always present back-stage. Meredith and her mates, for example, used glue to stick their tights to the insides of the toe shoes. The magic of Mother Gigone was that she was tall because she walked on stilts so that her huge hoop skirt could hide twenty acrobats underneath. All the audience knew was the delight when the acrobats burst out from the huge skirt. The little and sometimes the big girls, too, typically didn't sit still much. They would gather around the principals and touch their tutus, asking for an autograph or even for a point shoe. Between stage calls, it was either wait or rush. The girls played different games while waiting; one of the most popular was Uno, played on the floor. But everyone snapped to attention when a colleague was in trouble. It could be a wrapping of a sore foot or a quick change from one dance number to another, or a spraying of a girl's feet with hair spray to make her tights cling. When the curtain rose, all this energy and excitement transformed the show into a magic performance.

The support of the parents during the rehearsals and performances overwhelmed me. I was amazed by how the parents coordinated and organized their activities, helping the children do their best. The daily driving, back and forth to downtown Detroit, was tiring for some parents, especially those who lived far away. Some of the parents rented rooms in downtown hotels to give the dancers more time to rest. On the days when we had two performances, the parents took the children to nearby restaurants or they brought food to the theatre. Some of the parents even took a week's leave from home or work to either help watch over the younger children during practices and performances or to help with costumes, props, etc.

The little ones, 3-6 years old, performed just two minutes of the entire show, but their contribution was priceless. Their job was a very difficult one, because for the first twenty minutes of the show they had to lay absolutely still as presents under that ornamented Christmas tree until Drosselmeyer transformed the entire scene. Then they would come to life and present themselves to Clara. Lying still for twenty minutes is such a tough job. On one night, one of the little dolls, with the biggest, pinkest tutu, fell soundly asleep. As the other dolls got up, and marched off, she was left sleeping under the Christmas tree.

I was so pleased and relieved that the rehearsals had gone extremely well and that everybody had done their best. The relief didn't last long, however. The day before opening night, one of my key male dancers

Norman Stalzer, who was to dance the *Pas de Deux* for the matinee, the Harlequin and the *Pas de Quatre* for the evening performance fell off a horse and broke his arm. I had to shuffle the rehearsal schedules, accordingly replacing him with another dancer.

My talented student Meredith, whose debut as the Sugarplum Fairy the year before had been a test for her and for the prestige of my school, covered the matinee performances. For me, it was very satisfying to see how well the public accepted us. This year I promoted two other students from my school to the starring role of the Sugarplum: Maria Aversa and Kristen Quinn.

The success of *The Nutcracker* attracted more and more students to my classes at Marygrove College. During this session, Mrs. Lisa Simon from the *Oakland Press* wrote.

"In just a few short and 'happy' years, Lascu has changed the face of classical ballet in Detroit. Once an unknown Romanian émigré, Lascu is now a well-known instructor."

A NEW LOCATION

The landlord who had a deli next door needed additional space for expansion. His business was flourishing and our school was flourishing, also. Unhappy with his request to vacate, I told him that our lease allowed me to stay two more years. He desperately needed my space and offered me $2,000 for moving expenses. It was a nice offer, but I didn't have another place to move to. I promised him that I would do my best to find an equivalent space as soon as possible. After a month of searching, we found a good place in Bloomfield Hills. It was close to the Detroit Skating Club and a gymnastics center. It was only a ten-minute drive from our house. The landlord was happy and gave us the money that he had promised.

The new space had about 4,500 square feet with a high ceiling and we divided it into two studios. It gave us the opportunity to offer two classes simultaneously. For the parents, there was a good size lobby. There were also two dressing rooms for boys and girls, two bathrooms, and an office for Maria. Gene designed labels for all the doors and created a logo for the business cards, letterhead and envelopes. We built a protective space, an inside and outside entrance to protect against cold air when opening the door in the wintertime. We bought a new piano, and gave the old one to the grandchildren. Everybody was excited; the studio looked great.

The fall enrollment was overwhelming; students came from Detroit, all the suburbs, and even from nearby cities like Brighton, Flint, and Ann Arbor. It is a pleasure to realize how we were able to make our way in a new life in the free world. We traveled through roads and paths strewn sometimes with flowers and at other times thorns that made our hearts bleed. Despite these encumbrances in our lives, we survived. Now we had our own school! It was the crowning achievement of our longtime activity in the field of ballet in Michigan.

None of my students have became world famous, but their technical training and artistry made it possible for them to be hired by major companies throughout the world: Kenneth Levitt, Waverly Lucas have danced with the Harlem Ballet Theatre; Dmitry Mikheyenko at Florida's Sarasota Ballet; Conrad Belknap, at the Marrinsky Ballet Theatre in St. Petersburg; Alexandra Kochis at the Boston Ballet; Guillermo Resto at the Mark Morris Dance Group; and Meredith Dincolo.

After her eighth year in my school, I was not surprised that Meredith wanted to challenge herself. I felt a great sense of satisfaction when the symphony accepted my proposal for her to be promoted to a principal for three matinee performances. Meredith performed the role of the Sugarplum with not only technical precision, but with a wonderful youthful interpretation. Her parents had always jokingly told me that I was her second father and my school, her second home but it was basically true.

Meredith and her parents also decided to apply directly to the Prix de Lausanne, an international ballet competition held from January 26 to February 2, 1987, in Lausanne, Switzerland. I admired Meredith's determination and her parents' unconditional support. At the competition Meredith danced her *Giselle* variation beautifully and the public appreciated her performance enthusiastically. However, the jury didn't pass her to the second round. Diane, Meredith's mother, went to the jury to find out the reason why she hadn't passed and to ask for advice in general on her daughter's future dancing career. The jury members couldn't give Meredith's mother any reason for her daughter's failure because her technique and artistry had been very good. All they could say was that the shape of her body was too big for a professional ballet dancer. I was afraid that this unsuccessful competition would break Meredith's confidence for the future. But she was outstandingly strong and accepted this defeat as only a temporary one, considering it as a learning experience. She expressed her thoughts in a letter written to me on July 16, 1987.

"I just want to thank you so much for such a wonderful year. I enjoyed Switzerland so much and hope we can do it again. Thank you for all your time and effort; it has helped me so much."

Time proved that the jury had been wrong. Meredith became a well-appreciated professional dancer. She was accepted that summer to study at the School of American Ballet. In the fall she went to Italy to dance for Pope John Paul at the Vatican as part of a Catholic religious group. She danced successfully with the Hubbard Street Chicago Dance Company and is now with the Lyons Opera in France.

Some of our ballet school students were gymnasts, either from the nearby gym or acrobats who performed in *The Nutcracker*. Mr. Steve Whitlock, the director of the nearby gym, the Acronauts of Bloomfield Hills, asked me to teach a special ballet class for his gymnasts. I did so, and the result showed a dramatic increase in his gymnasts' scores in different competitions. The international competitions dramatically demonstrate the benefit of a very strong ballet background to Russian and Romanian gymnasts. Acknowledging this fact The United States Gymnastics Federation, decided to emphasize the classical ballet technique. Mr. Whitlock was impressed by my teaching and recommended me to the United States Elite Coaches Association. They invited me to be on their staff of the Junior Training Camp to be held October 3--5, 1986 at the Colorado Olympic Training Center in Colorado Springs. Excited about teaching our Olympic team, I accepted their invitation.

Iacob and the US Olympic gymnasts

It was a great challenge for me to meet personally and teach the best gymnasts in the United States. Their full attention given to my corrections impressed me. My teaching pleased everybody, and I was invited to return for the January 21-24 session, in Orlando, Florida.

THE UNFORGETTABLE VACATION

Summer was the best time for us to rescue ourselves from our everyday routine. We decided to take a vacation with our son and his family. Our destination was Hilton Head Island, Savannah, Georgia and then to Telluride in Colorado. Maria and I had spent our previous vacation at a Hilton Head Island resort and loved it very much; we wanted to share our pleasant experience with Eugen and his family.

We drove to the villa, and at first sight, we liked it. The villa included a dining room two bedrooms a kitchen equipped with all the necessary things for running a household and a big living room with large sliding glass doors. We could see the porch and the garden with different beautiful flowers, palm trees, and a pond.

My wife loved the sun and the salty ocean water, and every day she went sunbathing. She had the patience to get an equal tan over her whole body, often running into the ocean to cool off. I didn't have her patience to lie down and expose my body to the sun, so I played soccer, volleyball, or just ran on the beach. I would take her by the hand and run with her into the therapeutic ocean water. We swam together; I liked the crawl and Maria liked the breaststroke. We swam in opposite directions and then back and hugged each other. We enjoyed the ocean waves striking us, which massaged our bodies. We looked for the biggest waves and dove against them, so their overwhelming power would throw us toward the shore. We had no desire to be rescued from our bliss here in the ocean.

I was always the first to get out of the water and had the immense pleasure of watching her play in the salty blue ocean. I stood on the shore and waited for her to come out of the water. My eyes followed her every movement, swimming, diving, jumping and turning in the water. The culmination of my joy was when she came out of the water. I would watch her beautifully curved dancer's body. I remembered the time spent with her at the Mamaia Beach in Romania when her body dazzled me. She was now 57-years old but she had maintained the shape of her body, sculptured during her dance career. Silhouetted against the ocean, I admired her firm breasts, well-shaped legs and well-arched feet, formed by ballet training. Approaching the shore, she did some dance movements, turning her back on me jokingly, like a pampered child, and then she ran toward me and hugged and kissed me to our surprise, Gene, our son, had videotaped the whole thing.

My son's vacation time passed by quickly and it was time for him and his family to go home. The parting was difficult; Maria hugged and kissed the children, then we followed them with our car until they passed the bridge, connecting the island with the mainland. After spending another week sunbathing and swimming, we packed again and continued our journey to Telluride.

■■■

On our way we stopped in Savannah and looked for the Shallal family. One of their children, Audra, had studied privately with me when she stayed at her grandmother's home in Detroit. She benefited from my approach and returned many times to Detroit to take more classes with me. She asked me where I would spend my vacation this summer. I told her that we planned to go to Hilton Head Island.

I called Mrs. Shallal and we met in downtown Savannah. Following her in her Jaguar, we drove about twenty miles north of Savannah to a secluded ocean resort called Tybee Island. We carried our luggage to the third floor, as there was no elevator but it was a good workout. The apartment was small, with just one bedroom; we wondered what was happening. She saw our puzzled faces and explained the situation:

"We bought this unit two years ago. It is our place for temporarily relaxing after a heavy week of work, especially for my husband who is a surgeon. We are in the process of moving to a new house in Savannah, which is now a mess. I am sorry that we cannot have you in our new house at this time, but make yourselves comfortable, rest and relax, and I will come back tomorrow to take you for dinner."

After her departure we put on our bathing suits and lay down on the lounge chairs found on the balcony. We contemplated the beautiful view of the ocean and the bright sun preparing for the sunset. Great ships, as well as a steady stream of small fishing boats, passed by coming and going from the Savannah port. Tired from driving and the fresh air from the ocean breeze, we went to bed.

The next day the weather was not so nice; some rain clouds threatened our peaceful place. We went shopping to stock up on food for the coming days. We dressed for dinner and waited for the arrival of Audra's mother. She was on time and asked us if everything was O.K. Maria answered her with enthusiasm.

"It is wonderful; it is so quiet and peaceful out here. I love it."

She drove us to the Restaurant Windows in the Hyatt Hotel where we met her husband, who was waiting our arrival. The restaurant was a five-star restaurant, built near the Savannah River. Our table was right near the huge windows facing the harbor. The view included a magnificent display of the entire river with the motor and sailboats anchored in the port. We had a wonderful time and thanked them for their generous hospitality; then they drove us back to the apartment.

Early the next morning, we explored the beach where we watched the dolphins, playing and jumping in the water. We collected shells, but we didn't enter the water. Unfortunately, the water had been spoiled by fuel oil residue from the passing ships. We wondered where the other tenants from the apartments were but this riddle was solved when we went swimming in the pool located the opposite side of the apartments. It was a good-sized, clean pool and crowded with the rest of the tenants.

After lunch we relaxed on the balcony reading the Savannah newspaper and our books. It was so peaceful and quiet that we fell asleep. We woke up faced by a fantastic view of the sunset. It was incredible to watch how the sun was gradually losing its shape and the brightness of its beams. The color of the sky and the ocean water became a glowing red. The ocean looked like a huge monster that was devouring the sun. The nightfall slipped in step-by-step, and then everything entered into a total darkness. The only little points of light visible were from the anchored fishing boats and the passing ships. It was delightful; it made us feel that we were in a wonderland, created by the inner desire for an ever-lasting moment. Maria liked this secluded place very much; she was very happy, singing and laughing. Maria was lying on the lounge chair with her legs on the balustrade of the balcony, relaxed, overjoyed with the tranquility of the evening.

I faced Maria and I kneeled down next to her chair. I was so happy seeing her serene, and peaceful face. I gently caressed her face with my right hand and kissed her. She answered to my kiss and embraced me. I put my head on her chest, feeling the heat and smell of her sunburned body. We stood so, in the dark, quiet, peaceful night for a long time, listening to our heartbeats. The physical rhythm of our heartbeats was different. Hers was slower than mine, but spiritually they were beating in unison. We knew that every moment of our thirty-seven years together had been offered solely to each other, body and soul. These joyful moments with Maria always gave me new strength and confidence in my life. It was like an insurance policy; she would always stand by my side when I needed her. She caressed me with her left hand on my head, ears and back. Her movements were so sensitive. She knew that I liked this very much. I could feel the tip of her fingers transferring her love to my body and soul. I forgot where I was. I lost contact with the surrounding world. I was just with her: with her body, soul and her devoted love.

Unfortunately, the three days passed too quickly and we had to leave. We called the Shallal family, and thanked them again for their generous hospitality. We invited them to visit us in our house in West Bloomfield.

■■■

We studied the map and found out that from the state of Georgia we had to pass six states in order to arrive in Colorado. I don't remember the cities where we stopped to eat lunch, or the cities where we ate dinner, or the name of the hotels where we slept over night. We continued on our way and saw the sign for Telluride, a secluded winter sports area. In summertime, the town hosts art exhibits and jazz festivals. Wherever we turned, we could see the mountains, still partially covered with snow. The apartment was cozy, well furnished with comfortable armchairs. It was a pleasant surprise to find a Jacuzzi in the bathroom and a sauna nearby. After we made ourselves comfortable, we explored the city.

We took a walk down the main artery of the city, which was crowded with people. What especially called our attention was a building in the center of the town with colonnades and ornaments, resembling an ancient Greek architecture. It was an oddity among the other western-style buildings. We were told that it was a former bank where Butch Cassidy and the Sundance Kid committed their first robbery.

Beverly, Maria's friend, who had given us the key to her apartment, had told us that her daughter, Janice, lived in Telluride. We called her and she invited us for dinner.

We did some shopping: We visited an art gallery and looked for a present for Beverly, We found a decorative ceramic plate and hoped that Beverly would enjoy this souvenir from us. We left it on the dining-room table on a special support.

The following days we took guided tours up into the mountains in a 4-wheel drive jeep. The guide himself was the driver. The road was very narrow, winding, and full of bumps, and the car made a lot of noise, so it was difficult for me to videotape. The landscape was beautiful. We enjoyed the noise of the river that emerged from a powerful waterfall. It was a tiring trip; the compensation was that at least Maria had found some flowers. After the tours we were famished, so we went directly to a restaurant for dinner. Later, at the apartment, we enjoyed the sauna and the Jacuzzi; we had a good night's sleep.

We left Telluride, refreshed and very pleased with our stay. Since our itinerary was not fixed, I made a suggestion to Maria.

"We are in Colorado and we don't know when we will have another opportunity to come again; let's go to Aspen." On our way to Aspen, Maria suddenly said, "I saw signs indicating that close by is a Black Canyon."

"I never heard of it."

We stopped at a Texaco gas station, filled up, and found out that the Black Canyon was a great place to visit. Route 92 took us right there and we soon saw the huge sign with the inscription "Grand Canyon of the Gunnison National Monument." When we arrived at the rim of the Canyon, we both cried out simultaneously.

"It's fantastic, unbelievable."

It was like a gigantic black granite rock monument that rose from the bottom of the earth. We could see the river flowing below, taking its course, and lost in the far distance of the canyon. The rocks were impressive and steep. Indeed, it was an extraordinary sight. The walls looked like high skyscrapers alternating with tall churches. The "Cross Fissures Overlook" rim was yet another wonder. The rock looked as if it had suffered ruptures or fissures

Maria at the Black Canyon

as we do when we fracture our bones. "The Painted Wall" looked like a modern painting, with long, white, cordlike fibers of nerves hanging on the contrasting black granite walls. It was amazing beyond belief. The "Devil's Overlook" was quite a distance from the main route.

"My God, it is too deep and steep," Maria, cried out. "This is the reason why it is called the Devil!"

The Black Canyon visit was an excellent addition to our trip. For us this canyon was more dazzling, more monumental, more fascinating, more inspiring than even the Grand Canyon. Both canyons are great and unique in their way, but our favorite remained the Black Canyon.

Aspen was welcoming us, but we were not ready for it. We didn't even have a travel booklet with recommendations about where to stay, where to dine, what to do, etc. We followed the signs to the center of the town and stopped at the first hotel that we saw. The Boomerang was the hotel's name, a name that inspired us to stop. The name suggested to us that, like the Australian boomerang, satisfied customers returned again and again to the hotel.

July is off-season. Aspen is not crowded and there is little demand for rooms. I registered and found out that the cost was reasonable. We asked the receptionist for tour booklets to see how we could spend our time more productively and enjoyably in Aspen. Our first choice was a ride up a gondola to the mountains ski path. We walked to the Gondola station, but the schedule indicated that we were too early and we had to wait one hour before the first gondola departed. Hand in hand, we walked through the city. We browsed the chic shops and the colorful houses. We stopped at a shopping center, and then we walked to a park with benches, and lamps, which looked like regal crowns. Maria admired the flowers and a modern sculpture.

Maria at the Aspen Gondola station

Most of the people commuted on bicycles and the atmosphere were European. There were restaurants all over town with tables outside like in Italy or France. Flowers were everywhere on apartment balconies, hotels, and hanging along the streets. The hour passed quickly, so we had to rush back to the gondola station. The gondola was actually a cable car in the shape of an Italian gondola. Up at the top, there was a big restaurant where we had lunch. Through the big windows, we had a gorgeous view of the snow-covered mountains.

Soon it was time to head home to Michigan but Maria reminded me that I had promised her a long time ago that we would go to Colorado Springs. I liked this city and had told her about it in 1986 when I had coached the U.S. Olympic gymnastics team. I took Maria to the Olympic Training Center and to the grounds where the winter Olympics had been held. Then we headed to the Garden of the Gods, which contains a myriad of red rock formations. One particularly very huge rock stood apart. The position of the rock gave us the impression that it would fall over at any minute. The base of the rock barely touched the ground urging almost everyone to try to push it down. I tried myself, imitating the other tourists; but, of course, I didn't succeed. It is still an enigma and nobody yet can explain this phenomenon of nature. I videotaped Maria sitting under the almost falling rock. The sunset reminded us that night was coming, and we were exhausted from driving, sightseeing, and the fresh air.

"It is closing time, let's go," she said as she made her way toward the car.

We had a good night's sleep and the next day, we headed home. It was a well-deserved vacation, and we enjoyed it tremendously: At that time, however, I didn't know that this would be my last vacation together with my love, the partner of my life.

UNFORESEEN

We were planning to open our private ballet school at the end of August, so we still had time to take care of all the necessary things for the opening. We rewrote the school brochure and printed a new schedule we repaired loose bars, and cleaned the whole studio, especially the marble floor.

In life, however, things happen too fast. We barely solve one problem when a new one surfaces.

Every year before the opening of the school, Maria and I would go to the doctor for an annual check-up. This was the third year since either of us had had a sigmoidoscopy. The doctor explained that this involves inserting a flexible instrument into the colon, which allows direct examination of its lowest twelve to twenty-four inches, the area where tumors are most likely to develop. This test was the last test this year. I remember thinking that it would never end.

We are helpless when the pain is piercing us and almost forget it when the doctor, with his cool smile, tells us it is O.K.

My blood pressure and the results of the other exams done that day were good. He would let me know the results of the blood tests. I dressed and went into the waiting room to read a book, which I always carried with me. Reading a book, one page after another, made time seem to pass faster while I was waiting for Maria. But, after all, time was time, and I started to become impatient, thinking that my wife was staying too long for her tests. I didn't have any choice but to wait, but I couldn't read any more. I fixed my eyes on the door of the room where the test was going on. Finally the door opened, a nurse came out. As she closed the door, I approached her, anxious to find out the results.

"How are Maria's test results?" I asked her.

"The doctor will inform you about the results," she answered.

At that moment the door from the examining room opened again, and this time it was the doctor. There was no cool, smiling face, this time, instead a cool sad face. The vibes coming from the doctor's face increased the bad feeling I had had in my stomach. The doctor invited me into his office, and I waited to hear his findings. Doctors, in general, are not shy about revealing their diagnoses. On the contrary, they are proud to reveal their findings, good or bad, as proof of achievement in their profession.

So, without introduction, the doctor told me, "Your wife has tumors on the colon. My opinion is that she has to go early tomorrow morning to the hospital for a biopsy to find out if the tumors are malignant, and then we will decide what to do."

175

I was speechless and turned toward Maria who had just made her appearance. She was calm, but sad. I didn't know what to tell her; I couldn't find any words, so I just gazed into her eyes, trying to fathom her reactions to the devastating news. I sensed in her eyes an inner tension, that she was scared. I was too but I tried to hide it. As soon as we were out of the doctor's office and back in the car, she hugged me and cried on my shoulders. I caressed her hair; I took her tender face in my hands and kissed her weeping eyes. I just looked at her and still didn't know what to say. She calmed down after a while and we sat for a long time in silence. It was difficult to concentrate on my driving home as my mind, floating in a downward spiral, tried to sort out the situation. At home, I finally dared talk to her, and asked, "Did you have some pain or other symptoms lately that you didn't tell me about?"

"I didn't have pain. I just had difficulty relieving my bowels, and sometimes I had blood. I thought that it was from my hemorrhoids, which had developed during our touring performances in Romania. I never thought that this could generate tumors. Now that the doctor has found tumors on my colon, I am afraid that I might have cancer. My mother died of cancer."

It was awkward for me to try to distract her from her negative thoughts, but I had to say something. Her statement reflected the common medical opinion that a person inherits the susceptibility to cancer from his or her parents. I tried to tell her that this is not always the case.

"Your sister and brother are older than you are and they are fine. Let's wait until after the biopsy."

She didn't answer, and, as usual, before going to bed, we hugged and kissed. We lay quietly on our backs, glancing up at the ceiling, neither one of us could fall asleep. My mind and body were tense; my thoughts were running from one idea to another like an animal trapped in a cage and trying to escape. *Will the biopsy be O.K.? If not, what was I to do? What should I do? Should we go for a second opinion? I hoped it would be fine! But what if it was not? I felt powerless, I tried to relax and wait until tomorrow.*

The neurons in my brain, however, continued to repeat these questions over and over, an obsession without answers. I wished I were in her mind to find out her thoughts. I turned facing her and she was still in the same position but with eyes closed. I was not sure if she was sleeping or not, but the fact that she was no longer staring at the ceiling gave me a relaxed feeling, and gradually I fell asleep.

The next day we went to Beaumont Hospital and looked for Dr. Kedro. He was busy with another patient in surgery. The nurse guided Maria to the pre-op room for surgery, where she was preparing for the biopsy. I took a seat in the waiting room. The biopsy didn't take long, but for me the waiting was endless. The tissue for the biopsy was taken immediately to the laboratory, but that short time for Maria and me, waiting for the results was an agony.

Dreadful news: the results were devastating. It was positive, malignant- a word that frightens everybody, a word that threw us into a depression. Both of us were ignorant about cancer; we had heard about it but we had never given it much attention or taken a closer look at it. The doctor's face didn't reflect the gravity of the results; for him this was a routine examination. At that time, we didn't know about preventive medicine alternative cures, holistic medication, or macrobiotic cures. We looked to the doctor and awaited his verdict. Without hesitation he told us, "Mrs. Lascu, it is necessary to perform surgery and without delay." We were taken by surprise and shocked by this suggestion.

"Doctor! We would like to think about this, and we will call you and let you know of our decision."

He didn't like what I said. He replied in a very prompt manner and with a scary prediction, "Your wife's situation requires urgent surgery if it is not too late already, and I would advise you to talk to my assistant to schedule surgery for tomorrow."

With that pronouncement, he left us dumbstruck, followed by his nurse, for his next operation. We were emotionally down, scared, powerless, and tormented by the situation. We looked at each other and neither of us could say a word.

Finally I said, "Let's call Eugen, our son, and your brother and sister, and ask their opinions."

She agreed. We called them immediately, and they were hit very hard by the bad news; but they didn't know what was the best thing to do. We promised them that we would let them know our decision.

Maria was not afraid of surgery; she had had a hysterectomy in 1976. Then she had a tumor, but not a malignant one, on one of her ovaries. She had been a brave lady, and I remembered that she had gone with great courage into surgery. I still have the Quanta's mascot that I bought her after surgery. She had recovered well in a very short time, and, after that, the doctor had prescribed Estrogen for her. According to the information published today in many medical magazines, we know that Estrogen may cause cancer. In my mind, I connected this drug with the developing cancerous cells in her colon.

Whatever I thought might have possibly caused her malignant colon cancer, nothing could change the reality of the situation. I was unable to make an instantaneous decision about surgery. My thoughts were a way of trying to postpone the decision. I didn't know what was in Maria's mind because she was now silent. We really didn't know what to do, and we were both plunged deep into thought. The doctor's assistant approached us, interrupting our thoughts.

"Did you make a decision, because I have to schedule the surgery for tomorrow and inform the doctor of it."

"We didn't," was our answer.

"I don't want to rush you or to pressure you, but from what I deduced from the biopsy test, the situation is not rosy, and the cancer cells could spread to the whole body, which could become life-threatening. Therefore, the tumors should be removed immediately to give us a chance to eventually eradicate the cancer."

We both realized that we actually didn't have a choice. Maria looked straight into the assistant's eyes and told him with a raw and frightened voice, "So surgery for me is a gamble that I have to take in order to give me a chance to survive." I sensed the pessimism in her voice, but before the assistant could answer, Maria said with determination, "Let's do it."

That night, for the first time since the ordeal started, I was really tormented by negative thoughts. I felt helpless, lost, and wrapped up in thoughts that frightened me. My mind and body fretted all night, like a violent thunderstorm, sending rapid strobes across my brain. I had always made my decisions with a strong will, but now my mind staggered.

Did she make the right decision? What if the doctor doesn't handle it well? Should I try to change her decision or go along with it? How can I help her? Will she survive the surgery? Why didn't I do anything to prevent this illness? What should I do about it now? What is going on in her mind? Why didn't she tell me about the blood in her stool?

She was lying coiled up with her spine facing me, so I couldn't tell if she was asleep or not, and I didn't want to disturb her. I felt fragile in the grip of fear. I wanted my thoughts to calm down; I wanted to deny the terror in my brain. I wanted my thoughts to be as patient as a fisherman who stays at the water's edge for hours and days just to catch a fish. But my brain wanted quick answers and was unable to get them. I felt a sense of urgency to resolve the problem. I felt guilty and accused myself of letting her work too much. I felt anger and I wanted to blame somebody, but whom should I blame? I started to panic. My neurons lost their steady, homogenous thinking and divided into a contradictory dialogue between two different persons,

What are you going to do? Said the first one
There's nothing I can do now, said the second.
But you can't sit still and do nothing.
What can I do?

You are right, there's nothing, nothing, nothing you can do. Don't bring yourself down; try to relax, be patient, and wait calmly for the outcome. Problems are part of life and you have to work through them.

In my life I was strong and now I felt that I was a fragile human being; I had to deal with a reality about which I could do nothing. I tried to make myself believe that the outcome of the test was a mistake. I realized immediately that denial was a protective solution for myself, a way of not facing and accepting reality. I wished to have a magic ball, to envision the future, but I had to master the present circumstances by understanding them and waiting for the unknown future. I couldn't sleep all night and noticed that the daybreak had arrived.

We entered the hospital in the morning. Going to a hospital for a biopsy and then returning again for the surgery is nobody's desire. But this was not just any surgery; it was for a malignant cancer, a dangerous one. I don't like hospitals; they are temples for sickness. We met people in wheelchairs or walking alone. We didn't know what specific illnesses they had, but it didn't matter; for me, it was just an undesirable sight.

I couldn't guess what Maria was feeling; she walked with a steady pace through those endless passages. Her face expressed a strong determination to undergo this surgery as soon as possible. Arriving at the doctor's office, she had to fill out some forms regarding her medical history. She signed some papers declaring that she agreed to the surgery. The nurse advised Maria to give me her watch, earrings, rings and her purse. We hugged and kissed each other, and I wished her good luck. Then the nurse took her to the room where they prepare the patients for surgery. I accompanied them up to the door and we kissed again. I followed her with my eyes until the door closed and I was told to come back after noon.

My thoughts went back to the year when Maria had survived the hysterectomy, and she had taken up her teaching again with great enthusiasm. Her body had been strong as a result of her well-trained professional dance career. We had thirty-eight years of a happy marriage; she loved her entire family.

My son was working as a hospital administrator and inquired about Dr. Kedro. He was told that he was a proficient surgeon. This thought filtered through my mind and gave me a feeling of hope. After lunch, I returned to the hospital and the nurse informed me that the surgery had just ended and had gone very well; Maria had been a very brave patient. She was still in the recovery room, and I waited impatiently for the doctor. The doctor soon made his appearance with a satisfied smile on his face.

He shook my hand and told me, "The surgery took three hours, not including the preparation. Maria is fine and soon you will be able to talk to her. Maria's decision to accept the surgery was a good one because I had to cut about twelve inches from the colon to eliminate the tumors already found on the colon."

"I realize you did, technically, a brilliant surgery. However, my question is, were all the tumors eliminated?"

"It's too early to predict the future development of the cancer's cellular behavior, but I hope that I succeeded in cutting it all out hopefully it will not be necessary to give her chemotherapy."

His answer was not satisfactory for me, but I understood his limitation in being unable to promise me a definite positive outcome. He then informed me that he had to travel to Europe. In his absence, his associate would take care of Maria. Not long thereafter the nurses came with the hospital gurney on which Maria lay quietly with closed eyes. I went near the gurney; the nurses recognized me and stopped for a moment. I bent over Maria's face and kissed her. Slowly, she opened her eyes and showed a smile.

"Mammy scump (dear), how are you feeling?" I asked her.

She blinked her eyes and very carefully did a little nodding with her head. I understood that she was O.K., but weak. She was still under the influence of the anesthetic. The nurses continued their way to her room and asked me to wait outside the room until they had transferred her to the bed. I followed them, and, from the threshold of the door, I watched the whole transfer process with the different tubes and wire connections. The head nurse took her blood pressure and gave her some medication. Finally, I was allowed to enter the room.

I grabbed a chair and sat near the bed gently touching Maria's hand. Slowly she turned her head toward me, and I saw in her eyes that she was glad that I was there. I took her hand and kissed it; then she touched me with her other hand on my head. Her touch made me feel strangely protected and overwhelmed me with love, realizing it was she who needed to be protected at this, difficult moment. We just looked at each other; and I asked her if she needed something. She answered by nodding her head. Soon she was asleep. I was eager to find out more details of the surgery from her, but she was not yet ready for such a conversation.

As I explored the hospital where I would be spending so much time, I became depressed. The hospital was a sterile, stinking, fluorescent hell.

When she woke up Maria stretched out her arms to me, so I bent and hugged her. What a joy to see her make such a radical improvement. I was so happy being in her arms that I forgot that I was in a hospital. A nurse interrupted our short idyll and proceeded to carry out her routine procedures. She asked me to leave the room. The associate doctor also stopped by to examine her. He was pleased with her progress, and, as he left the room, he told me that thanks to the strength of her body she would have a fast recovery. It was getting late and the nurse advised me that it was time for me to go home. I hugged and kissed Maria, and run to our dance studio to teach with a happy feeling. The children and parents loved Maria they were anxious to hear how she was doing. I called Gene, Traian and Annie, and I updated them about the surgery. They were pleased and told me that the next afternoon they would stop by the hospital to visit.

In the morning, I returned to the hospital for a short visit before going to teach at Marygrove College. We did our usual routine of hugging and kissing. I found her more invigorated than the day before. I left to go to my classes with a relaxed mind, promising her that I would be back at noon. After my last class, I stopped by a florist and bought fresh red roses, her favorite flowers, before I rushed to see her. I couldn't go into her room immediately because that was exactly the time when the nurse was doing her routine check up. The nurse finally opened the door and told me that I could go in. She said that Maria was strong and wonderful, and she was glad to have her as a patient. The nurse admired my flowers and said Maria would enjoy them.

Indeed Maria, smiling, took the flowers from me, admiring, smelling, and held them to her breast.

"Thank you; they are so beautiful and fresh," she said. Where did you find them?"

"On Woodward Avenue, close to the hospital. I will bring you the same every day."

"I like them very much, but you don't need to spent so much money. You are my everyday flower, and I am happy to see you."

That afternoon, the time passed by quickly; Eugen and his family came to see her, later Traian and Olga, and then Mary and Walter Lazar. Annie, her sister, lived out of state called to check in. During the following days, the children with their parents from our school took turns bringing sweets and flowers and different stories. Maria was happy to be surrounded by so much attention, and thanked everybody, promising them that soon she would see them at the school. By the end of the week, her hospital room was a garden with flowers, candy and chocolate display.

The doctor's associate was right; Maria recovered fast. I massaged her feet and legs and gradually she started taking walks up and down the hallways of the hospital. She gained strength every day. At the beginning, I helped by supporting her during the walk until she got the confidence to do it alone. After ten days she was released from the hospital but could not return to work for at least three more weeks. At home, I continued to massage her legs and feet in the morning; we took our daily walk through the neighborhood and we did some elementary ballet movements, like *demi-plié* and *battement tendu*. During this time, we also began to look into alternative methods for curing cancer. We bought books with true stories about people who were cured through the macrobiotic method: *Living Well Naturally* by Anthony J. Sattilaro, *M.D.* and Tom Monte, *Recovery from Cancer to Health through Macrobiotics* by Elaine Nussbaum, *The Cancer Prevention Diet, Michio Kushi's Nutritional Blueprint for the Relief* and *Prevention of Disease* by Michio Kushi with Alex Jack.

After reading Mr. Kushi's book, we thought that macrobiotics could help Maria cleanse her body from any eventual residue of the cancer cells, and for me, it would prevent it. We learned that the macrobiotic movement has an international organization called the United Nations Macrobiotics Society. They had referrals to local counselors, physicians, dietary and other health care professionals.

We called the headquarters in Boston and they recommended Mrs. Bonnie Breidenbach from Grosse Point Park, she was specialized in Macrobiotic Education. She detailed a strict daily dietary plan for Maria. She asked Maria to record what she ate and report to her every week. Mrs. Breidenbach also advised Maria to take macrobiotic cooking classes, until she learned how to cook that way until then she advised Maria to eat at macrobiotic restaurants. Maria followed the instructions rigorously.

We went together to eat at a macrobiotic restaurant. The taste of food didn't appeal to her, but Maria consumed it anyway because she believed in its positive effect on her illness. I understood that it was very difficult for her to change her eating habits after so many years. It was difficult for me, too, but that experience helped me to understand how important it is to have self-control. Maria also enrolled in group therapy offered by the Center for Attitudinal Healing.

Sometimes hard times can bring out our best and motivate us to move forward and upward to higher levels of living, loving, and growing. The doctors pointed out repeatedly that she had a strong physical body and that her recovery was noticeable from day to day. Maria realized that she was in a slump, that this was the time for endurance, for struggling through and relying on her own survival skills.

She asked me to take her to the school to meet the students and their parents where she was received with, tenderness love, warmth and excitement. She felt great satisfaction and delight when she realized that the students and parents respected and missed her. I sensed that the welcome by the students and parents infused her with positive energy. She was elated and accepted the joy of the moment. She was not yet able to teach but watched classes and conversed with the students and parents. That day, she felt a purpose in her life once again I saw a meaning and beauty around her. I was happy to see her enjoying herself and I hoped that being here would accelerate the healing energy throughout her body. I wondered how soon she would be able to teach or drive the car by herself.

We never know how long a recovery takes. We didn't know why things happened the way they had with us. I just said to myself that my wife's recovery was an ongoing process. Time and patience would be needed to open the way to unknown results. My hope was that she would have trust in her strength and enough patience to go through the slow recovery process. For all of us who loved her and stood by her, it was a challenge to support her in this process. She repeated her visits to the school many times and gradually started to teach. At the end of the term she presented her open classes for the parents and guests. After the class, the children and parents overwhelmed her with flowers and gifts. In the meantime, I called my friends in Germany and asked them to find medication or a doctor or a hospital that could cure cancer. They loved Maria dearly and promised me they would do their best.

One day returning home from my classes I found her very depressed.

"What's wrong mammy scump (dear)?" I asked her.

She started to cry. I didn't insist on an answer. I didn't know the nature of her depression, so I let her calm down by herself. She looked out through the kitchen window admiring the garden that she had so beautifully created and loved, and with a low voice she told me, "I will die."

I was shocked by her words; I held her shoulders with my hands and looked at her. I saw real fear in her eyes for the first time.

"Mammy scump (dear) why are you saying that? Did something happen at the therapy class?"

"Yes," she answered.

"What, tell me about it," I asked.

She hesitated for a second then continued, "Some of the participants of the therapy class had missed three weeks already and I asked the coordinator of the therapy where they were. The coordinator said that they had died." This answer hit me like a bullet.

"Each person is a different case; you are recovering fast, and your strength grows every day. Don't be so hard on yourself," I said.

She started to cry again.

"Why is this happening to me? Tati scump (dear) this is terrible. My feeling is that I will die and I am sorry that I have to leave you behind." We hugged each other and stood for a while in silence. It was time for me to go to our school to teach my classes, so I told her to take a nap and relax.

The next day I called Maria's counselor, Mrs. Breidenbach, and told her what had happened at the therapy class and about the devastating effect it had upon my wife. I told her that Maria didn't want to go back to these classes. Her answer was that Maria was very sensitive, and she should cease going to these therapy sessions. She advised me to contact the Kushi Foundation in New York City and ask for an interview with Mr.Michio Kushi, a support person for the macrobiotic way of life. She warned me that it was very difficult to get an appointment with him and that he was very expensive, but I should insist on seeing him.

I pleaded the gravity of my wife's situation to Mr. Kushi's secretary; I told her that my wife was depressed and that she desperately needed help. To my grave disappointment, the secretary informed me that Mr. Kushi was already booked for the next month; the first available appointment would be the three days at the end of June. I accepted the dates without hesitation, and then she informed me that the interview would cost $1000. I had to make a deposit immediately of $200 and then I called the travel agent to reserve our tickets.

In the meantime, my son told me that his godfather had created with great success a drug that had cured cancer patients in Romania. "A new hope" I said to myself and told my son to contact him right away in order to work out the details of getting the drug. My son called his godfather in Romania, informed him of Maria's illness, and asked him to send the medication, urgently. Eugen's godfather explained that he had to order some ingredients of the medication from Switzerland because it was not available in Romania but as the medicine was ready he would send it to us.

In the newspapers, I found information that in Mexico there was a place called the Clinic Paso del Norte where they cured cancer. I called them and they sent me booklets and application forms. It was a comprehensive plan for a two-year series.

The classes at our private school had kept Maria going, but I could sense her depression ever since the event from the therapy class, which was still present and affecting her.

We continued to eat the macrobiotic dishes prepared by Maria based on the instructions given by her counselor. Maria gradually resumed her joy with her grandchildren and devoted much of her free time to them, hugging them more frequently, as never before. She held them tightly to her chest, caressing them and kissing them as never before. It was an obsession; her eyes reflected a sadness that I had never seen. She acted as if she were a lens of a recording camera. Her steady gazing eyes wanted to preserve the children forever in her mind. All this actions stemmed from her depression that didn't go away, generated by the feeling that she was going to die. I looked forward to the appointment with Mr. Kushi, with the hope that he would be able to change her feelings. Also I looked forward with great hope to the Clinic Paso del Norte in Mexico. Unfortunately, neither plan was implemented.

Three days before our departure to New York to see Mr. Kushi, Maria started to complain of pains in her stomach and gradually lost her appetite. The pains were tremendous, more and more constant, and the situation became critical. I called Dr. Kedro, but he was out of town. I called 911 and they took her to a nearby hospital's emergency room. They diagnosed that she was constipated and gave her some medicine and sent her home. She started to lose weight, and her eyes became jaundiced. I was scared and called 911 again; this time they took her to another hospital's emergency room. I called my son at his office and informed him what had happened; I also called Traian, Maria's brother, who came right away and stood by me in the waiting room. It was obvious that I should call the Kushi Foundation and cancel our much-awaited appointment.

After about two hours of waiting with nobody coming out to tell me what was happening with Maria, I lost my patience. I asked the security guard to let me into the emergency room. The guard denied my request, but I didn't give up; I told him that I was her husband, that I had waited too long and that I must talk to the doctor to find out what was happening. He finally softened and let me pass. I could hear the moans of the suffering patients, but I wasn't sure which were Maria's.

Occasionally a nurse or a doctor appeared, but neither of them came to the door where I was waiting. Again I waited about an hour or more, and again I lost my patience. I approached the first doctor who appeared. I introduced myself and asked him where Maria was. He couldn't tell me; there were too many patients to remember, but he was very kind and told me that he would check. He disappeared behind the curtains for a while when he appeared again he asked me to follow him. He led me to her bed; she was awake. I kissed her and then I asked the doctor about the diagnosis. He said that he didn't know exactly, but that the jaundiced color in her eyes was a sign that her liver was in trouble. He had already called the chief surgeon who had agreed to come to the hospital as soon as possible. I was worried; what he told me didn't sound good.

"Do you think that it could be a new operation?" I asked him.

"I don't know; please have a seat and wait until the other doctor arrives. He will tell you what has to be done."

Lost in the turmoil of my thoughts I sat on a nearby chair. I forgot that Traian was sitting outside in the waiting room until the security guard told me that somebody was asking for me. Traian was anxious about what was going on. I hesitated going back into the waiting room because I was not sure that the security guard would let me in again, but I wanted to talk to Traian, so I asked the guard to let him in. Of course, he refused explaining that he had already made an exception for me. He agreed to let me come back, so I advised Traian to go home and I would update him as soon as I talked to the chief surgeon.

Traian left and I waited...waited...waited. This was a time when I simply didn't know what to do. I had to struggle through my feelings of frightened, uncertainty, helplessness, anger and hopelessness. I had no clear perspective. I felt a sense of urgency. I wanted to get from the doctors a sense of security, of knowing what was going to happen, but nobody was around to talk to me. Many people went in and out from the emergency room; but I didn't know which one was the chief surgeon, and nobody called me in.

I lost my patience again, and I asked permission from the security guard to talk to one of the doctors on duty. I waited; finally, one of the doctors came into the waiting room. It was the same one with whom I had talked before. I asked him if the chief surgeon had arrived; his answer was negative. I told him that I would like to be near my wife. He guided me to her; once again she had already been moved to another spot and she was sleeping. I wanted to be a magician to take away all her suffering, but I was powerless. At this moment I hoped that doctors and things outside myself held the key to her recovery. Absorbed in my thoughts and resigned to my powerless situation, I went back to my seat and waited. Not too long after, a gentleman with a portfolio under his arm suddenly opened the door and passed by me in a hurry. I ran after him and stopped him. I introduced myself. He shook my hand and introduced himself. He was the chief surgeon of the hospital. He asked me to wait until he could examine Maria; then he would let me know his diagnosis.

I didn't have choice, so I waited again another hour or more. For me it was stressful, endless waiting. When he finally appeared, he still didn't have a clear diagnosis. I can still see his face, which reflected an uncertainty. He told me that at this point he couldn't determine the problem. He needed to open up the previous surgery to find out why she had these pains. I wasn't satisfied with what he told me, and I asked him why he couldn't do a cat scan or X-ray to find the cause. His answer was given in a very authoritative manner.

"I have to see for myself what was done in the first surgery and then we will go from there."

"When are you planning to open up the surgery?" I asked.

"Tomorrow morning." He then told me that I should go home and wait for his call after the surgery.

I was tired and staggered by the day's events so I went home and updated Gene and Traian. I didn't eat and went right to sleep. For the first time, that night, I actually lost my trust in medical science. I woke up with a headache. The stress and maybe the fact that I hadn't eaten the previous night were taking its toll. I ate and took a Tylenol tablet from Maria's supply and tried to relax in the armchair, waiting for the phone call from the doctor. It was already past 10:00 A.M. and I couldn't stand it any more. I grabbed the phone and dialed the doctor's office in the hospital. His secretary answered. I told her who I was. She told me that the doctor was still in surgery and as soon as he was finished, he would call me. I was on thorns, so after more than an hour of waiting, I called again. The answer was the same. I was restless, my headache wouldn't go away, and I took another Tylenol.

I paused in my office as I wandered throughout the house feeling helpless. I sat at the table trying to make some plans for my classes, but I couldn't concentrate. It was noon and still no phone call. There was no sound at all in our big, empty house. The windows facing the garden were open and I looked at the neighbors' roofs, chimneys, and cars in their driveways, their gardens and their flowers. My thoughts went to my dear wife who loved spending hours in the garden, planting flowers. I walked to the window and said hello to one of my neighbors. She asked me about Maria and wished her a fast recovery.

The phone rang. I excused myself from the neighbor and rushed to the phone. It was my son who wanted to find out the results of the operation. I am always happy when my son calls me, but this time I was disappointed because I expected the doctor's call. I told him that I had lost my patience that I had made the decision not to wait any more. I was leaving for the hospital. He agreed to join me and we decided to meet at the entrance.

The hospital was a big red brick building in downtown Detroit. I took a panoramic view of the huge area to know how to orient myself for the future. Soon Gene, arrived and we entered the lobby together. We looked for the information desk that was in the center of the lobby where the lady told us that the visiting hours were just in the afternoon.

"I am a patient's husband and he is my son. My wife was, or maybe she still is, having an operation. Please let us in. We want to see her or to talk to the doctor."

She looked on the computer screen and found Maria's name, but she didn't have a room number. Then, she called surgery and she was informed that Maria was still in the recovery room, which was on the sixth floor. She gave us directions to the elevator. I was furious at the doctor for not having called me. My son calmed me down by suggesting that maybe he had called while I was on my way to the hospital but later we found out he hadn't called at all.

On the sixth floor, a nurse guided us to the recovery room and told us to wait until she found out if we could see her. She informed us that the doctor was still in surgery with someone else, but we could wait in his office. The doctor's office was on another floor, but with the nurse's help we found it. I asked the secretary why she or the doctor hadn't called me at home. She excused herself by telling me that the doctor had been busy with other patients. Waiting is a notion that I never liked, but now I didn't have a choice; so I had to get accustomed to it.

The spring term had ended at Marygrove College, and Dance Detroit was just beginning rehearsals for a trip to Japan from which, I had withdrawn. Our private dance school was preparing for the annual open classes for the parents. I had spent time in the afternoons choreographing and rehearsing a full-length production of the *Swan Lake* with my students, so in the mornings I had the time to wait.

For a while I chatted with my son, dissecting the new situation. Was the first surgery a failure? Or were the cancer cells spreading through Maria's body? My son's opinion was that the jaundice in her eyes was connected with a failure in the liver, possibly by a virus, and not necessarily from cancer cells. This was our uneducated speculation, and we were still hoping for the best.

The waiting process finally ended; the doctor made his appearance. He shook my hand and I introduced my son. He repeated the well-known excuse that he had other unexpected emergencies, and then he invited us into his office. As a man who doesn't have much time, he came right to the point without compassion.

"The situation is not so good; the cancer cells have attacked the liver. But, we have a chance to stop it eventually if we proceed with another surgery on the liver."

I said to myself, where did I hear these words before? Oh yes, the doctor who did the first surgery said the same. It looks like these doctors come from the same school; they like to cut as much as possible regardless of the real outcome. Neither of them told us to try alternative solutions.

"Doctor, aren't there other solutions besides surgery, such as drugs, or different methods?"

"In her case, I don't think so," was his answer.

I decided to tell the doctor about a medication that was recommended to my son:

"Doctor, my son found a source of a medication for curing this terrible illness with good results, and we would like to try it on Maria."

"Even though I don't have any knowledge about this particular medication, I will allow you to administer it to her, if you believe that it will help her." But he reaffirmed his opinion that Maria should have more surgery.

Maria was never out of my mind and I was envisioning her lying on her so-called recovery bed, struggling for survival.

I fell deep into mental talking; many thoughts passed my mind. My positive thinking was that the doctor's proposal for more surgery opened a new hope for us. But dark thoughts also came to my mind, that this was just a delusion. I couldn't make up my mind if this doctor's proposal was right or wrong. I wanted to identify the reality, but I wasn't able to. My thinking walked through the complex labyrinth of my brain trying to find an answer. I couldn't give an answer to the doctor; I had to see and talk to Maria first.

Gene thought that I was absent-minded and interrupted my thoughts.

"What are you thinking? The doctor is waiting for an answer."

"I am sorry, Gene. My mind wandered to Maria and I think that we should postpone the answer until we consult with her after the recovery."

Then I addressed the doctor and asked him if we could see Maria. He told us to follow him. He took us to the recovery room, but Maria was no longer there; she had been taken to her designated room. After we found out the room number the doctor guided us to her. I touched and kissed her hand but she seemed to be sleeping. She was still under the effects of anesthesia. The doctor advised us to go home and have a good sleep and come back the next day, and he would meet us in her room.

I was overwhelmed by the day's events and discouraged. The thoughts in my mind were coming at me pell-mell. Problems and conflicts had always been part of my life, but I had found skills to solve them. Now I was powerless, depressed and disappointed that I couldn't find the right answer. I needed something, to make my negative thoughts go away and to bring order into my pell-mell thoughts.

I loved classical music. One of my favorites was the Beethoven's *Fifth Symphony,* which I had on a tape in my car. Listening to this music with its message of hope over fate always gave me a powerful feeling, a boost in my work, an optimistic view of the future. I inserted the tape and the sumptuous vibrating waves of the music gradually wrapped around my thoughts bringing them into a floating serenity. I arrived home with my mind surrounded by good thoughts for the next day.

I left in the early morning for the hospital. Maria was awake and welcomed me smiling, but the room was crowded. The nurse, who at that moment was changing Maria's IV, barely let me kiss Maria. The nurse told me that I had come too early; this was the time when they are busy with the patients. Indeed, doctors with their assistants bustled around her. So did the nurses with different assignments: blood pressure, medications, taking blood, etc. I was merely a spectator to this performance that was unusual for me.

Soon the doctor arrived making his daily rounds. He examined Maria's chart and told me that everything was going well. He asked Maria how she was feeling. Maria's answer was different from his conclusion; she complained that she had pain, pointing to the surgery. The doctor assured her that this was the normal result of the last surgery and the pain would go away. Addressing his assistant he told him to give Maria some painkillers, and she should start short walks with the help of an assistant. He also explained to Maria his findings after the surgery and his opinion that after she gets her strength back, she should have further surgery on her liver. Maria was terrified, just as my son and I had been, the day before. I took her hand and told Maria that she shouldn't give an answer now; she should wait until she has a complete recovery. She squeezed my hand as a sign that she agreed with me.

"I still have pain through my whole body," she told the doctor. "I don't think that my mind is ready to understand what's going on. Let me feel better and then you will explain to me again your findings from this last surgery and we can discuss what the best approach should be."

"O.K., Maria, we will talk again, and in the meantime we will do our best to help you recover as soon as possible."

Maria's breakfast arrived. The doctor left, asking me to walk with Maria every day and as often as possible. I was in the hospital every day and massaged her arms and legs, and then together we did our walking. We took three walks a day, and every time we increased the distance. Then she started to walk by herself many times a day. Her strength improved considerably. The week passed swiftly; the nurses and doctors were gratified. Maria was feeling much better. She was eager to talk with the doctor, and the doctor was eager to do the surgery.

Maria asked me how the open classes were going and how her students were doing. I told her that her substitute teacher had prepared them according to her instructions. I also informed her about the *Swan Lake* rehearsals, which were dedicated to the tenth anniversary of the Lascu School of Ballet. I told her that everything was going well, and all the parents and children sent their love and their best wishes for her recovery. They were looking forward to seeing her at the performances. She gave me a hazy smile and told me that she felt that she would not be able to attend the performances, and to wish everybody from the school good luck and success.

The West Bloomfield Community Education sponsored the *Swan Lake* performances. The performances indeed went well and the audience was pleased; we videotaped all the shows, but I was sad and so was everybody else that Maria was not present. She had prepared and rehearsed the little ones for that ballet. They did a very good job, and they missed her. Everybody missed her. This was the first time that my wife was not present at a major performance of mine. She was superstitious and during each performance, she would hold her fists tightly together till it was over. I was always eager to find out her critique after each performance. Her opinion was the most important and most valuable for me. She was sincere, and straightforward, and that helped me to see any shortcomings in my work. I was always aware that her love for me was genuine, and her help was a sincere dedication to my life.

Several days later while my wife was still hospitalized, the doctor arrived for a conference with both Maria and myself. We listened again to the doctor's elaboration of the critical situation. This time he was more bold and straightforward with us. He explained that all the x-rays and the blood analyses showed that the cancer cells had definitely attacked Maria's liver. In fact, he told us that she actually didn't have a choice. The surgery was her only a hope but not a guarantee. It was just another attempt to stop the spreading of the cancer cells. Often problems with people can be negotiated and worked out, having a variety of options. In our situation, so far, there were just two options, surgery or waiting. How frustrating it was for us, to want to move forward to the end of the tunnel and then find out that we may never get there. There was silence in the room; Maria looked at me. I sensed that my wife wanted to talk to me without the doctor being present. I broke the silence and told the doctor to leave us alone and we would let him know our decision.

Maria started to talk first. She arrived at the conclusion that she would give the doctor one more chance to save her if possible. But her conclusion sounded pessimistic. I didn't feel any strength behind her decision, which was normally uncharacteristic of her. It sounded more as if she didn't care any more about the outcome. I tried to change her shaky thinking by telling her the good news that the alternative medication had arrived and she should start taking it.

"Do you think that I should not undergo the new surgery and take the alternative drug, instead?" she asked.

I didn't answer right away; her question surprised me and at the same time confirmed my feeling of her overwhelming pessimism.

What if? I imagine that my life is a huge river, and I am at the mercy of its strong whirling gyration. I try to swim to get out of it to go to the shore. The strong flow of the water overpowers me and takes me down the waterfall. I manage to grab a branch and for the moment I am holding it, but I don't know for how long. I returned to reality.

"Mammy scump (dear), the doctor said that the surgery is a new hope, and so the new drug can also be a new hope," I told her. "We hope that both can change the course of the illness."

"Let's try it, and let's hope for the best," she told me as she took my hand.

The surgery took eight hours and exhausted Maria's body, our patience and our minds. She was held longer than usual in the recovery room. They let me see her, but she couldn't answer my questions. Her eyes were closed, and she didn't react to my touch. I asked the nurse in charge of Maria what was happening, why didn't she give any sign of life? The nurse explained to me that during that kind of prolonged surgery the more anesthetic administered, the more time the recovery takes. But she assured me that Maria was fine and pointed to the monitors that showed her pulse and heart beat status, which were good. The nurse suggested that I go home to relax and not worry or be concerned. I should come back the next day; then I would be able to talk to Maria.

I went home but I couldn't relax. I was worried. I was again in a slump, unfocused and with feelings that I couldn't sort out. In spite of the nurse's assurance, I was down, obsessed by bad feelings. Maria always answered after the previous surgeries in one way or another by a blink of her eyes a nodding of her head or a squeeze of her fingers. This time there was nothing. I was unclear about what I was experiencing, and it was difficult to foresee the outcome. I was confused and I couldn't find my place.

I went to the window and looked out through the dark night. I saw my neighbor with his family in their kitchen having dinner. It was a pleasant image and I envied them for that. I wished to be in the kitchen myself having dinner with Maria. But I was alone and troubled by my turbulent thoughts. I started to walk through the house, and I found myself in front of the stereo system. Then I remembered that Beethoven's *Fifth Symphony* had helped me to envision beautiful images before. I inserted the tape and turned up the volume as loud as I dared to without disturbing the neighbors. I dropped on the bed, facing the ceiling, and listened to the music. This time even Beethoven's majestic music couldn't distract me from my worries; it had a relaxing effect, however, and I eventually fell asleep.

I woke up early the next morning and I saw that the stereo was still on. I realized that I had fallen asleep during the symphony. I took a shower, had my breakfast, and drove to the hospital. I was delighted to find Maria awake, but she looked tired. I took her hand and kissed her. She squeezed my hand, but she didn't smile. I asked her how she was feeling. She didn't answer, just nodded her head imperceptibly, as if she would say, so-so. I was glad to see by her eyes that she was conscious and could hear my voice and feel my touch.

The doctor was satisfied with his work, but her recovery was very slow. When she had the surgery before, she was able to walk after the first day. Not this time. She needed help to get up, to be transferred onto a chair as the nurse changed the bed sheets or washed her face and combed her hair. I resumed my massaging of her arms, legs and feet with the hope that she would soon be able to walk.

Maria had many visitors, but she liked the ones with great big jolly smiles and good humor. She didn't like people feeling sorry for her. Visitors came without interruption: Gene, his wife Mihaela and their twin children, Marie and James; Traian and his wife Olga; Annie, Maria's sister; our friends Mary and Walt Lazar; and many parents and their children from the school. The room was again transformed into a show place with a variety of flowers, boxes with chocolates, and lots of cards with recovery wishes. She hugged and thanked everybody, but she didn't have her usual charming smile and enthusiastic expression.

She had to take painkillers more often and needed help moving from one side of her body to the other. She had difficulty doing it by herself. Her calls for the nurse were hardly ever answered, and this made her suffer more and more. She complained to me that during the night she had been ringing the bell desperately, and nobody had come. I informed the doctor of this situation and he answered that during the night there were fewer nurses on duty. I told him that the situation was the same during the day. He was surprised and said that he would investigate the matter.

I didn't have the patience to wait for his investigation. I told him that I would like to have an additional bed put in Maria's room so that I could sleep there and help Maria anytime she needed it. He promised that he would talk to the administration. My request was granted. The next day I found a bed near Maria's and I moved into the hospital to become Maria's permanent nurse. This gave me an opportunity to observe and assess the real situation. She was very weak; her movements were slow, and she couldn't tolerate being in the same position very long. Therefore, her request was very often to be changed from one position to another. When she rang the bell for a nurse to help, it took an eternity until a nurse showed up. Maria didn't want me to help her, because she was afraid that I would hurt my spine by lifting her so often. She reminded me that I had had a spinal injury before. I told her that I would be very careful when I lifted her. I guessed that her awkward positions were unbearable, so she didn't protest any more when I helped her. I massaged her legs, arms and whole body, as many times as she wanted it.

The doctor recommended certain breathing exercises with a special apparatus provided by the hospital to prevent pneumonia. She didn't like to do the exercises, so I had to insist and convince her of their importance for her recovery. It took another week until I could take her for a short walk. Her walk this time was very slow and shaky; I had to support her all of the time. I asked the doctor why she hadn't regained her strength like before? Doctors always find answers, and, typically, the chief surgeon asked me to have patience. He told me that the growth of her liver to its former shape would be a long process. As soon as this happened she would regain her strength. This was another of the doctor's uncertain explanations. Could this be another new hope?

Living in the hospital, I had the opportunity to observe the daily routines of the doctors and nurses. Whatever their duties were, they were done mechanically. Missing was the necessary warmth and tender attitude toward patients. The chief surgeon who had done the operation on Maria never came to spend enough time with her in order to find out what was bothering her. His visits were short and technical, and I was the one who ran after him to tell him what was really going on. The food came on time, but sometimes Maria didn't touch it.

One day, Maria expressed a desire to watch the videotape of *Swan Lake* taken during our performances at the school. She was pleased with what she was able to see, but after 10-15 minutes she became tired, and we had to change her position in the bed so she could rest. I was worried about why she was so weak and asked the doctor. This time he couldn't find a new explanation; he just said that he didn't know, and he would order some new tests. If necessary, he would order a cat scan, and then he could tell me the reason. The blood tests showed that she had developed an infection, so they started to give her shots of a strong antibiotic. Also, a specialist in infections was consulted, and he recommended also a cat scan be done to find the source of the infection.

The next day, she was taken early in the morning to the lower level where a cat scan would be done. The nurse told me that I should wait for her return. I did, but after two hours of waiting, I lost my patience and asked for directions to the cat-scan room. I found Maria in the lobby of a cat-scan room in line with other patients.

"Are they taking you back to your room?" I asked.

"No, they didn't do the cat scan on me yet."

I went to the information desk and asked the nurse, "Why don't they take Maria back to her room and plan the cat-scan for another time?"

She disappeared behind the door of the cat-scan room; it took a while before she finally made her appearance. The doctor said that Maria should wait because her cat scan was planned for that day, and it had to be done. In spite of my anger and frustration, we waited two more hours. When I complained to the doctor about holding Maria for five hours in a waiting room in her weakened state, I was confronted with an evasive answer.

"It is not I who performs the cat-scan; I just recommend it. I can't control their schedule; it is not my responsibility."

"But she is your patient, and you have to supervise what's happening to her. I am worried about her shaky recovery and consider that holding her more than five hours in a lobby has made her worse." I answered angrily and spoke with a raised voice. He calmed me down, apologizing and promising that he would do his best to see that such a thing would not happen again.

Her cat scan didn't have the answer they were looking for. The doctor just told me that the liver was almost back to its former size, and the treatment against her infection would continue until the antibiotic had the desired curative effect. I felt that his answer was not honest, and that he was hiding the reality of Maria's condition. He was in a hurry, as always, but I followed him out of the room and asked him for an appointment for the next day. He agreed, but he didn't know his schedule for next day and advised me to contact his secretary.

Maria's health didn't improve. On the contrary, her movements were slower; she refused to walk, she became agitated, and showed no interest in what was going on around her. She accepted my presence, and she liked the massage on her legs, but I couldn't persuade her to take a walk with me. She asked me again to show her the *Swan Lake* videotape. I remembered that she couldn't watch more than 10-15 minutes, so I selected the portions where James and Marie, our grand children, were dancing. She enjoyed it and smiled.

She rested for a while, and then she told me that she liked my choreography in *Swan Lake*; she asked me to sit on the bed near her and then she hugged me and kissed me. I told her that everyday I would show her more of the videotape. She nodded with her head and said that it would be wonderful. I was so happy that she once again appreciated my work, but watching her dimmed my happiness as she tried to smile and at the same time struggled with terrible pains, which throbbed through her whole body.

The next day, Gene and I met with the chief surgeon, but he was late as usual. He didn't sit; rather he started to walk around in his office, looking at us now and then. He gave me the feeling of awkwardness that what he had to tell us wasn't good news. Finally he stopped walking and said.

"Mr. Lascu, I don't want to delude you," he said. "I will present to you the conclusions of our entire staff about Maria's present status. I have done many surgeries in my career and I don't usually fail. This time her illness, the cancer, has beaten me; I couldn't keep pace with it. I tried my best, but through all my experience as a surgeon, I have never encountered such an aggressive cancer. The cancer is spreading through her body at an unusual pace. Maria is still alive due to her fantastically strong body. Also, I want to inform you that during the last surgery, I noticed a healing effect of the medication that your son recommended. However, the medication also couldn't keep pace with the already spreading cancer. At this point our advice is to take Maria home and let things take their natural course. I want to let you know that everybody who took care of Maria loves her dearly and admires her for her beautiful character and the courage that she has displayed in our hospital."

The doctor's presentation shocked us and made clear that there was no more real "New Hope," that it was just a matter of time. Deep inside me, I still had hope that her strong physical body would override the aggressive cancer. The doctor informed Maria that she would be discharged to go home and wished her all the best. The nurses all came to say goodbye to her. Maria offered everybody the chocolate candies and some of the flowers she had received from her visitors. Gene, my son, rented a bed similar to the one in the hospital and placed it in our master bedroom. He also, employed a skilled nurse from the Renaissance Health Care to take care of Maria. As her condition worsened and her pain became unbearable, the nurse gave her morphine shots to temper the suffering.

It was on a Saturday that she expressed her desire to see the grandchildren. I called Gene and he complied; he said that they would come over as soon as they were dressed. I told Maria. She was glad and asked me to hand her a mirror, and a hairbrush. She wanted to look good for the grandchildren. She adored them and missed them. They had grown beautiful and had reached the age of four. Their mother dressed them exquisitely; they looked gorgeous. They now stood in front of the bed and didn't know what to say or what to do. Usually they ran through the house or in the garden. This time they felt the solemn aura in the house. There was a silence in the room. It was a threat that could not be ignored, the threat of what would come to take Maria into the infinite unknown.

Maria devoured the children with her eyes and began to show the outline of a smile. Her eyes were sparkling brightly and beamed toward them. Maria reached out her hands inviting them to get closer to her. Marie went to the right side of the bed and James to the other. They both took Grandma's out stretched hands. Maria pulled them closer to her and hugged and kissed each of them. It was a heart-breaking sight; I felt a tug on my heartstrings. Maria was taking her goodbye from the children. I left the room and started to cry. After a while Mihaela and Gene hugged and kissed Maria and than took the children and left. I saw them to the door and hugged and kissed everybody.

Maria called me; I returned to the bedroom with a forced smile on my face. She told me that she was thirsty and that she would like a glass of water. I gave her the water.

Then she said, "I had a very good time with the children. They are beautiful and adorable, and I am sorry that I can't take care of them any more. My strength is gone."

"You will recover, and your strength will come back again."

She smiled and said nothing, and then she hugged me and kissed me all over my face. I took her face in my hands and kissed her many, many times; then I said.

"I love you, and I will love you for ever."

She pulled me to her chest, hugged me, and we remained embracing for a while. Then she asked me to help her find a comfortable position on the bed and told me that she was tired and wanted to rest.

The next day in the morning I woke up to a sunny day; it was a Sunday. I went to Maria to give her the everyday massage. Usually I started with the right leg. I asked her to give me her right leg; she gave me, instead, the left leg. When I asked for the right arm she stretched out her left arm. I realized then that she was not able to control her body, that the cancer cells had reached her brain. I finished my massage and brought her breakfast, which she refused. I told her that she had to eat to get back her strength, but she didn't answer. The nurse arrived and gave her the shot of morphine and changed her bandage. She tried again to offer Maria breakfast without success.

"Don't you like the breakfast? I asked her. "Do you want something else?" No verbal answers, just a shake of her head as negative. We tried several times to talk to her; she looked at us, but no answer. Toward noon she closed her eyes and remained quiet. The nurse checked her pulse and Maria was still alive, but the nurse suggested that Maria should be taken to the hospital. I called emergency 911, and Maria was again in the hospital.

The doctor examined her and told me that my wife was in a coma; he didn't know how long it would last. He also told me that I could speak to her because she might hear me or I could play her favorite music. Gene and his family came to see her; so did Traian. We all talked to her and played Beethoven's *Fifth Symphony*, which was also one of her favorites. She didn't open her eyes and didn't talk to us any more. My hopes that her strong body would bring a miracle vanished. On August 20, 1988, she left us forever. She was just 59 years old.

Her desire was to be cremated and her box with ashes was deposited at the White Chapel cemetery in the city of Troy. Was it a coincidence or destiny? The chapel was built in the same year she was born, 1929. Only my family, Traian and his family, and very close friends were present. In her memory one of her friends, Beverly Cohn, read to us her thoughts and experiences with Maria:

"When I was requested to say a few words in memory of Maria, I was indeed very honored. I watched her at school. She was a caring teacher, always ready with a pat on the back at our accomplishments. A knowing look when criticism was necessary. We all loved her, from the youngest to the eldest. I was the eldest. I saw the love in the home between Iacob and Maria. Her pride in her grandchildren was monumental. Her land abounded with flowers; she loved nature. She was a quiet listener, ready to interject when the time was right. On reflection Maria was unique in that she was a caring person with great insight. She excelled in anything she undertook. She had the quality of fortitude and courage. My observation of her made me aware that she was a loving and compassionate wife, an understanding mother, and a loyal loving friend. She has gone before us. We could not all conveniently start together, and why should you and I be grieved at this, since we are soon to follow, and know where to find her."

Maria loved flowers, and I took care that in front of her box, fresh flowers were permanently present.

THUNDERBOLT

I knew since our last meeting with the doctor that her illness was terminal, but I didn't expect that it would take her away from us so quickly. It shocked my balanced life; she was my devoted love, my friend, and companion. I believe that the heartbeats continue to pulsate, as long we are alive with no reason to know. However the heartbeat stops when the reasons unknown to us have no more power. We were together thirty-eight years and we lived a wonderful life. I wondered what my future fate would be. Every minute in my life I wanted and needed to be with her. She took care of me. Now my balance was gone. I tried to withhold my tears, but I ended up sobbing loudly. I grieved for losing my most invaluable partner from my life. My thoughts were drained of hope and optimism. I felt that my grief was devouring me and that I wouldn't be able to hold on any more; I had to follow her.

Sometimes, I started to take a walk from my house without setting a goal or time. Cars passed by and the people from the subdivision who knew me greeted me. The sun was too hot that morning, and I found myself turning into the nearby woods to protect me from the burning heat. I saw the clouds moving through the tops of the trees, and I feared that the trees would fall and crush me. I stopped and waited; I had the feeling that I would like to be crushed. *Go on, get out of here,* I heard my mind crying, and exiting the woods I started to accelerate my walk until I felt exhausted. My muscles gave in and I fell down on my back on the grass of an open wide lawn; I lay still, breathing in release, and feeling empty and hopeless, I felt the pressure of the air on my chest.

Maria and I were two people who had the same purpose in our lives. Everything in the house reminded me of her tasteful touch. I could hear her laughter; I could see her unique beautiful body in the garden bending over the flowers and smelling their fragrance. I could remember that for her birthday I always gave her roses, the same number as her years. I could remember the music that she loved so much, the aria from the first act of the opera *La Bohème*, "Che gelida manina," which we had listened to so many times together.

The panic of the future surrounded me; I felt crowded and overwhelmed by the task of work that I had to face alone. These were moments of extreme stress and emotional struggle. To make it through it all, I had to relax and breathe deeply and relying on my survival skills. I had to see the beauty of my family and friends; in them, there was purpose and meaning for my future.

Yet in the middle of my grief, I couldn't gain perspective. The gift of clarity had not yet arrived. I had to let go of my belief that my life had ended with the loss of my dearest and replace it with a belief that I could walk through this difficult journey. I had to trust in myself, that "being" was sufficient and let go of my need to figure things out. I had to learn to let things happen naturally and let events, and my participation in them, fall into place. I could go with the flow, unburden the turbulent feelings from my shoulders, and let the power of nature ease me into wherever I needed to be. I had to reestablish my relationship with my grandchildren, which I had lost during my intense non-stop working. This was an essential task, which grew with every passing day.

I couldn't know how long it would take to accommodate myself to this new way of life, but I knew it was unreasonable to expect that it would be overnight. During that turbulent time I was unable to fulfill my contract with Oakland University's Department of Music, Theatre and Dance. I was supposed to teach in their Summer Dance Workshop, but I couldn't concentrate on the necessary preparation for my classes. I didn't have my usual strength and courage to carry on. It had never happened before. I was depressed, and I felt guilty about my inability to fulfill the contract.

"It is unfortunate," said Traian, my brother-in-law "that a lot of people choose compulsive and addictive behaviors, like alcohol, drugs, sex and other relationships for relieving the pain. Sooner or later people discover that these are only temporary pain relievers, which don't solve the problem. There is a better way to stop your pain, namely, to face it and feel it. When you are ready to accept nature's help, you will have the courage to feel the pain and let it go; then the pain will move you forward. One thing leads to another and you will get better. Jacky, life goes on and gets better with each new decision; you have your family, the grandchildren whom Maria loved dearly."

I understood that hard times and stressful times were part of my life and I had to grow and move forward. It was my choice to use my energy to work through my issues or to refuse to grow. I also understood that even though I am a sturdy human being, in many ways I could be fragile and must accept changes and loss; sometimes in this process, I could encounter temporary setbacks. Hard times could motivate and mold growth; they could bring out my best and propel me forward and upward to a higher level of living and loving. The stress on me was physical, too. The pain in my back returned more often.

As usual after Labor Day, we had started rehearsals for the 1988 *Nutcracker*. The entire cast and myself had decided to dedicate this 1988 *Nutcracker* season performances to the memory of Maria. In the lobby of the theater we set up a special display with Maria's picture. Each performance had radiated with the homage paid to Maria. The guest artists had known Maria personally, from their previous guest appearances with us. They offered their condolences to my family and me and dedicated their outstanding performances to Maria. In the past I had always watched the performances together with Maria. She would sit near me, holding her fists clenched during the entire performance. At this performance, her seat next to me was empty, as it remained for all the following years.

The success of the 1988 *Nutcracker* had thrilled me and, at the same time, it was over-shadowed by my tremendous grief. I was pleased with the performances and thanked everybody. That made me happy and gave me hope of eventual recovery from the tremendous grief I suffered. The desire to uphold the high quality of *The Nutcracker* performances reminded me of Maria's constant encouragement throughout all the years that she was near me. The next *Nutcracker*, I thought, should be the best. It will be the 15th anniversary, and I had to survive my grief. I had to organize and mobilize the best crew for that event.

It was the time to open the doors of my school for the fall-winter session. Mihaela took Maria's place as secretary of the ballet school. I promoted the best students from the advanced class who expressed a desire to teach ballet. They took over Maria's classes. Contributions toward a memorial scholarship in Maria's name were made to The Michigan Ballet Foundation, (MBF) Inc. This non-profit, tax exempt organization, was first conceived in, 1987 by an enthusiastic group of dance lovers interested in promoting local and regional classical ballet throughout Michigan. Maria's signature on the papers filed for incorporation, dated November 22, 1987, attests to the fact that Maria was a member of the first Board of Directors.

Some of the primary goals of the Michigan Ballet Foundation were to encourage qualified students to pursue dance careers; provide scholarships for promising students; promote talented ballet dancers in local, national and international competitions. The Board of Directors of the Michigan Ballet Foundation then decided to organize a classical ballet competition dedicated to Maria Lascu. The foundation established three awards: first place award of $1,000; second place award of $500; and third place award of $250.

For the first Maria Lascu Memorial Scholarship Awards Competition, the Board also organized classical ballet master classes. For that purpose they invited the world-renowned ballerina from ABT, Miss Cynthia Harvey, and Sean Lavery from the New York City Ballet. The competition and the master classes were held on May 20 and May 21, 1989. Both events were held in the studios of the Lascu School of Ballet. The visiting ballet masters taught wonderful classes and they were also the judges who selected the talented students to be awarded scholarships. I watched with pride when my most talented students competed for the first Maria Lascu Memorial

Scholarship. The event was very successful, attracting students from all over Michigan! Unfortunately the MBF later dissolved so the annual Maria Lascu Scholarship Award Competition was canceled.

The stress on me continued to be not just emotional but physical, too. Since the annual check up when Maria, was diagnosed with cancer, I continued to go every year to the doctor to screen my health. One morning after I shaved, I accidentally touched my right breast and I felt a lump about the size of a pea. It was painless, but I didn't like the feeling of it. I had another lump on the back of my head and two under my right upper arm but the consistency of those lumps was different from the one on my breast.

At a check-up in May, I showed the lump on my right breast to my holistic doctor, Gurudarshan S. Khalsa. He examined it carefully. He was as concerned as I was and recommended going for a surgical consultation. He didn't recommend a specific doctor so I had to find one. I called St. Joseph Mercy Hospital in Pontiac and I was referred to Dr. Gary L. Perrault and made an appointment.

I don't remember the exact day or hour of my appointment, but I remember that it was in June. It was always an ordeal for me to go to a hospital. This time the ordeal was increased by the fear of the outcome. I climbed the steps of the hospital, entered, and looked around until I found his office. Dr. Khalsa, my family physician, had found my general health to be very good, so I went with some confidence to the appointment. Dr. Perrault examined the right breast and extracted some fluid from the lump. He told me that it was definitely a tumor, but he couldn't say yet if it was benign or malignant. We wouldn't find that out for sure until the extracted fluid from my lump could be processed at the laboratory. A chilling feeling went through my body as the storm slowly approached me. He instructed his secretary to make another appointment for two days later.

I remember the days of agony waiting for the results of Maria's biopsy. Now I went through similar feelings again. What if the laboratory test shows that the lump is malignant? My next appointment was disappointing. The technicians at the laboratory couldn't make a clear determination, so they suggested that the doctor perform a biopsy. They also recommended x-rays and an ultra sound.

The biopsy was scheduled for August 25, 1992 at St. Joseph Mercy Hospital in Pontiac. I was taken to a dressing room and instructed to undress and put on a special hospital nightshirt. I was taken to a big room. It was crowded with other patients on similar stretchers.

"How long is the waiting time?" I asked the nurse.

"About ten or fifteen minutes."

I looked around, trying to analyze the faces of the other patients. Their faces didn't reflect their illnesses, but they looked as worried as I was.

According to the clock on the wall, fifteen minutes had passed a long time ago. In a one-hour period, two patients were taken for their surgery or biopsy. Nobody was around to ask why it was taking so long. Finally a nurse showed up, and I addressed her.

"Should I go home and come another day?"

"No! No! There was an emergency and you will be taken soon," she replied.

Her interpretation of "soon" was equal to one more hour of waiting. I was finally taken into the surgery room and I was anaesthetized. When I woke up, the nurse told me that Dr. Gary Perrault had performed the biopsy. Gene, my son, drove me home. The secretary told me that I would be called as soon as the results came from the laboratory.

Agonizing days followed with the same old question of "what if?" After three days the secretary called and told me that the doctor had the results and wanted to see me. Doctors are always pleased with their surgeries and Dr. Perrault was also pleased with his surgery as well with the healing process. I can still see the doctor walking toward the door and inviting me from the examining room into his office. He told me to have a seat in front of his desk. He placed himself in the comfortable chair and started to talk as if he was pronouncing a death sentence. He explained to me that all the results of the biopsy, x-rays, and ultrasound had come in and they showed the following results:

"The biopsy specimen measured 3 by 2-cm and the cut section showed a gray-white tumor mass measuring 1.4 cm. There was a gross extension of the tumor to the margins, as well as microscopic extensions to the margins. The margin of the neoplasm was infiltrated. In conclusion, the final diagnosis of the right breast biopsy was Infiltrating Ductal Carcinoma, in other words, cancer."

I was stunned; I couldn't believe it. A thunderbolt struck me! It hit me like any natural disaster strikes when it arrives unannounced, unexpected; it could destroy me. At first, I didn't realize the full impact of the illness because I couldn't believe that it was happening to me. But there was no doubt about the trauma.

Years had passed since Maria was taken by cancer. I knew that this disease was running a wide circle around the whole world but I took the attitude of denial.

"This diagnosis is a mistake," I told the doctor. I don't believe it. I feel good and never have I complained of any pain in my breast."

He stood up, and on his desk he spread all the results from the ultra sound and papers signed by different doctors from the laboratory, attesting to his diagnosis. I stood up also and examined the results of the biopsy. Fear gripped me. I knew that this fear was far more than the fear of an animal biting. After Maria's death, I had always secretly known in my heart that this moment would come; I just didn't know when. I always trembled with fear each time I read in the newspaper of people dying from different forms of cancer. I lowered my head as a sign of acceptance of my "guilt." I stood there silently. All at once I felt that my numberless days were numbered. He asked me to have a seat again as he did the same. With a calm voice, he started to deliberate the "sentence." He said that I was not the first one and I would not be the last one to be diagnosed with cancer. He encouraged me by telling me that the current modern literature about medical and surgical procedures regarding cure for breast cancer cure showed positive results. I was impatient to hear his recommendations so I interrupted him.

"What treatment are you recommending for me?"

"Because of the proximity of the lesion to the areola complex, and the presence of tumor at the excisional margin, I recommend modified radical mastectomy as the best procedure. After the surgery, I also recommend radiation treatment. Also, I am urging you to not neglect the treatment of this very serious disease, which may still be in an early and treatable stage."

My reaction to his recommendation was a question to myself, was that the only method to cure my illness? Should I decide now what to do or should I seek other opinions? I was confident that there were other possibilities, so I should not make a hasty decision. I decided that I would look first for other opinions. I told him that I would think about his recommendation, and I would call him and let him know of my decision. I requested the documentation of the biopsy results and left the room.

I left the hospital in a rush, not knowing what to do. I tried to be calm and concentrated on my driving home. In front of the doctor, I had kept a strong presence of mind. At home, I couldn't find my place. I was bewildered; I felt the blood rushing to my head. I went to my study and dropped into the recliner. The pounding in my head grew louder; my temples throbbed. The hammering in my ears wouldn't stop. The images of the hospital, the doctor with his smiling death face, and the results of the test would not go away. I felt the need to vomit, to expunge the fear that had settled into my stomach. The unknown aspect of the future scared me. It was the truth that I didn't want to recognize. The pain in my stomach was knifelike; the sounds in my head were cracks of thunder. For a moment, I forgot where I was.

I knew that trauma was everywhere; I was not singled out by nature. Trauma had a way of finding me, and I was not prepared for it; it had power like nothing else. It forced me to be with it and work with it, maybe for the rest of my life. I didn't know where to look for an alternative treatment. I didn't even know whether or not the cancer could be treated. I knew that each individual's cancer was personal, and the treatment should probably be different. I felt that I had just undergone some mental and physical changes. I could not prove it; I am not a scientist but I thought that the illness, which hit my body, was probably a result of my shattered immune system. Because we are surrounded by nature and we are part of it I believed that I possessed a survival method we all human beings have I didn't know how long I would survive. I was conscious that I was a mortal human as were my fellow men. I could die at any moment; I was at the mercy of the power of nature that surrounded me. I looked desperately for people who could help me to survive and who could push my mortality as far from the present as possible. I found these people, in my son and his family.

I looked into exploring the power of nature, which I believe provides a natural healing power to our bodies. I looked into other people's traumatic experiences by reading the books they wrote about their recoveries. I learned from them that if I could survive this tremendous fall, I would not be frightened anymore. My old ways of living died, and I was in the world in a new and different way.

When I found out the terrible diagnosis of malignant cancer, I had to call my son and warn him not to spread that horrible news. I didn't want people to have pity and give me all kinds of advice about the surgery. I wanted be responsible for my own firm decision regarding treatment. I didn't know yet how I would fight the cancer in my body, but I was determined to find out the best way. Thinking of my son and his family, tears came to my eyes but I quickly brushed them away. My heartbeat was normal; it seemed to be feeling nothing. Was this self-observation a reflex of terror or some deep denial of the inevitable?

The first doctor that I consulted was the parent of one of my students, Dr. Anibal Drelichman, M.D. F.A.C.P. He was an oncologist. I told him the whole story and presented the documentation. His opinion was the same as Dr. Perrault. The second doctor I consulted was from Beaumont Hospital, Dr. James Catto. His evaluation was slightly different. He wanted to be sure that the lesion was benign. Therefore his recommendation was that first he should perform a subcutaneous mastectomy for gynecomastia through a circumareolar incision with a permanent histology evaluation of the submitted specimen. If the lesion was benign, that should be sufficient operative treatment of the problem. If the lesion were malignant, a formal mastectomy would be appropriate. His assistant handed me a form of Patient Acknowledgement of Informed Consent to sign it if I decided to undergo the surgery. I told Dr. Catto that I would consider his recommendations, and I would notify him regarding my final decision. I was disturbed by the doctors' unilateral approach toward this disease. They were not even willing to talk about an alternative approach. I was made despondent by their narrow view of this disease, which has killed millions of people in the world.

My only alternative-- and my last hope-- after the devastating prognosis by the three doctors, was to go back to my holistic doctor and ask for his advice. I had confidence that he would encourage me to try other venues. But once I was out of the hospital, my confidence teetered; I wasn't sure what Dr. Khalsa's position would be. He met me, in his office. I liked his office; it was a large room with a big desk crowded with a lot of papers. He invited me to have a seat as he looked for my medical records and pulled out a sheet of paper. He handed me the paper; it was a letter from Dr. Catto. I recognized the letter because Dr. Catto had also sent me a copy. In the letter, Dr. Catto informed Dr. Khalsa that he had examined me; he described his conclusions and his recommendations regarding my illness; he also described me as a candidate reluctant to follow his advice. Dr. Khalsa looked at me. I felt that he was uncomfortable about giving his opinion, so I asked him.

"What would you do in my situation? What is your advice for me as an holistic doctor?"

"It's hard for me to give you advice; I am not an oncologist or a specialist in cancer treatment. This is the reason that I sent you for a surgical consultation. If the doctor's conclusion is surgery, I think that you should follow it. One of the causes of cancer is stress. We live in an era of both stress and many dreadful diseases. Mr. Lascu, you went through a very difficult time, losing your spouse, and you are working too much. New machines, computers, tests, new vaccines and inoculations are invented every day. The diagnostic capabilities are available to doctors at a greater speed than we can find the cure. But I can give you some guidelines regarding your situation. In case you decide not to have the surgery, I still advise you to undergo radiation therapy. I recommend reading some books concerning stress and diet, which could help you achieve a faster recovery. I also recommend that you consult Dr. James A. Thomas, from Ann Arbor who specializes in counseling terminally ill patients. Finally, I will give you a list of vitamins you should take."

Dr. Khalsa was cautious, but at the same time he tried to help me. I wasn't discouraged by his conclusions because I understood that he had to avoid a confrontation with his peers. In spite of the fact that I found myself cornered by three highly recommended doctors and confused by an evasive answer by my regular doctor, I was still not convinced that I had to follow any of their advice. I questioned myself again, wasn't it worthwhile to follow the impulses that lived inside me? Yes, I believed in myself. I asked myself over and over again what invisible and unpredictable route should I take? I knew that my life and my soul were spacious enough for everything in it. As soon as I was out of Dr. Khalsa's office and back on the bright sunny street, I had two thoughts that were competing each other.

The first thought was glum and projected the fear that I was sentenced to spend my few remaining days driving back and forth to the hospital for radiation and chemotherapy treatments if I would even be able to drive. I knew that fear was a person's first enemy. I knew that my father, fifty-nine years old, had died of stomach cancer, and my mother at eighty-two of uterine cancer. I knew that my wife had had cancer and the surgery hadn't helped. What could I do to overcome the fear?

The second thought was like a throbbing shining star, which predicted a brighter future. My mind told me that I should not run away; I should defy my fear and then I would be free to do anything I chose. My mind told me to let my body take its course naturally and use alternative holistic treatments to cure my illness. So I had to choose between these two ideas. One, I could accept the doctors' recommendations without rancor, and undergo the surgery of the modified radical mastectomy. Second, I could use my willpower to reject whatever in my life I did not wish to accept or whatever I was convinced wasn't right for me.

The second thought won. I firmly decided, No! I would avoid the surgery, the chemotherapy and the radiation, and I would mobilize my body's energy to fight by natural means. The dreadful images of Maria's ordeal and suffering wouldn't disappear from my mind. The multiple surgeries she went through didn't help her survive. I admitted to myself that each case could be different. In my case, I thought if the cancer cells were aggressively spreading in my body, no surgery would help. I didn't want to mutilate my body; I chose the breast conserving treatment.

My determination was to avoid surgery. I called my son and told him my decision, and I asked him to contact the doctor from Romania to send me the drugs that he had previously obtained for Maria. I was determined to use these drugs in spite of the fact that they hadn't helped Maria. My judgment was that for Maria they had arrived too late. Maybe they would be late for me too, but I had to try them. My son agreed with my decision and flew to Romania to bring the medication to me as fast as possible. I bought the books that Dr. Khalsa recommended and in the meantime I contacted Dr. James A. Thomas from Ann Arbor and made an appointment with him. I had two counseling sessions every week. The run to Ann Arbor was difficult for me because I didn't want to miss my classes at Marygrove and my own school. Therefore, my counseling sessions with the doctor were after lunch; I ate during the drive to Ann Arbor. I found the sessions with Dr. Thomas boring and not helpful to me, so after two months I gave them up.

In the meantime, I looked forward to getting the medication from Romania. Not too long after, Eugen arrived with a provision of medication for two months. The recommendation from the Romanian doctor was to take them for two years. In the short time of Gene's visit to Romania, the doctor could prepare just two months supply and he didn't have sufficient ingredients to prepare more. Most of the substances necessary to prepare that medication were imported from Switzerland. He promised Gene that he would do his best to make sure that the rest of the medication would arrive in time.

Parallel with taking that medication, I changed my lifestyle. I exercised in my home every day; I walked every day, and I listened to audiotapes learning to relax and meditate. Also, I studied several books which Dr. Khalsa recommended regarding what kind of food I should eat to improve my immune system, to help my body fight against the cancer cells. Food became an important part of my life. Gradually I eliminated all kinds of meat, dairy products, and eggs from my diet. I also reduced dramatically my intake of sweets. I never liked to shop for food, but I changed my perspective. I discovered that choosing a variety of the best food that was at the same time good for me was a pleasant challenge. I started to eat to be alive, rejecting the opposite idea that I was alive to eat. I read books about people who were successful in their fight against cancer.

I remembered Dr. Khalsa's advising me to have radiation therapy even if I refused to have surgery. I asked my son to find a good radiation specialist. Gene had done his one-year fellowship at Beaumont Hospital and was familiar with all of the departments. He recommended Dr. Vicini. I made an appointment and he did a comprehensive examination of my breast, took a pertinent history, and did a complete physical of me. He asked me how I felt and if I noticed any changes on my breast. I told him that I felt well and I hadn't noticed any skin changes in the breast, nipple discharge, pain, decrease in appetite, weight loss, or other constitutional symptoms. Also I didn't have any complaints regarding my cardiovascular, musculoskeletal or neurologic system. His conclusion after my physical examination was favorable. I quote his physical findings:

"Mr. Lascu is alert and oriented x 3 and in no apparent distress. Vital signs are stable. He is afebrile. There is no jaundice noted. There is no supraclavicular, infraclavicular or cervical adenopathy. The lungs are clear to ascultation. The heart is RRR. The abdomen is soft, nontender and without evidence of mass or organomegaly. There is no swelling in the extremities. The right breast shows a scar in the 6 o'clock position that is well healing without evidence of infection. There is no skin changes noted in either breast with arm extended above the head or pressed to the hips. There are no masses palpated bilaterally in either breast or in the axilla."

I was glad that he found me in good shape, but he subscribed to the diagnosis of the others three doctors. He advised me to undergo the radiation therapy regardless of whether or not I had surgery. I accepted his opinion and I agreed reluctantly to undergo the radiation therapy. I was scheduled to see Dr. Keidan, the radiation therapy specialist. He explained to me the risks, benefits and complications of radiation therapy. I understood that there would be erythema, hyper pigmentation, loss of hair in the treated area, and some fatigue as well. He also made me aware of the risk of rib fragility and possible pathologic fracture.

What a frightening picture was being unfolded! I wanted to tell him on the spot that I had changed my mind, but instead I asked when the first session would be? How fatigued would I be after each session? Would I be able to teach? He couldn't give me precise answers to my questions because, he said, he had to see what effect the first session would have on me. Then I could decide if I was able to work or not. His answer shook my resolve and put again in doubt my previous decision to undergo the radiation therapy.

I went home with a tormented mind. How could I resist so much professional pressure? How futile was it to rely on the natural power of my body to heal myself? The strength of my belief started to weaken, but the next day I was strong again in my natural belief. I called Dr. Vicini and told him that I had decided to postpone the radiation therapy. I told him that the school year had started and I would be very busy. He was very understanding but used the opportunity to remind me that this was a very serious illness and I should reflect more on it. I promised him that I would call him as soon I had more free time.

During these endless visits to so many doctors, I had completely forgotten to call Dr. Perrault back. He had probably lost his patience because on September 9, 1992, I received a letter from him in which he reminded me that the modified radical mastectomy would be the best procedure, but it should be performed within two weeks of the biopsy diagnosis. At the end of his letter he wrote.

"Since I have not heard from you since our last conversation, I am concerned that you do not neglect treatment of this very serious disease, which may still be in an early and treatable stage. I would urge you therefore, to please not delay any further treatment of this disease. I would also be happy to provide you with several names of qualified surgeons and cancer specialists. Please do not hesitate to call for any further assistance that we might provide for the treatment of this very serious disease."

The letter surprised me and I examined it carefully. I rejected his idea that mastectomy was the best procedure. I considered it a narrow view in the ongoing debate between one and another new treatment in the modern era. I stood firm in my decision. I didn't answer his letter, but he called me. During our conversation, he told me again his former recommendations. I told him my decision, that I would pursue other treatment modalities that do not require surgery. He didn't like it.

After Labor Day, I resumed my daily routine, teaching at Marygrove College in the morning and teaching in the afternoon at my private school. I felt well and continued to practice my new life-style. Dr. Perrault was persistent and wrote me a second letter on October 27, 1992. In general, he repeated the same advice given me previously, but some of his statements in that letter bothered me. I quote, "I would like to again emphasize as I have in the past repeatedly and per our last phone conversation that the only chance to cure breast cancer is to excise the cancer before it spreads outside of the breast. I feel very strongly that the only chance for cure in your situation would be to excise that residual tumor either via lumpectomy with auxiliary dissection followed by radiation treatment or via a modified radical_mastectomy. I feel very strongly based on the current medical and surgical literature that this is your only chance for cure and that by pursuing other modalities you may forfeit your chance for cure, since this disease may still be in an early and treatable stage. In closing I would urge you Mr. Lascu to please not delay any further the treatment of this very serious disease."

Two things disturbed me: first, the words **only chance**. I considered that this repeated phrase reflected his stubborn attitude. I believed that he should have consulted other valuable, universally recognized literature that opposed his view. Many books, articles in magazines, and newspapers had described a variety of methods that have cured cancer without surgery. Maybe he had already read them, but he did not believe in their pronouncement, recommending that cancer could be cured without surgery. The second was the new option that he offered me **via lumpectomy with auxiliary dissection surgery**. So even in his beloved literature were different choices. I felt that the second letter was just another doctor's attempt to perform a new surgery. He probably liked to perform a lot of surgeries as often as possible. It was his choice, not mine. Definitely, his beliefs and mine about cancer treatment were completely opposite.

As I write these words about my illness, eight years have passed since I was diagnosed with a malignant cancer. I still have the fear of the unknown. I don't know that I am cured. I don't know if I am rid of the cancer in my body. I know that I am feeling well and that no new or recurrent lumps have appeared on my breast.

Periodically, I went to Dr. Vicini for his evaluation. He always welcomed me in a friendly manner. He wasn't mad at me because I hadn't followed his advice to undergo the radiation therapy. When he checked for lumps on my body and ordered special blood tests and x-rays concerning the cancer, he was satisfied with the results and told me that I was free of cancer.

The moment I learned that I had cancer I wanted to quit working or, at least, to reduce my workload. I am grateful to the people who shared their life experiences in their books or articles regarding their victories over cancer, using alternative methods. I am grateful to all the people who influenced my decision to avoid the surgery. My health improved, which gave me trust in myself to continue on in my beliefs, and I decided not to give up my work. Several years following Maria's death, a profound influence on my decision to try an alternative cancer cure was the tragic experience that Maria went through. Her legacy for me actually saved my life during my own bout with cancer.

I couldn't ignore that horrible ordeal that she went through. I didn't want to go through the same hell; I'd rather choose to live with my body intact, as long it would be my destiny.

I remembered about some yoga exercises from my trip to China in 1956, all that was required to practice them was my willingness. I thought that I had to try them. Maybe these exercises would help to ease my recovery. I can make no claims that I was objective or that my impulse to start doing the exercises was based on scientific research. Despite all the scientific research and medical advances of the twentieth century, I thought that I had to explore new paths to good health.

The exercises had done wonders for my breathing, and I felt robust in my lungs. Besides the physical changes, the exercises improved my mental attitude, and I became calmer, clearer, and had a more relaxed state of mind. I felt an improvement in the balance between my body and mind, which gave me a new hope, and a good, deep, overall feeling. I became a believer that there was a connection between emotional pain and physical pain and that several health problems could be related to negativity, to feelings of anger and bitterness. I was convinced that my mind had to play a part in any long lasting changes in my physical condition.

I also believe that this change depends on each individual person who should actively participate in his or her health care. I believe that people have to assume the responsibility to maintain and improve their well being, creating new solutions for changing their lives.

I have asked myself if something positive came from my illness and general life experience? Yes, I felt that I learned more about myself and about life in general. We are surrounded by nature and we are part of it. I believe that for every problem the nature has an answer.

211

INTENSE COLLABORATION

Some days we had both matinee and evening performances of *The Nutcracker*. On those days, I went to a nearby restaurant for lunch. After one matinee, I went to lunch with Margo Cohen who danced the role of Clara's mother in *The Nutcracker*. We discussed various topics regarding the performance and other ideas; she asked me why I hadn't choreographed other productions with other major artistic institutions. I told her that for that I needed a professional company. She listened intently and asked why I hadn't already incorporated a professional ballet company?

"I don't have a financial sponsor. I knew from my life experience in both Romania and the United States that men who own banks or have other sources of wealth, or men with high political status are the most powerful people in the world." She didn't accept or reject my statement.

She just said, "It's difficult, but not impossible." How much money would it take to incorporate a professional ballet company?"

I wasn't prepared for such a question, so I told her that I had to think about it. Margo told me that her husband saw some of the performances; he was very pleased with the whole production. He could help me, to achieve my dream if I was still interested.

"Do think it over, and tell me if you would like me to mention it," said Margo. I told her that I would be pleased to present my ideas to her husband.

I met with both of them after another matinee performance, and I repeated my case to him. He already knew the basic outline of my ideas from Margo, but he listened to the details with patience. After I finished, he asked me to present him with a detailed budget for whatever was necessary for starting a professional company.

I did, but then I got an evasive answer regarding the professional ballet company. Instead, he offered an alternative: I could start working with the Michigan Opera Theatre (MOT). The idea to incorporate a ballet company would be tabled until later. I was happy with his suggestion of collaboration with MOT because I had choreographed the ballet sections from *Rigoletto*, *Die Fledermaus* and *La Traviata*, for them in the past.

Mr. Cohen informed me that he had already talked with Dr. David DiChiera, the general director of the Michigan Opera Theatre and I should expect to be contacted soon.

After I was called, I met with Dr. David DiChiera. He asked me if I was interested in choreographing the ballet sections from the operas *King Roger*, a Polish opera by the composer Karol Szymanowski, and Saint-Saens' *Samson and Delilah*.

I was interested in his offer and accepted it. I thought that this would present me with a challenge and it would help me in my recovery from grief. The more reality I had to cope with, the easier it would be for me to live without denial. Instead of dwelling on a future without my dear Maria, I would begin thinking of my future work. I told David that I would like to have professional dancers for these ballets, and I described my idea for a professional company. This time, I suggested to him that it would be good if MOT had such a company.

He agreed with me that I should audition professional dancers from all over the nation. I was pleased with his decision and as soon as we signed the agreement, I proceeded to call for auditions. Some of the dancers came for their auditions to the Lascu School of Ballet; others sent me videocassettes. I had good dancers and they responded very quickly to my choreographic requests. The outcome of my work was very satisfactory. The public rewarded my work with an enthusiastic outburst of applause.

Nancy Malitz, *Detroit News* Music critic, described my work as follows:

"With the pragmatic and effective choreography by Iacob Lascu, who knows how to design movement that fits the talents of his dancers such as the super-flexible Amy Toth, the third act had a wow factor."

Resuming the collaboration with the MOT proved to be successful and opened a new era of creativity for me. I tried to be occupied outside my home, as much as possible. I taught classes at Marygrove College from 8:00 A.M until noon and at my private school in the afternoon from 4:00 P.M. until 9:00 P.M. Final exams for the Marygrove College students kept me busy at home, too, preparing the questionnaires based on the syllabus. At my private school, the open classes were an important event for the students and particularly for the parents. Of course I continued miss Maria who was always present at all of my open classes. At home, after the open classes, we would discuss the results of our work for the past year.

I had even branched out into the medium of popular music. Aretha Franklin called me to give her private ballet classes and to choreograph for her and six dancers. I choreographed dances to a variety of songs; one dance was a medley for her up coming tour and other performances. In addition to working with Aretha Franklin, I also gave private classical ballet lessons to two ice-dancing couples on the United States World Figure-Skating Team: Eve Chalom and Mathew Gates (two-time United States Silver Medallists) and Elizabeth Punsalan and Jered Swallow (five times U. S. National champions and seventh in the world).

This was my eighteenth year of collaboration with the DSO. Dance Detroit and the DSO ended a successful season in 1992 with *The Nutcracker Ballet*. The crowd filled the 5,000 Fox theatre seats for all the performances, and the DSO was very pleased. Their revenue grew substantially.

As I predicted, the hunting for more revenue to squeeze from *The Nutcracker Ballet* productions, continued. Mark Volpe, the DSO's executive director, reported to the press in November 1992 that the 1991 season of *The Nutcracker Ballet* at the Fox Theatre had grossed $1.5 million. Some 75,000 people saw the twenty-one performances. But for the DSO, that revenue was not enough; they wanted more and more. It became a central point of focus of the DSO's administration and the booking agent from Brass Ring Productions. Overwhelmed by the immense success of the 1991 season they decided to add four more performances to make a total of twenty-five. As in the past, I pointed out that twenty-one performances was a great achievement, and that they should not increase the number of performances. If they felt they wanted more money, they should later add one each year and advertise more aggressively. They didn't listen to my recommendations. I warned them that the usual DSO promotion and advertisement campaign was not substantial to attract that many more people to the performances. Time would prove who was right.

I informed Mr. Cohen of the results of my meeting with David; but, at the same time, I reminded him that I had presented him with a budget for a professional ballet company. I initiated a meeting on January 10, 1992, where I invited people who were interested in creating and sponsoring a professional dance company. The people present at that meeting decided enthusiastically to create a professional ballet company. At the same meeting, we nominated and elected members to form an executive board of directors. The board elaborated the following resolution:

"Be it resolved that a ballet company is created under the name of the Metropolitan Ballet Theatre hereafter referred to as "the company". The founding members of the board of directors of the Metropolitan Ballet Theatre, Inc shall be recognized as follows: Brad and Claudia Stroud, Eugen and Michelle Lascu, Ray and Jill Rinke, Joe and Julie Valentic, Iacob Lascu, and Robert Diez d'Aux."

It was a nice beginning, but the events that followed widened the different opinions about the future plans and leadership of that MBT Company and I resigned from the board. They went their separate ways and I went mine.

After my success with the ballet for the opera *Samson and Delilah*, the director of the MOT, Dr. David DiChiera, asked me to stage the ballet *The Sleeping Beauty* and, at the same time, the ballet sequence for the opera *Aida*. In The *Detroit News*, reporters Nancy Malitz and Barbara Hoover announced some of the future plans of the MOT's Director Dr. David DiChiera:

"MOT will add a new layer of complexity to its operations by creating a Detroit-based ballet company to perform *The Sleeping Beauty* in 1993 and continue working under MOT auspices. The main reason for creating the subsidiary is to maintain the momentum of ballet in the spring. A MOT ballet company will lend credibility to the multi-arts fund-raising effort and could attract new financial support."

It was a practical approach, according to DiChiera. It was a way of building a local institution with local dancers. It would give opportunities to local dancers to be part of such a company. The idea expressed by DiChiera was right; it reflected my old dream of opening the door for local, talented dancers.

I auditioned dancers from all over the country for *The Sleeping Beauty* and *Aida*, and I selected a group of fourteen couples, talented professional dancers and some of the best dancers from my private school and from Marygrove College. When I selected them I looked for dancers who had a similar style. Later, when I saw them together at rehearsals, I was pleased with the selections. They learned on fast.

The Cohen team and the Dayton Hudson Corp. had become the sponsor of *The Sleeping Beauty* and later of other full-length ballets. I had been glad that they had opened the door to the MOT and challenged me with an opportunity to display my creative talent. It had been a new exposure, a new experience.

The Metropolitan Ballet Theatre had auditions at the same time and celebrated their first performance. But their celebration didn't last long. The reality was that the MBT was poorly financed. Their expenses were much greater than the donations and the income from the performances. The dancers were not paid on time and later not at all. Their second ballet *Giselle* was planned but abandoned for lack of financial support, and the company disbanded.

Michael Margolin, special writer to *The Oakland Press*, interviewed MOT's General Director Dr. David DiChiera who gave him his opinion as to why the MBT collapsed:

"He [David] wanted to move 'step by step, slowly' to create a ballet company. Metropolitan Ballet Theatre 'moved too fast...immediately developing a full structure ballet company...and moved away from [their] commitment to Iacob Lascu."

DiChiera wanted a ballet company to feed his grand opera productions with dance talent and choreography. He was right by mentioning that Mr. Stroud and Mr. Valentic moved away from their commitment, but later DiChiera did the same.

The opening night of *The Sleeping Beauty* was on May 28, 1993 at the Masonic Temple. At my suggestion, MOT invited Karen Kain, Margaret

Illmann, Kimberly Glasco and Serge Lavoie, principal dancers from the National Ballet of Canada to dance in *The Sleeping Beauty*. In addition to the regular performances, there was a morning dress rehearsal performance planned for the schools in the Detroit metropolitan area. For that performance, the roles of Aurora and Prince Florimund were interpreted by two of my students, Kelly Knechtel and Dmitry Mikheyenko, both very talented dancers. By promoting two students from my private school to dance in principal roles, I opened up the possibility for talented local students to become professionals.

Introducing one ballet production in every season could be an embryo for a ballet company in the city of Detroit. The success of the ballets from *Aida* and *The Sleeping Beauty* strengthened my collaboration with MOT, and we signed a new contract to stage *Cinderella* for the next season.

As soon as I was finished with *The Nutcracker* season, this new challenge waited for me. *The Cinderella* performance knocked on my head. This was the first time that *The Cinderella* ballet would be staged in Detroit. The sets and costumes were borrowed from the San Francisco Ballet. Auditions were held at my private school and I screened other dancers by watching the videos they had sent. Some of them who had danced in *The Sleeping Beauty* were returning. For the role of *Cinderella* I invited one of my favorite principal dancers, Evelyn Cisneros from the San Francisco Ballet fans of the DSO *Nutcracker* would remember her as a frequent and exquisite Sugarplum Fairy and from Germany Catherine Batcheller of the Stuttgart Ballet. Catherine also danced the role of the Fairy Godmother, alternating with my student Ami Elizabeth Smith. The Prince was Wolfgang Stollwittzer, also from the Stuttgart Ballet. Leslie Dunner was again my choice for conducting the MOT Orchestra.

To build up the financial base for the MOT's ballet productions, the Friends of Ballet was busy generating support for the grand performance of *Cinderella*. For that purpose, Margo Cohen hosted a cocktail reception. I was invited to the party as the guest of honor. For the same purpose of generating money for the *Cinderella,* the Friends of Ballet organized an art exhibition at the Gallery Office Center in Southfield, entitled "Once Upon a Time…Happily Ever After." The opening of the exhibition was on April 8 where MOT ballet buffs joined artists and art buyers. The Forbes-Cohen/Nemer Associates and Xerox Corporation were the sponsors of this exhibition by more than one hundred Michigan artists. Hundreds attended the opening and purchased much of the art. The proceeds would defray *Cinderella* production costs.

For a while, I was concerned that Evelyn Cisneros couldn't come on the date when we began our rehearsals. She was busy dancing *Romeo and Juliet* in San Francisco. I found a solution; I choreographed all the dances

Evelyn would have to learn, with Catherine Batcheller and Wolfgang Stollwittzer and sent Evelyn the video. Catherine, who also danced the role of *Cinderella*, picked up the choreography very fast; my idea to send a video of Catherine to show Evelyn the choreography would have been scary if Evelyn were not such a fine professional artist. My concern evaporated as Evelyn agreed with my idea.

"It's part of my job as a professional performer to learn things quickly."

Evelyn joined us two weeks before the opening and I was amazed that she had learned all her parts displaying a wonderful bodyline and expressed it very naturally. She just needed to go through the partnering parts with Wolfgang. Evelyn commented on my choreography to Barbara Hoover from the *Detroit News*:

"The music has apparently inspired him and created ambitious choreography. There's a lot more dancing, more dance steps in each variation than we did in the San Francisco *Cinderella*. *The Pas de Deux* has six or eight lifts, we did only three or four in San Francisco."

To Susan Hall-Balduf from the *Free Press*, Evelyn said, "The choreography is very musical and technically demanding. He has very specific ideas about where he wants steps and where he wants pantomime. But he is also very generous. If something is too fast or it's not comfortable he'll make changes."

The performances were held at the Masonic Temple. I was overwhelmed by the quality of the whole company and I was pleased that I didn't disappoint the audience, the MOT, the sponsors, the dancers, or even the critics. I thought that with my *Cinderella* ballet production MOT had proved that it could put together a fine production. This was enough reason to hope that an annual ballet production would become a tradition for MOT. Susan Hall-Balduf, *Free Press* Dance writer, commented in her review of the *Cinderella ballet.*

"Choreographed and directed by Iacob Lascu, this was MOT's second homegrown full-length ballet, and it wowed. Lascu is locked into staging the DSO's oh-so-annual *Nutcracker*. He has said he would like to do something more interesting. This was his chance, and he made the most of it. In particular, the second act *Pas de Deux* between the young lovers had the audience mesmerized; springtime at the ballet. Now there's a tradition that deserves to be annual."

MOT's Artistic Director David DiChiera felt uplifted about the company's dance venture and its success. Ticket sales grew from the previous year and proved that MOT could build up a ballet audience gradually as we had done with the annual *Nutcracker*.

In her article entitled "That was the year that was," Barbara Hoover wrote in The *Detroit News:*

"In May, Michigan Opera Theatre proved it's serious about getting into the ballet business with its second annual production, a polished new staging of Prokofiev's *Cinderella*, choreographed by Iacob Lascu, of Detroit Symphony *Nutcracker* fame."

Encouraged by the *Cinderella* success, the MOT planned Tchaikovsky's *Swan Lake* ballet for next spring. These annual ballets were intended to be the beginning of a growing dance arm for MOT.

I thought that I would have time to relax and enjoy the view of the lake from my condominium windows. In reality I was pushed into another lake, The *Swan Lake* ballet for the MOT. For the evening performances of *Swan Lake*, the former principal Bolshoi ballerina Valentina Kozlova danced the role of the heartbroken Odette and the dazzling Odile, the prince was Serge Lavoie. Janna Berman and Anthony Randazzo, both principals with the San Francisco Ballet, danced the matinee performances. This production was another milestone in my life. The public enthusiastically received it. I proved again to the people who were sponsoring that performance that I had enough talent to create more than just *The Nutcracker Ballet*. Even the director of the MOT David DiChiera, surprised me with a short but eloquent thank you note:

"Iacob, I'm very pleased with the cast and your choreography. Congratulations, here is to your success."

This third production with the MOT confirmed that the Metropolitan Detroit area had talented dancers capable of building a ballet repertoire. Here I was after three great full-length ballets; I proved it and I am thankful for the challenges presented to me. I had a great sense of personal satisfaction.

In the past, Maria attended all of my performances. She loved my performances and hoped that some day I would be able to choreograph for a professional company in the United States. I had a great feeling of satisfaction that I could fulfill Maria's hope, even though it would not be completely gratifying because she was not present. I had missed her in the seat near me in the audience. I also missed her criticism and encouragements at the rehearsals. I missed her lovely smile, the hugs and kisses after each performance. Even though I couldn't see her, she is always in my mind, heart and soul.

For the MOT 1995-1996 season, I decided to choreograph the ballet *Romeo and Juliet*, with music by Sergei Prokofiev. Still at that time Dr. David DiChiera showed absolutely no sign that he intended to terminate our collaboration. On the contrary, his actions encouraged me to believe that he wanted to consolidate our relationship and develop a permanent MOT ballet company. I was pleased when I received an invitation from Mr. and Mrs. John Boll to join them and Dr. David DiChiera at their home on Sunday,

December 3, 1995 to hear about the exciting future of ballet at the new opera house. Mrs. Margo Cohen, the main ballet sponsor was also present; actually Margo drove me to the gathering. I was curious to find out what the future of ballet would be at the new Detroit Opera House. David invited me to sit near him, facing the other guests.

First, David talked about the happy event, the opening of the new Detroit Opera House and his vision to combine the opera's repertoire with ballet performances. He also announced that the next ballet that I would present after the *Romeo and Juliet* would be *Giselle*. He introduced me and asked me to talk about the upcoming *Romeo and Juliet* performance and my vision for the dance company. I was confident that this gathering would bring a new breeze for the Detroit dance audience.

Returning from the winter break, I launched myself with excitement into exploring the beautiful music of Prokofiev's *Romeo and Juliet*. The score challenged me to reflect on my own interpretation of the passions and the violence of that fateful story. It was a long journey for me to prepare, research, and find my own way of translating the flow of the music into movement. The broad dimensions within the music invited me to energize myself and develop many choreographic possibilities. I emphasized a more dynamic development of the story, and I gave a fresh color to the choreography in order to express the intensity of the conflict in Prokofiev's brilliant score.

For the role of Juliet, I invited Kimberly Glasco, principal dancer of the National Ballet of Canada, and Caris Natalie, principal dancer from the Netherlands Ballet Company, Amsterdam. For the role of Romeo, I invited Aleksandar Antonijevic, principal dancer of the National Ballet of Canada, and Alexander Gouliaev, principal dancer from the Netherlands Ballet Company. Tybalt was Dmitry Korobeinikov and Mercutio was Kenneth Larson, alternating with Johann Persson.

The audience was enthusiastic. I was glad to have had the opportunity to choreograph that wonderful story based on such an exquisite musical score. I was very pleased with the production; it was one of my long-time dreams fulfilled.

The year of 1996 marked a change in the cultural history of Detroit. On April 21, 1996 was the Gala Opening of the Detroit Opera House. The commemorative program included photos of people who had contributed in many ways: financially, performing, choreographing, or directing during the twenty-five years of MOT's existence. I was thrilled seeing myself in one of these photos, standing near Morry Cohen and David DiChiera. I thought that this was a nice form of recognition for my dedicated work for MOT. So I was disappointed when I found out later that their actions or statements were only formalities and not genuine.

Each season the collaborations had brought a larger audience, something that gave us the satisfaction that we were on the right track. Totally immersed in the rehearsals for this latest ballet, I was pleased that everything was going very well and the dancers were doing their best. I was accustomed to the media, the newspapers and TV, who showed up to interview the dancers, the conductor, and me.

This time it didn't happen that way. The media interviewed both of the principals and Dr. David DiChiera at my private ballet school. Contrary to previous years, I was not invited to be part of the interview. It was a normal procedure to let me know at least what was happening in my own studio. Thus, when I was not notified, it ignited a suspicious spark that all was not right. I felt that something was going on behind my back.

In the past, David was always ready far ahead with the MOT repertoire for the next season. Back stage, I asked him when we should meet to discuss the dates and other details regarding the next ballet *Giselle*. His evasive answer conveyed a different attitude toward me from that of the past. It was no longer the friendly Iacob. I was the stranger Mr. Lascu. Avoiding a specific answer, he left saying he had to talk to the board of directors. This was another sign that my collaboration with the MOT was ending.

Time passed; it was very clear to me then, that I would not choreograph the ballet *Giselle*; I was never given a reason from David why I would not be choreographing *Giselle*. Convinced that Margo Cohen knew the reason. I asked her what was going on but she repeatedly avoided telling me the truth. So I approached her husband, Morry, who finally told me frankly that I would not be choreographing any ballet for the next season because the ballet production cost too much.

I wasn't satisfied with his answer. I didn't pursue the subject further realizing I was misled in my hope of forming a local ballet company. From that experience I learned the importance of a written document that verbal commitments and the combination of a handshake do not matter. I was naïve and conducted myself for something my parents had taught me. This was my thought at that time and still is today.

With MOT, I proved that I could successfully choreograph other ballets besides *The Nutcracker* and that the talent pool of ballet dancers in Detroit is deep enough to support major productions. I remain forever grateful to Mr. and Mrs. Cohen for sponsoring me, for giving me the opportunity to present to Detroit Metropolitan audiences four full-length ballets and allowing the local talent to proved themselves to this community. I am also grateful to Dr. David DiChiera for all my collaborations with MOT.

TWENTY YEARS

I pulled myself through this entire busy schedule, but with more and more difficulty. I had moments when I wanted to abandon and quit everything, Marygrove College, my private school, *The Nutcracker*, collaboration with MOT. This overloading of my tasks, this eternal worry of resolving problems favorably, and the grief over Maria's death devoured my body constantly. I didn't give up; I ignored the pressures and let my mind wander and dream.

When I was hit by the thunderbolt of my cancer diagnosis, I told just a few people about it. I isolated myself; I didn't talk to people of my pain. I didn't want them to regard me as a suffering creature that passes by begging for help. While the hurricane of cancer raged through my body, I didn't stop working. I continued to effectively run my school, *The Nutcracker* rehearsals and performances with the DSO, and the *Cinderella* with the MOT. The people around me didn't notice that my body was under siege by a ferocious enemy and that I was fighting with all my immune system against it. No one ever guessed what I went through every day.

However my main stress came from the rehearsals for *The Nutcracker*. I had to spend Saturdays and Sundays at the rehearsals instead of having a quiet, relaxing weekend after a heavy week's workload. I had to deal with so many children and complex parents with their endless requests to excuse their children from rehearsal or complaining that their children didn't get the part that he or she had dreamed of.

I was fine; I followed what I had learned and slowed down my activity. I let the Ballet Mistress Marie Aversa, conduct the majority of *The Nutcracker* rehearsals. I was pleased how she conducted the rehearsals. The twenty-five excellent performances were a great achievement for the company. Her exigency and perseverance resulted in their high quality performance. Then after this season Marie Aversa left to dance with the Ohio Ballet and than I appointed Mollie Casey as Ballet Mistress to take her place.

Fortunately for the 20th anniversary of *The Nutcracker,* Marie Aversa returned to Detroit to celebrate the occasion with us. I was relieved when she accepted the position of Ballet Mistress again and conducted the majority of *The Nutcracker* rehearsals. She knew about my illness and took most of the burdens off my shoulders by helping me overcome some of the stress in my work. She knew all the dances very well and took care to maintain the style of my choreography. Her expertise, gained after so many years of *The Nutcracker* rehearsals, allowed me to miss many rehearsals.

She prepared the 20th year *Nutcracker* with care and dedication, obtaining from the dancers the maximum artistic quality.

Marie Aversa stood by me giving me moral support encouraging me to fight the illness. She was a good Ballet Mistress devoted entirely to her work, and was dedicated to *The Nutcracker Ballet* that she loved so much. I will always remember and cherish my collaborations with her and I am thankful for her support during my difficult time.

As in previous celebrations, the parents took the initiative and organized different committees for each task: T-shirts, pictures of the whole cast in the program booklet, etc. For the opening night the parents' committee invited all the Claras who had performed during these twenty years. To see all the Claras again was an emotional evening for me. I hugged every one of them and admired how nicely they'd grown up. Some of them had gotten married and came with their husbands and children. One of my special guests was Joan Baxter, who, twenty years earlier, had recommended me to the Executive Director of the DSO, Marshall Turkin. She resides now in Chicago, but came to the celebration.

Iacob with Darci Kistler and Damian Woetzel

The first performance was a gala. I was honored by the presence of Merrill Ashley and Ben Huys from the New York City Ballet for the role of the Sugar Plum Fairy and the Prince. Cynthia Harvey from the American Ballet Theatre for the role of the Snow Queen and Damian Woetzel from the New York City Ballet. On this occasion, the State of Michigan Special Tribute, signed by Governor John Engler, was presented to me. The Mayor of Detroit, Dennis W. Archer sent a letter of congratulations.

When the applause ended after the last performance, I could envision for a moment Maria on the seat always reserved for her, near me. But the vision faded and I went to my dressing room. After the last performance I thanked everybody and quickly went home. I wanted to be alone with my thoughts. Without Maria I couldn't enjoy these accomplishments accumulated through so many years like I had in the past. They were fruitful results obtained together with Maria. She was no longer with me to share the success. We had been married for thirty-eight years and even after seven years; I had not yet learned to adjust to the emptiness in my heart. I missed her very much and in my room alone my mind was only with her. In my distant memory, an image came to life of Maria in a Bucharest museum dancing to the music of Enescu's first *Romanian Rhapsody*. She danced it brilliantly. She was the one who helped me and inspired me all the time. The competition was very tough and I consider that what I achieved here in the United States was the recognition of my talent and hard work. I thought that I was lucky, too.

I never fully understood the financial intricacies that determined the DSO's move of *The Nutcracker* to the Detroit Opera House (DOH) in 1996. Management told me that the rent at the DOH was lower than the Fox Theatre. Since the financial end of things was not important to me, I accepted the move with great confidence that on the larger DOH stage, the dancers would be able to move in a more relaxed manner. The individual dances and the entire production would look better.

However, the DSO had already rented sets and costumes from the American Ballet Theatre (ABT) without consulting me. When I learned this, I informed them that our sets and costumes were very nice and there was really no need to change. They explained that they wanted to present a new production with the move to the new opera house in the hopes of increasing ticket sales. "Dance specialist", DSO General Manager Paul R. Chummers wanted me to make changes to my choreography. He even asked me to create a new production to go with the new sets, suggesting that they would have to take other measures should I refuse. Taking that to be a warning, I was offended by his insinuation that *The Nutcracker*, my work of art, was all of a sudden unacceptable.

Despite the controversy and without a signed contract, I began rehearsals after Labor Day as usual for the upcoming *Nutcracker,* warning the DSO that without a decision soon I would stop the rehearsals. The DSO was pressed by two facts: they had already spent too much money renting sets and costumes and there was no time for them to contract another company for the production. After endless negotiations between the DSO and myself they finally presented me with a contract for eighteen performances.

The DOH has an audience capacity of about 2,500 half the size of the Fox Theatre. To compensate for the difference, the DSO jumped the number of performances from 13 in 1995 to 18 in 1996. The new sets were strongly advertised but not the production itself. When the ABT sets arrived I found that I detested them because the sets narrowed the space for the dancers. I did my best, but it was most difficult, especially in the first act, to choreograph the large cast.

The smoke puff made by the symphony in the press and on radio and TV about the new sets and costumes didn't have its desired effect on the audiences. It was obvious to me that if the management had let me continue with our beautiful former sets and costumes, the house might have been sold out like it was in earlier years when the public fell in love with the 1975 production. I believe the mistake of advertising the sets and costumes and not the production, the ballet company, the choreographer, and the local dancers contributed to the diminished attendance.

More than 850,000 people enjoyed my *Nutcracker* in the 23 years it was presented. However there were millions of people who hadn't even heard of it because the marketing hadn't attracted them to the holiday tradition. For numerous reasons the media coverage in the press, and on the radio and TV had been poor. While there were households of families who knew all about the major sports teams in town, they knew nothing about ballet. It is my belief that ballet performances if consistently and well promoted would attract enough people to be financially viable.

It had now been nine years since Maria's death and I was gradually becoming aware that again my life was too intense, too stressful. In my dressing room after *The Nutcracker* my thoughts wandered as always to Maria. Her seat in the theatre was again empty and I missed her so much, especially at that crucial moment in the dispute with the DSO. I needed her advice to find the right solution for the future. Maria was always my best critic and inspiration. When she was alive I discussed all my creations with her. A highly trained dancer herself, she had a keen sense of beauty and harmony and I valued her professional opinion. Now, I felt strongly that she was standing by me and agreed with my decision not to change my production. I felt an infusion of something in my mind, a thought which came from her:

Dear Tati, hold on to your principles; don't give them up. Enjoy what you accomplished professionally and socially and take care of yourself. Remember that in your experience you learned that during your work you met very kind and helpful people who appreciated your talent and your work. At the same time you met very nasty people who used their influential political or financial power to get what they wanted. They appeared to enjoy their power over you. But fortunately the people with compassion and a loving human spirit helped you keep your balance to survive with dignity and health. Leave DSO and MOT to their fates and you follow yours. You will be happier at this time dedicating your future to your son and his family. Follow your fate.

The thoughts accompanied me home and made me think just how and when to implement them. My decision would not only affect the DSO, but Marygrove College and my private school.

THE THREE DECISIONS

The first decision was to deal with Marygrove College. By 1998, I would have completed twenty-five years of working at that institution, and I thought that this would be the best time to retire. I wanted to retire gradually and I talked to the dean of the possibility of working just part-time in the 1997-1998 school year and to retire completely in June 1998. It was approved, and I started enjoying my semi-retirement from Marygrove. At the annual spring concert of Dance Detroit I choreographed for Marygrove College *Meditation*; a *Pas de Deux* danced beautifully by Marie Aversa and Stephen Hadala, based on the music of Jules Massenet.

The following year, in June 1998, my complete retirement from

Professor Emeritus

Iacob with Gene (his son) and his wife Mihaela and the twins, Marie and James

Marygrove College began. I looked in the mirror at my destiny and I couldn't believe that I had spent twenty-five years at Marygrove. The 1998 Spring Concert was a special tribute for my retirement. At that concert I did my last choreography for Marygrove College. It was an excerpt from the Rachmaninof concerto for piano and orchestra, *The Rhapsody on a Theme of Paganini,* my first choreography done for Dance Detroit when I came to the United States. After the performance, there was an afterglow party, also in honor of my retirement. At that party, the dean, teachers, former colleagues, students and former students expressed their recognition for my twenty-five years of service at Marygrove College. The dean concluded that during these years I had done a great service to the community of Detroit. At the annual graduation ceremony, I was awarded the title "Professor Emeritus." Marygrove College also honored me with a retirement dinner attended by all my family and friends.

My second decision was to close my school or to transfer it to somebody else. I kept this decision to myself until the end of the 1998 summer session. Of the three decisions this was the hardest. I loved that school; I set it up together with my wife. Many hours of hard work were invested with great results. The Lascu School of Ballet had become well known. Its reputation had spread all over Michigan and the nation.

Every year, I held open classes at the end of the term, which always culminated in a performance for the public. But this year, it was not just a usual closing performance. It was a celebration and, at the same time, a farewell from my school and my students. This was an important year in my life, the twenty-fifth anniversary of our immigration to the United States. I hadn't planned it that way; it was just a coincidence.

The program presented was entitled *Metamorphose*. I demonstrated to the audience the transformation of the students from a pre-dance class to an advanced one. The highlight of the program was *The Verdi-Massenet Suite* danced by the advanced class. In that suite, I included the *Pas de Deux* danced at the Marygrove spring concert, the *Meditation*, but this time it was danced by Katherine Nason and Stephen Hadala. The program was exceptionally warmly received with ovations, cheering and prolonged applause.

Then it was my turn to perform, which was a very difficult task. I had to make my speech, announcing the painful news that I was closing the school. I had scarcely started my speech, telling them that I was celebrating a twenty-five year anniversary, marking my arrival in the United States, when a tornado of applause broke out. The endless applause became a standing ovation. I felt a lump in my throat and I couldn't continue my speech; I cried. As I swallowed, I saw myself as a young man, a long time ago when I first started to dance and then later when I became a teacher and a choreographer. Year after year, I stepped into a studio and everyday did the technical classical ballet classes followed by rehearsals. Year after year, I taught and choreographed for different companies in Romania, China, and Peru and in the United States. I never could dream in Romania of having my own classical ballet school because it was impossible under the communist regime to own your own business. In the United States, the spirit of free enterprise made it possible for me to dream and implement it. Now my mind and my body were filled with emotions generated by the parents' recognition of my achievements during the past twenty-five years. It took me a long time to calm down, to be able to continue my speech.

I introduced Traian and his wife Olga and publicly expressed my gratitude to them for their comprehensive help, of my family and me to immigrate and start a new life in the United States. I thanked Mihaela and Eugen for their constant support in running the school. I thanked all the teachers who had helped me to achieve the excellent reputation of my school.

My third decision was to hold firm to my principles not to surrender to the pressures from the DSO to create another *Nutcracker*. Financial sponsors of some of my productions, a politician, and even a top-level administrator at Marygrove College advised me to create a new *Nutcracker*. Well meaning as they were, they didn't understand the nature of my artistic integrity. *The Nutcracker* was my work of art, my masterpiece of originality. It had successfully stood the test of time beginning with four performances in 1975 reaching 25 performances in 1992.

I liked my *Nutcracker*. It was part of my emotional creative process for which the DSO and others opinion had no equivalent. Each of the 23 years, the children, the dancers, the principals all changed, but my production had the same high quality of cohesiveness, beauty, charm, and dramatic presentation. I always felt an intense excitement watching it. I was and still am very proud of my *Nutcracker*.

If I gave in to the pressures of the DSO and others, I would be giving up that originality and I, as a choreographer, would be the real loser. Not for a single moment was I tempted to give up my beliefs. Through the testing of this experience, I learned to understand my own power and that doing the right thing always wins.

Many people asked me if I based my career on reviews or influential political and financial pressures. My answer was a categorical, "No"! I refused to do that when I lived in a communist country, and I refused to do it in a capitalist country. I didn't expect to endure the same pressure, political and financial in America. I do not choreograph for the press, their critics, politicians and influential financial powers. This new situation revealed to me how insecure I was in the new free world, in general, and, in particular, *The Nutcracker* when I no longer had my good fairy connection. I understood that wherever I was on this planet in communist Romania or in capitalist United States I had to have good connections to open the door for me.

Originally when I came here in 1972, I thought I would continue my work in the United States where I had left off in Romania. But, the reality was that I had to prove myself again and I found it difficult for me at first to find my place in the Detroit dance community. Indeed I had to work all day long with passion, giving the maximum of my talent and nagging people to do extra rehearsals, while often enduring teasing because they thought I worked too hard.

For me it was the feeling, the emotions created by the choreography. What I create are my ideas, beauty and entertainment, for the satisfaction of the people. This is who I am and this is how I choreograph. Some people were going to appreciate it and some were not. I could not apologize for something I believed in. I had to stand my ground with an inflexible will, opposing unjustifiable demands. *Talking it over with Maria in my thoughts, and she agreed with me.*

Even though I chose to exercise my artistic freedom and refuse to choreograph a new *Nutcracker*, I didn't leave the United States as I left Romania in similar circumstances. I am concerned about the loss of individual rights over the last quarter century in the United States and the violation of personal privacy. Even though I am bothered by these changes in this country, I preferred to retire in the United States, which is still the most wonderful country in the world.

Life has taught me that tolerance is like grease. It takes the friction out of everyday life. There were people who helped me and then abandoned me: I disagreed with them but I could understand them. They didn't keep their commitments. I fought for truth and I wanted it to surface immediately; I learned that truth has no special time and I must wait for it even if it never arrives.

I asked the DSO to make the decision and let me know so I could inform the dancers. The decision continued to be put off. Again, the DSO called me to another meeting to persuade me to choreograph a new *Nutcracker*. Again my artistic creativity was on trial. I could only speculate that the real reason behind this continued pressure was an excuse to terminate the collaboration. At the same time, the DSO told me.

"It is a very good production, but it is old; you have proved to be a talented choreographer and we have confidence that you can create a better one."

I answered, choreography, as any other artwork, if it is good does not get old. It is your mind that has created a wrong opinion, influenced from outside sources. I believe that in your subconscious you know how good my *Nutcracker* production is, but your interests dictate otherwise.

I had expected that the DSO would wait to celebrate 25 years of successful collaboration, but I was wrong. I listened to their arguments but I wasn't able to understand the motives that lay behind the discussion. I understand that it's very simple to donate money to an artist or arts organization and think of oneself as having done a noble thing. Unfortunately, sometimes such an act has a selfish motive such as to be noticed, to stun, to entertain, and to impress others, to be liked or admired.

But, it is important to realize that one's donation and one's display of charm, love, and kindness is no substitute for artistic competence.

Finally, in May 1997, I signed a contract for twelve performances of *The Nutcracker* at the Detroit Opera House. The DSO verbally let me know that the 1997 *Nutcracker* would be the last.

Stepping out of the hall and closing the door behind me, I felt a sense of relief. I couldn't give a name to the feeling but it was one of solemn quiet. I was the winner, not the loser. I was proud that I was an independent person, with my own judgment and ideas. Only I knew the discipline, the effort, the tension, and the strain that it took to produce such a superb *Nutcracker*.

That fall, I dedicated all my talent and skills, as usual to honor my last contract with the DSO. Remembering the days and nights Maria and I spent in research and preparation in order to create the steps and the choreography for *The Nutcracker*, I thought how I had selected the children and the young talented dancers. There were moments when I was exhausted but did not permit myself to even admit that I was tired. I just continued the rehearsals with the eternal demand for greater perfection.

Soon, Mr. Chummers informed me that the DSO would publicly acknowledge my twenty-three years of fruitful collaboration. Also, he told me of the opening night gala planned as a tribute to my work and me. Various personalities were to be invited. I asked him to make the results of the meeting public immediately.

Nothing was announced. I was mad because I knew that I must tell the dancers when we began rehearsals that this would be the last *Nutcracker*. Despite my insistence, they delayed the announcement. Eight days before opening night, the DSO called an urgent meeting. There, they presented a press release to me. Outraged that they wanted to make this announcement just before opening night, I protested and told them that they should have done it when we signed the contract. Now, it was too late and they would have to wait until the final performance.

Not comprehending what a devastating effect this would have on the cast just before opening night, the DSO expressed the belief that the press release would encourage more people to buy tickets to the performances. Reading the news release, which contained complementary words about Dance Detroit and me as well as inaccurate information about the situation, I asked them to make the corrections. I couldn't stop the release from being sent but I could delay it until we could let the dancers know directly. I didn't want them to find out from the press.

Some reporters were present at the Saturday rehearsal. I told the DSO Public Relations Representative Miss Jill Woodward, that she could read the press release after the rehearsal. Afraid to do so because she knew she would be booed, she asked me to read it.

Grudgingly, I read the release to those in attendance, it was dated the December 4, 1997.

"After 23 years of highly-successful collaboration, the Detroit Symphony Orchestra's production of *The Nutcracker*, featuring choreographer Iacob Lascu and Dance Detroit- the resident dance company of Marygrove College, will take a final bow at the end of this year's run at the Detroit Opera House, December 12 through 21, 1997. We are very proud to have been associated with this fine production, which has meant so much to so many. There will always be a special place in the hearts of the thousands of Michiganians who saw this particular choreography, and to those who danced it. Mr. Lascu's artistic vision has brought the magic of this legendary ballet to more people than any other dance production in the history of our state. 23 years is a very good run. When we began discussions about a new production, Mr. Lascu indicated that the current one was still his favorite and he was not prepared to create another one for us at this time. Iacob Lascu, the choreographer and creative director behind this long-time Detroit favorite, said, 'this ballet has been very important to me, and I have enjoyed working with the Detroit Symphony for over two decades. Many excellent young dancers have cut their teeth on this production, and gone on to professional careers. I am very pleased with our accomplishments'."

After reading the DSO release to the 1997 cast I address them, telling them that this would be my last year at the helm of the show. I am proud of my *Nutcracker*. I think it's one of the best! My words were received with a burst of prolonged applause and tears from more than 120 people in the crowded and now overheated dance studio at Marygrove College. With a lump in my throat and tears in my eyes, I withdrew.

At that historical rehearsal the emotional moment was soon transformed into rage. The children, the dancers, the parents were outraged, and besieged the members of the DSO administration present as well as the reporters.

In the *Free Press*, Mr. David Lyman quoted some of the parents' comments about the DSO decision:

"How indecent of them to come and make this announcement less than a week before these children have to perform."

Other parents saw the decision as a further sign of the diluting of the local cultural community:

"This production has been very successful. To change it like this, with an out-of-town company, is really an attack on the culture of the city."

I understood their heartbreak over the DSO decision and I was deeply moved by the overwhelming support of the cast and their parents' defense of my dearest ballet.

Barbara Hoover, in her review in the *Detroit News*, pleasantly surprised me too.

The Nutcracker - Snowflakes

"His touch will be missed. Lascu has a fine eye for beautiful patterns, which crop up most obviously as the Snowflakes dash back and forth in precise lines, their zigzaggy skirts flying under showers of stage snow. They're as exquisite as the famous Wilis in *Giselle*."

Opening night, the dancers, and I expected that we would be honored with the presence of Mayor Dennis Archer of Detroit as DSO Public Relations Representative Jill Woodward had told us. The mayor, however, did not show up. So, the DSO quickly arranged a curtain front ceremony for the final performance where one of Archer's secretaries read a proclamation dedicated to me, Iacob Lascu. With it the DSO presented me with a framed photo of the Snowflakes.

That moment was an empty one, but I was happy that night if only because I had not surrendered my ideas. No reward or recognition could have been greater than the appreciation of the general public who had supported Dance Detroit and me through 23 wonderful years. The devotion offered by so many talented artists, and the sacrifices made by so many dancers and their parents for the productions will never be forgotten.

For these final performances, the dancers worked whole-heartedly, brilliantly, with talent, poise, dedication, and with their faces radiating the pleasure that they were part of a production that had conquered the hearts of nearly a million people for nearly a quarter of a century. The dancers conducted themselves like professionals as always and danced brilliantly for all the performances. It was a wonderful cast and production crew.

This annual tradition, no matter how much work it took, never lost its quality, beauty, and excellence. It was an exciting thing to see people coming back, year after year. It was also a great satisfaction for both the audience and especially for me to watch the same dancers year after year, progressing from parts as little dolls to the highest junior corps de ballet and finally into the roles as principals. Twenty-year old Stephen Hadala began his *Nutcracker* career as an acrobat, and for this final season, he danced the Prince. Later, I was thrilled to find out that the Pittsburgh Ballet accepted him.

Every night and afternoon, I watched the performances, deeply absorbed by their beauty. I will always cherish the dancer's talent, beauty, charm, freshness, enthusiasm, dedication, and devotion to my productions. They brought great joy and happiness into my life as well as the audiences they entertained.

I went home fulfilled with the outcome of these last twelve performances. I never in my life felt such contentment in my heart. The next year, the DSO imported another company with a new *Nutcracker* and the following year, they discontinued the annual tradition. According to Mr. Douglas R. Cornelsen, a member of the DSO orchestra, in his article published in the professional musician magazine *Keynote*, "The reason given for terminating *The Nutcracker* Ballet was high overhead." The "new" was not the key of the high overhead, but the inept marketing of *The Nutcracker Ballet*.

The Nutcracker Ballet had become one of the best-loved holiday traditions in Detroit and would not be soon forgotten. It was part of Detroit because Detroiters were part of *The Nutcracker*. I had also tried with MOT to develop a tradition. But I was disappointed and thwarted in my attempt. I believe that later certain political motivation abetted management's action against me. This belief of mine was seconded by another source of opinion according to Mr. Douglas Cornelsen in his article published in the *Keynote*.

Everything that I have done professionally in my life blossomed from my natural talent, nurtured by hard work. Was my professional life an accomplishment, a victory? No! It was just my way of my life, a part of my life, as was the loss of my wife. With all my experiences and projects behind me, I was confident that my retirement would bring me new possibilities, exploring new venues and activities. I was asked if I regretted or missed my work. My answer was simple: I don't miss it and if I had known how much I was going to enjoy it, I would have retired sooner.

The year 2000 had a hot summer, just like the one forty-seven years ago when my parents, my two brothers and I moved to Timişoara. We were a happy and united family. It was also a hot summer fifty years ago when I married Maria. Today the whole world has celebrated the second millennium but I couldn't celebrate our golden anniversary. It is the year 2000 and I look back on my life as a time past; I have lost my parents, my brothers, a lot of friends and Maria, my dear wife who gave me the greatest happiness that a human being could imagine.

Retired, I would finally have time to relax, see my grandchildren, and friends more often. It would be a change in lifestyle and a slowing of the gears, which had been shifting too fast for me. For a time, I thought that I was alone, that everything in my life had been lost and ruined. But the experience accumulated in my life gave me wisdom, strength, patience and a permanently optimistic view. At the same time, I now have the courage to try to change anything that I can. I have the judgment to make decisions between what I can change and what I cannot.

I know that I will pass through my life just once. I feel as if my past has been just a preparation, and the future is committed to the memory of a woman whom I loved dearly; I trusted her reality and her dreams. Maria and I traveled a long way together, sharing the experience accumulated in two different philosophical, ideological, economical and political societies.

Maria loved dancing. As we talked so many times about our rehearsals and stage experience, she told me that for her, being on stage is a complete isolation from the every day activities as she feels free to express anything she wants at that moment on stage. She prepared her dance characters, entrusted to her by the choreographer, in a manner that was greatly admired by everyone. Every step, every gesture was studied and meticulously rehearsed over and over until she had to leave the studio. Everyone who watched her said: it is very good - but for her the road toward achieving perfection never ended. I realized during my dance career that her way to study did gradually infused my work. Her dedication to the art of dance was unmatched by any other dancer in the company. Being with her all the time in the studio and on stage I was surrounded by her talent, which touched me deeply and had a profound impact on my work.

Many times, the head of the dance department asked her to conduct rehearsals or to teach classes, but she refused. She liked the act of dancing, the classes, the rehearsals and the performances, but she never expressed a desire to teach or to choreograph. I myself asked her many times to start teaching or choreographing, but she was always evasive and said: "I am not suited for that; I just like to dance."

But her flow of talented and creative ideas was pouring into my work, as I started to teach and latter to choreograph. I never really understood her on this respect. I just accepted it as a gift from her unconditional love for me.

In the United States of America, when the opportunity opened for me to resume my profession, she was also offered to teach. After many pleas by others and myself, and after she realized the difficulty of our situation as newcomers in the U.S.A., she finally but grudgingly accepted to teach children at Marygrove College's Continual Education Program and later at our own ballet studio. She also accepted to teach classical ballet at a private school. At the end of the term, the school's director asked her to choreograph a dance for the children. That distressed her very much. Once home, Maria reminded me that she never wanted to teach or choreograph in the first place, and that she grudgingly accepted to teach only due to our struggle for building a new life in the new world. She didn't even want to go back and teach at that private school because of the choreography request. I told that I will do the choreography and she would stage it. I just asked her to give me an idea of the level her class was at and how many students were in that class. But, as before when I was choreographing, her talent started pouring out excellent new ideas again. In the process of looking for music, I presented to her many recordings and she chose the score she liked most: the ballet *"La Boutique Fantasque"* by Gioacchino Rossini, arranged and orchestrated by Ottorino Respighi. I told her again that I will do the choreography but she needs to be part of the process. She reluctantly accepted. We started to select excerpts from the chosen ballet music and proceeded to divide the scenes according to the number of dancers and the idea she herself suggested: the girls should have dolls in their hands and dance for them and with them. We succeeded to assemble a nice dance that had great success. This episode reflects once more our artistic collaboration in which she never wanted to take the front seat. However, she always helped me with her love and dedication in succeeding with my creative process.

Looking back at this beautiful relationship, I just marvel about her inner creative choreographic talent that she never wanted to develop on her own. I couldn't then and I can't now find an explanation for that. I just believe that her unique character to devote herself to the person she loved made her act that way. For me one thing is certain. I couldn't have achieved the results of my work without her uninterrupted talented stimulus.

I cannot forget Maria. I encountered my soul mate in an artistic military company. Our wedding party was made up of just two witnesses and us. We didn't have a honeymoon, but our whole life together was always like a honeymoon. It was magical, exploring each other and finding new, beautiful vibrations that kept us going and made us losing ourselves into each other. Her aura is present in the house. It is empty and silent without her. Wherever I look, her taste of decorations in the house is obvious.

In the summer, we sometimes sat on the back yard deck watching the flowers planted by her or the squirrels running through the garden. She poured me a glass of cranberry juice that she knew I loved a lot, and always kissed me.

Mondays were the days that I worked in Flint from late afternoon until 9:00 PM.

"I will miss you," she always said before I left. "I'll be back," I said taking her hand and kissing her; "you are always with me" pointing my index finger at my heart.

But now I don't have her anymore. Her loss has created a vacuum in my life. It shouldn't have been like this. She was beautiful and young when the illness took her away. I remember the stricken sensation that came over me and how frightened I was that she was going to leave me and I'll have to rebuild my life without her. I fell in love at first sight and loved Maria all my life; and still love her, even though she is no longer with me.

We were two lives in two worlds. We shared our ideas and work. We shared our triumphs and our defeats. We walked together by holding hands. We shared the pleasure of our hands' touching and cared for our bodies in health; we looked after our bodies when they were weak. We shared our earnings and expenses, our food and drink, the house, the cars, and the vacations. We gave our son our unconditional love and tried to be his role model. We learned to compromise in our life, sharing our love and trust, which kept us together. She was the miracle who completed my life.

In my life, I learned that a man without purpose is depraved. The future will open for me a new way, a new purpose, and a new goal; whatever else I do, I can dedicate the rest of my life to protecting Maria's desires and dreams, the family, which she loved with an infinite passion.

I will do my best to accomplish that; it is what I have left yet to do.

About the Author

Iacob Lascu was born in Romania where he became a well-known Ballet Master and Choreographer after extensive studies in classical ballet, character and folklore with renowned Romanian and Russian Masters.

As Ballet Master and Choreographer of *Ciocîrlia, Rapsodia Romînă* and *Dance Detroit* and as Assistant Choreographer and Ballet Master of the Romanian Opera, he created over 130 choreographies. He received a Gold Medal at the 1955 International Festival in Warsaw, Poland and Orders and Cultural Medals on four occasions.

Immigrating to the US, he continued to perform at the same artistic level and was recognized by the Michigan Senate five times for his overall contribution to the arts. He received the title of Professor Emeritus from Marygrove College in 1988.

Printed in the United States
925700003B